101 PROJECTS FOR YOUR MODEL RAILROAD

ROBERT SCHLEICHER

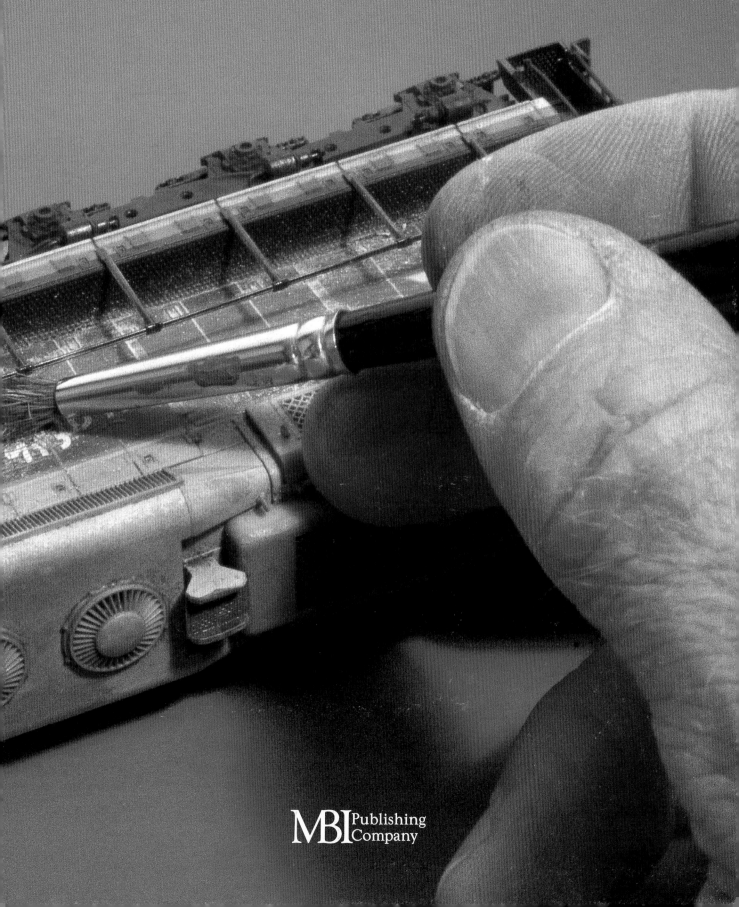

MBI Publishing Company

Bob Schleicher has spent his entire life as a journalist, author, and magazine publisher in the hobby industry. His writing has appeared in *Road & Track*, *Boy's Life*, and several other publications. The publisher of *Model Car Racing* magazine and author of MBI Publishing Company's *Racing and Collecting Slot Cars* and *101 Projects for Your Model Railroad* lives in Niwot, Colorado.

First published in 2002 by MBI Publishing Company, Galtier Plaza, Suite 200, 380 Jackson Street, St. Paul, MN 55101-3885 USA

MBI Publishing Company books are also available at discounts in bulk quantity for industrial or sales-promotional use. For details write to Special Sales Manager at Motorbooks International Wholesalers & Distributors, Galtier Plaza, Suite 200, 380 Jackson Street, St. Paul, MN 55101-3885 USA.

Library of Congress Cataloging-in-Publication Data Available
ISBN 0-7603-1181-1

Front cover:
Model railroading is one of the most evolved, exciting, and diverse hobbies around. You can fill a 60x100-foot building with a rail-by-rail re-creation of a real railroad, or you can detail a single locomotive while sitting at the corner of your kitchen table.

Frontispiece:
Your model railroad needs a setting—a place or places that you can create with as much care and accuracy as you devote to the locomotives and rolling stock that you weather and superdetail.

Title Page:
Weathering is just one aspect of model railroading that allows you to develop and apply the skills of a visual artist. It also requires some special techniques, most of which you'll find in this book. Try them all, and discover those that work best for you.

Back cover:
By taking advantage of tools, techniques, and materials that have resulted from years of trial and error, you will make your experiences in the model railroad hobby even more fulfilling.

Edited by Dennis Pernu
Designed by Katie Sonmor

Printed in Hong Kong

CONTENTS

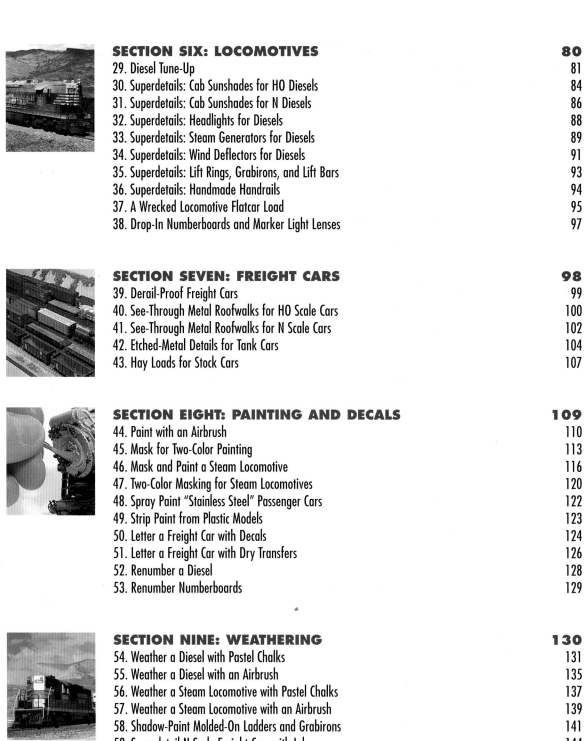

INTRODUCTION

UNDERSTANDING THE INFORMATION BOXES

Each project in this book features a preview, so you can decide more quickly if you want to devote the time and/or money necessary to properly complete the project—as well as discern whether you have the necessary skills. Each preview includes the following:

TIME: This is a rough estimate of how long it will take a modeler with the skill to use plastic cement and a hobby knife or razor saw to complete the simplest version of the project. In many cases, the skills and techniques learned in these projects will become integral to your future in modeling or operating.

TOOLS: I've tried to list everything you'll need for each project, from tweezers to scissors, as well as more specialized tools like hobby knives, razor saws, soldering guns, and more. You'll enjoy the project more if you really do buy the proper tools, rather than attempt to get by with pliers and a bread knife.

MATERIALS: There is always a lot of controversy over which cement is best for any given project. I'll tell you what works best for me, but you are free to choose. Choose your cement with care, however, because it may etch plastic, be too brittle, or have some other characteristic that could ruin the finished work. Paints are also an area of considerable choice. Some modelers prefer acrylic enamels, others lacquers, and still others synthetic enamels. In addition, you may have specific brand preferences. I suggest you stick to paints for modelers wherever possible, because their pigments tend to be somewhat finer than those in general-use paints—and the colors offered are better suited to modelers.

COST: Note that each dollar sign is the equivalent of $10 so that anything less than $10 receives a single dollar sign. We live in inflationary times, but I have tried to estimate within $10 the cost of each project, always assuming you will do your own labor. There are some techniques, like soldering and two-color painting, that you might want to trust to an expert. Experts usually charge by the job, and their time and cost may not be even remotely close to what I suggest. They may feel the need to be more thorough and, thus, consume more time—or they may know shortcuts that save time.

TALENT: Oh boy! Almost everyone in this hobby thinks he or she is an expert modeler—and who knows, maybe they all are. My rough estimates of talent are based on how many years you have actually been building model railroad–related projects. Time alone, however, is no indicator; I know modelers who have been building for years and have never drilled a hole or used a soldering iron, and still others who have never seen an airbrush or applied a decal. Here are some of my criteria:

BEGINNER: No learned skills beyond assembling a plastic kit with tube cement or shoving pieces of snaptrack together. May have operated trains on track nailed to a piece of plywood.

NOVICE: Has used liquid cement for plastics, painted with aerosol cans, laid flexible track on cork roadbed or Homasote with nails or spikes, and has wired a model railroad with at least one reverse loop. May have built a model railroad with open-grid benchwork and simple plaster scenery.

EXPERT: Already knows how to solder, how to use an airbrush, and how to apply decals. An expert model railroader has also hand-spiked at least one turnout, mounted beneath the table switch machines; wired a layout for multiple-train operations; built scenery from Styrofoam and/or plaster; and constructed benchwork with multiple grades and levels.

SCALES: This refers to the size of the model relative to the real thing. HO scale is the most common model railroad scale, with models 1/87 the size of the real thing. N scale models are 1/160 scale, or 1/160 the size of the real thing. S scale models are 1/64 scale, O scale models are 1/48 scale, and G scale models are 1/32, 1/29, 1/24, 1/22.5, or 1/20.3 scale, depending on the manufacturer.

SPACE: I've listed the size of the finished model. If the project is a diorama or a complete model railroad, I've listed typical ranges of sizes.

TIP(S): The not-always-obvious techniques that make it easier to complete the project.

WHY? In most cases, because you want to. If there's something that (in my opinion) is really special about the project, I'll share that opinion.

COMPLEMENTARY PROJECTS: These are the other projects in the book that use similar techniques. Projects that need to be completed before this project, or that need this project to finish the model, are also listed.

SECTION ONE
GETTING STARTED

Model railroading is one of the most popular hobbies in the world, and one of the oldest. It's what the business world refers to as a "mature" hobby, in that it has reached its peak but continues to thrive. In the case of model railroading, that "peak" means that you can buy just about any car, locomotive, or structure you wish, ready-to-run or as a simple plastic, cast-resin, cast-plaster, or laser-cut wood kit. Even track is available complete with ballast and built-in switch machines that allow the turnouts to be moved from mainline to branch-line, either manually at the switch or by remote control. Further, train control has been refined so that you can operate dozens of trains on the same track with digital command control (DCC) systems. In short, the time it takes to build a complete model railroad has been reduced to better match today's hectic lifestyles and relative lack of leisure time.

This book is not intended to be an introduction to the hobby, nor is it an instructional for building a complete model railroad step by step. There are already dozens of such books out there, including my own *The HO Model Railroading Handbook*, *N Scale Model Railroading Handbook*, *The Large Scale Model Railroading Handbook*, and *Fun with Toy Trains*. The purpose of this book is to help make the hobby even more enjoyable by dividing it into projects small enough to be completed in an evening or two. It is also intended to offer shortcuts that can make the hobby far more pleasant by helping you avoid "blind alleys," while taking advantage of techniques and ideas that have resulted from years of trial and error. Most of the photos have previously appeared in *Railmodel Journal*.

GETTING STARTED

PROJECT 1 • CHOOSE THE RIGHT RAILROAD

 Time: Lifetime

 Tools: Your call

 Materials: You pick 'em

 Cost: $$$

 Talent: Novice

 Scales: HO, N, S, O and G

 Space: Between 6x10 inches and 60x100 feet, depending on whether your passion is for toy trains, model railroads, or real railroads

 Tip: Build or buy whichever models make you proud to own them.

 WHY: For the sheer fun and pleasure of it all

COMPLEMENTARY PROJECTS: 2, 3, 4 and 101

1 You can pick any time period and any part of the country for your model railroad. Ed Patrone is modeling a railroad of his own creation set in the gold rush country of California's Sierra Nevada foothills in about 1950.

Model railroading is perhaps the most evolved, exciting, and diverse hobby you can find. You can fill a 60x100-foot building with a rail-by-rail re-creation of a real railroad as it operated on a particular day in time and call yourself a model railroader, or you can buy a single locomotive or a single car and still call yourself a model railroader. You probably fall somewhere between these two extremes, although a 60x100-foot "dream layout" is do-able for anyone willing to share his or her efforts with other members of a model railroad club.

START HERE

Your first "project" will be to determine what it is about miniature trains that you find so appealing. Briefly, model railroaders' interests fall into one of two very broad categories: toy trains or railroad prototype models. While both can be defined as "model railroads," there is a difference. For our purposes, consider yourself a toy train enthusiast if what you really want to do is relive the joy you got (or missed) from toy trains (Lionel, Marx, American Flyer, Athearn, Tyco, et al) when you were younger. If, however, you want to summon the good feelings you experienced watching, riding, or just reading about real trains, scale prototype models will be your choice.

Modern low-production tooling techniques have made it possible for model manufacturers to produce very limited runs of cars, locomotives, and even buildings, making the choices very broad, indeed, among both toy trains and scale models. You can, for example buy reproductions of just about any toy trains made from 1900 to 1960. You can also buy ready-to-run replicas of nearly every full-size steam or diesel locomotive, freight car, and passenger car that ran on any real railroad at any time in the last 100 years.

3 Like many model railroaders, Paul Brennecke could not decide on just one railroad or one specific era, so he created his own "Grande Road," based loosely on the Denver & Rio Grande Western, for his 9x15-foot N scale layout.

2 Bob Davis elected to re-create a portion of the Pennsylvania Railroad, circa 1955, on his 20x20-foot HO scale layout.

I deliberately make a distinction between toy trains and scale-model railroads because, for many of us, our real love is either toy trains (or whatever we call them) or real railroads (that we want to replicate in miniature). In truth, the vast majority of "model railroaders" confess both a love of toy trains or scale models and a passion for real railroads. Most model railroaders simply buy and operate whatever appeals to them.

SORTING IT OUT BY SIZE

Once you pick a size you should stick to it, so that all of your models are comparable to one another and to their prototypes. Again, you can stop anywhere you want along the spectrum from toy train to prototype scale model. In order of popularity among model railroaders, HO (1/87) is the most commonly selected scale, followed very closely by three-rail "O gauge" (more or less 1/48 scale) trains like Lionel, MTH, K-Line, Atlas, and others. These are followed by G scale (1/32 up to

1/20.3) and N scale (1/160). S scale is about halfway between HO and O, a compromise allowing fairly large models in medium-size spaces.

If you pick G scale, for example, you can run just about anything on the track, from tinplate 1930s-era "Gauge 1" 1/32 scale models to exact-scale replicas of 3 foot, narrow-gauge steam locomotives in 1/20.3 scale. These G scale models are all massive and require a lot of space just sitting still, let alone while operating on a layout—which is why most are run on outdoor "garden railroads."

At the small end of the size spectrum are N scale models. N scale offers the chance to run nearly full-length trains in scenic settings that can more accurately dwarf the models than larger scales. N scale's major drawback is that you really do need to be "good with your hands," just to get derailed cars and locomotives back onto the track, let alone to lay the track. N scale is possible for anyone, thanks to simple plastic rerailer tools and snap-together track products; ready-to-run cars,

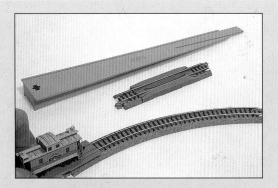

4 N scale cars and locomotives can be difficult to put back on the track. Kato and Con-Cor offer plastic rerailers, simple little ramps that roll a derailed car or locomotive onto the track in an instant.

5 For many model railroaders, the passion for the hobby is based on real or dreamed-of experiences with toy trains—like these Lionel three-rail freights—circling a Christmas tree.

locomotives, and buildings; and even ready-to-run coffee-table layouts.

HO scale is a compromise that allows the models to have much of the "heft" of O scale while still being small enough to operate in a space not much larger than N scale. HO scale probably offers 10 times more choice of products than in any of the other scales. This makes it easier to pick a favorite real railroad, a favorite time period, and maybe even a favorite area of the country, and still know you can buy just about anything that ran on the rails. HO scale is often (but certainly not always) the choice of modelers who want to create complete towns and portions of real railroads set in specific time periods. This vast array of equipment means you can buy exact-scale replicas of your favorite cars or locomotives from nearly any real railroad.

HOBBY DISCIPLINE: AN OXYMORON

Model railroading is a popular hobby because it includes something for everyone. The trick is to sort through all that stuff so you don't end up with a room full of model railroad cars and locomotives that cannot possibly be melded into a complete model railroad . . . or even several model railroads . . . or even a coherent display.

The majority of modelers revel in operating their favorite real railroad equipment, even if there is a certain incongruity in seeing Santa Fe diesels pull a New York Central train or watching 1880 steam locomotives run beside 1980 diesels. But this is very much what model railroading is all about: It's your hobby, and only you know what you want to buy. And it's a hobby that has all the product you can imagine, providing all the freedom to choose all that pleases you.

GETTING STARTED

PROJECT 2 • DO YOU NEED A LAYOUT?

Time: Lifetime

Tools: You decide

Materials: Your call

Cost: $$$

Talent: Beginner

Scales: HO, N, S, O and G

Space: Between 6x10 inches and 60x100 feet

Tip: Discover whether your passion is for toy trains, model railroads, or real railroads.

WHY: To watch 'em run and to run 'em

COMPLEMENTARY PROJECTS: 1, 3 through 21, and 84 through 100

1 Scale models of nearly every real railroad locomotive, freight car, and passenger car are available, often ready to run. These HO scale Bachmann models are shown on an 18x48-inch, 1870s-era diorama at the Union Pacific Museum in Union Station at Ogden, Utah.

All it takes to become a model railroader is an interest in the hobby. But if you don't go beyond the printed page, you will miss nearly all the hands-on and visual pleasures the hobby has to offer. Your next question might well be, "Do I need a model railroad?" Dozens of the best-known authors in model railroading do not have anything that resembles a model railroad layout. Others don't have more than a handful of cars and locomotives.

WATCHING 'EM RUN

Experienced model railroaders attach a variety of words, most of them derived from the world of "real railroading," to the experience of running a model railroad. It all comes down to the simple truth that nearly everyone likes to watch trains run.

The first step of this project is to make the decision that you want to watch them run. Next, you need to decide if you want to watch them run in your own home or if you are willing to join a club and watch them run on the club layout.

THE MODEL RAILROAD CLUB

Many model railroaders build and collect dozens, sometimes hundreds, of cars and locomotives, but do not own a model railroad layout. These folks belong to some type of model railroad club. The traditional model railroad club rents a huge

13

space in an empty warehouse, store, or even in the basement of a real railroad passenger station. The not-so-obvious advantage of joining a club is that you can apply only the skills you have learned to help the club build and operate the layout. And those skills can be as simple as finding the time to spend at the club on "construction" nights. Usually, one or more club members, who are experienced carpenters, build the benchwork. Some know how to lay track and love doing it, while the first love of other members is the electronics or computer hardware and software to make the layout run. Others have skills and knowledge in the scenic arts, locomotive building and tuning, or operating real railroads and applying those methods to the club. Some want the power of being an officer, and others are just plain know-it-alls. The point is there's certainly room for you, because even the experts need hands-on help—and the know-it-alls need someone to talk at.

LAYOUT SPACE

The traditional model railroad occupies most of a basement, attic, or garage. If you have the space for a layout that size—in fact if you have even a 9x9-foot spare room—that's the place for your model railroad. If you don't have a spare room, basement, or attic, books and magazines are full of ideas on how you can share the space in a guest room or with the family car (depending on which room you choose, of course). Years ago, such layouts were built right into the house. With today's more mobile society, most modelers design their layouts so the table (or benchwork) is divided into segments no larger than about 3x6 feet. Such layouts can be considered "movable" rather than "portable."

FLOOR-LEVEL LAYOUTS

A third option is to simply run the trains on the floor. If you use G scale or Lionel-size three-rail track, this works almost as well as running them on a tabletop. Although, I do not recommend it for N scale, thousands of Japanese modelers use Kato and Tomy track for room-size layouts laid right on the floor in a single evening, operated on, then reboxed and returned to the individual members' homes. HO scale sectional track with built-in roadbed like Bachmann's E-Z Track, Life-Like's Power-Loc Track, Kato's Uni-Track, and Märklin's track work well enough on the floor if the floor is hardwood or tile, or has short-pile carpet. Atlas track is not rigid enough for use on the floor. Don't even try to use any HO track without ballast on the

2 This is a portion of Mel Johnson's 2 1/2x12-foot module re-creating a typical town on the Union Pacific Railroad in the 1930s. His layout is kept in operation at home along a shelf in a spare room. Mel belongs to a modular model railroad club, and his module is combined with others to create a larger (20x20-foot) oval layout for train shows and conventions.

floor. A compromise is to lay the track on a 4x6-foot board that you can store under a bed or upright in a walk-in closet.

LAYOUTS ON SHELVES

If you do not have an entire room available for a layout, you can build a wonderful layout along just two walls. At worst, try to find room for a 2x8-foot space for a modular portion of a larger layout. If you can negotiate for two, three, or four of the walls, build the layout on 4-, 6-, or 8-foot-long and 2-foot-wide shelves and bolt the ends of the shelves together so the layout is portable. Then, if the room must be vacated for guests or some other reason, the layout can be stored on edge in the garage.

3 The massive O scale layout of the Denver Model Railroad Club fills half the basement of Denver Union Terminal. Like many club layouts, this one has been in existence for over 50 years. It was recently rebuilt with new track and scenery techniques.

(Another choice is to build a 2x4-, 2x6-, or 2x8-foot modular railroad as described in Project 3.)

You can build a complete model railroad in any scale from N to G on a shelf as small as 1x4 feet. As a self-contained unit, however, this shelf can hold only enough track, even in N scale, for back-and-forth switching. For some folks, that's enough. It's a great game to move cars in and out of trains and to spot them (leave them off) or pick them up from industries. Small layouts like this are, in fact, the backbone of the hobby in Great Britain. The British have perfected the art of shelf-style layout designs. Many of their layouts are just 8 to 12 feet long and made from 2-, 3-, or 4-foot sections, each 12 to 24 inches wide. Usually, 2 or 3 feet of one extreme end are hidden with a false front and used as a "fiddle yard." Trains enter this yard from the visible portion of the layout and are rearranged or "fiddled" by hand to return the "next day" with a new consist.

If you're really stuck for space, consider building some dioramas depicting, for example, an industry, and two or three tracks on a 1x3-foot piece of 2-inch-thick blue insulation Styrofoam. Protect the edges with strips of 2-inch baseboard. The diorama can be completely detailed and someday it may become part of a larger layout. Many modelers build a dozen or more such dioramas before they ever find space for a complete layout.

PROJECT 3 • PORTABLE OR MODULAR?

 Time: Lifetime

 Tools: It's up to you

 Materials: Again, your choice

 Cost: $$$

 Talent: Novice

 Scales: HO, N, S, O and G

 Space: Between 2x4 feet and 60x100 feet

 Tip: First, discover whether your passion is for toy trains, model railroads, and/or real railroads.

 WHY: To watch 'em run and to run 'em

COMPLEMENTARY PROJECTS: 1, 2, 4 through 21, and 84 through 100

1 Tom Fetters is actually modeling another model railroad. He is re-creating the Delta Lines, a fictitious railroad that the late Frank Ellison built in O scale in the 1930s and 1940s. Ellison wrote about the Delta Lines in illustrated articles for *Model Railroader* and *Model Builder*, two magazines that are no longer published. Tom is building each of the famous Delta Lines' fictitious towns on roughly 1x6-foot modules, which he will link together in a permanent shelf-style, N scale layout.

Wise model railroaders design even the largest layouts so they can be disassembled for moving, because that just might happen. If you consider it likely you will move, you might want to design your layout so it can be easily disassembled and built in segments small enough so it can be transported, with each segment or unit light enough for just two people to carry. Project 3, then, is to decide the general shape of the layout. Do you want to run it around the walls on a shelf, for example, or would you rather it occupy a massive table in the center of the room?

Any model railroad that can be taken apart into movable segments can be considered "portable," even if it's "permanent." A modular model railroad, however, is designed so the individual segments or modules can be connected to a variety of other segments or modules, perhaps even ones built by others.

To make a modular layout design effective, then, the joining ends must be built to some standard so your module will interface with everyone else's module.

THE BEST SIZES FOR PORTABLE LAYOUT SEGMENTS

Usually, that means the layout should be divided into segments no larger than about 3x6 feet. A shelf-style layout placed around the walls of a room is the most preferable layout if you have a spare wall or two. Because the average person cannot reach more than about 3 feet, the maximum width of a shelf layout is limited. For maximum realism, however, the shelf layout should be placed at eye level so the horizon is just inches above the tabletop. At that height, you can only reach about 2 feet unless you stand on a stool. The maximum width of your shelf-style layout, then,

2 Steve Abernathy has re-created Juliette, Georgia, on the Southern Railway for this 4x4-foot outside-corner module. The module is operated as part of a group of other HO modules. The town was made famous in the movie *Fried Green Tomatoes*.

3 A small portion of an NTRAK layout at a National Model Railroad Association annual convention. Only about 40x40 feet of model railroad (about 20 modules) are visible — just a small segment of the massive layout. It is common for three or four 100-car trains to circulate these layouts at the same time.

should be between 2 and 3 feet. The length of the segments can be as much as 8 feet. You can fill any size room with these 6- to 8-foot-long shelves. If you can work completely around the room, you won't need anything wider than that 2 to 3 feet. If, however, you need to include reverse loops or turns, the "shelves" may need to be as wide as 5 feet for an HO scale layout.

The alternative is, of course, to build a freestanding table that you can walk around—or, at least, walk around three of its four sides. You can still divide a 4x8-foot layout into two 2x8-foot segments placed back-to-back to make it easier to move and store. If you want to operate the layout above a bed, consider 4x6 feet for a peninsula-style layout. You can then store the layout beneath the bed when it's not in use.

MODULAR MODEL RAILROADING

The alternative to the traditional model railroad club with its permanent layout is the modular model railroad club. Each member of the club builds his or her own segment or module of the whole layout. The modules are all built to precise dimensions and designs so the ends of any module will join (interface) with any other module. The modules are then used as "building blocks" to assemble an oval-shaped model railroad or, if there are enough modules, an N- or M-shaped layout. Modular layouts can be as small as 4x8 feet, but most are 8x12 or larger.

The largest group of modular layouts in the world belongs to members of NTRAK. These folks sometimes assemble layouts from modules owned by members who live in the same town, as well as at regional and national model railroad conventions and at shopping malls. These layouts can be 100x200 feet and larger, incorporating hundreds of modules 2x4 feet and larger. The simplicity of the design has caught on, and modules are currently ready to be combined into club-size layouts from all around the world. The NTRAK group is limited to N scale modeling, but hundreds of HO, S, and even O scale modelers have used the design to build their own modules. If you are going to build a modular model railroad, even if it's just a "portable" layout built of joined segments, purchase the *NTRAK Manual* for $1.50 and the *NTRAK How-To Book* on module construction for $10 (NTRAK, c/o John Cook, 15913 Brawner Drive, Dumfries, VA 22026-1416) to see how NTRAK does it.

HO, S, O, AND G SCALE MODULAR RAILROADS

There is no equivalent worldwide group of modular model railroaders in HO, S, O, or G scale. There are, however, clubs in nearly every major city that operate modular model railroads on the NTRAK concept—they simply limit their layouts to include only modules that belong to members. You can see examples of all sizes of modular model railroad club layouts, including NTRAK, at the National Model Railroad Association's annual conventions. The convention sites change from year to year, but you can obtain site, date, and registration information from the NMRA (4121 Cromwell Road, Chattanooga, TN 37421).

PROJECT 4 • SELECT CITY, MOUNTAINS, OR PLAINS

 Time: Lifetime

 Tools: Your choice

 Materials: Your choice

 Cost: $$$

 Talent: Novice

 Scales: HO, N, S, O and G

 Space: Between 6x10 inches and 60x100 feet

 Tip: Keep diverse scenes separated by backdrops—it's the transitions that eat up layout space.

 WHY: So you can see your trains in the environment of your dreams

COMPLEMENTARY PROJECTS: 1 through 3, 5 through 21, and 84 through 101

Decisions, decisions, decisions. Once you've decided what kind of trains you want and that you want them to be on a tabletop, the third decision is "Where?" Your model railroad needs a setting, a place or places that you can model with as much accuracy as you apply to the trains that you model to roll through that scenery. If you are a railroad prototype modeler, you have already selected a town or towns and the countryside where your selected real railroad ran, and you've probably even picked a year, if not an exact day, that you want to re-create. For most model railroaders, however, selecting a specific place can be a puzzle. Here are a few pros and cons.

1 John Hotvet located his 20x40-foot model railroad in the attic of his home. Like mo[st] experienced modelers, he built the benchwork to accommodate the hills he envisioned when he designed his track plan, thus allowing plenty of space for mounta[in] scenes like this one.

SCENERY FOR TOY TRAINS

If you are re-creating scenes of toy trains from your childhood, a simple winter village is the place to start. For these layouts, you can simply shop Christmas decoration and gift stores and select from an endless array of winter scenic material and buildings. Firms like Department 56 offer ceramic buildings that are about 1/64 scale, close enough for most three-rail layouts. Other companies offer slightly smaller buildings that can be used for HO scale. You can, of course, use any of the plastic buildings sold for "serious" HO, N, S, O, or G scale models and simply rest them on a layer of white felt to simulate snow. For snow, you can also use Woodland Scenics "Soft Flake Snow" or unscented talcum powder held in place with artist's matte medium.

MODELING MOUNTAINS

The first choice of many modelers is to set their railroad scenes in the mountains. Mountain railroading is truly spectacular, but it requires far more space than you might realize. Think about it: if a mountain slopes upward at 45 degrees, it's going to take a foot of tabletop for every foot it rises above or falls below the tracks. And 45 degrees is steep for a mountain. What many modelers do is make the slopes far steeper, often close to 90 degrees. A steep slope can be reasonably realistic if you texture it with a rock face so it looks like a cliff, but just how much of your layout do you want running along cliffs? Mountains are at their best on really large layouts with space for a 4- or 5-foot-wide "shelf" along the walls and peninsulas 10 feet or wider to allow space for the mountains to soar above the trains and cascade below the tracks.

FARMLANDS IN SCALE

Farmlands are nearly as difficult to model as mountains, but for exactly the opposite reason: there's no place to disguise the horizon. If you want to re-create flatlands, build your layout on shelves that are near eye level so the rear edge of the layout really is the horizon. One solution is explained in Project 91. For maximum realism, you will still need some type of subroadbed to elevate the tracks 20 scale feet or more above the tabletop.

THE CITY AS SCENERY

If you really want to cram a lot of scenery into a relatively shallow shelf, model a city. The industries, stores, offices, and apartments can be as high as you like to effectively disguise the horizon, and they can require as little as 3 or 4 inches of depth. You can even elevate adjacent tracks on stone or steel viaducts to squeeze in more track.

ROLLING HILL HEAVEN

For most modelers, rolling hills are the scenic treatment of choice. Rolling hills happen to be the places where most real railroads are located for the simple reason that there are more of them in the places where real railroads are built. Rolling hills can be covered with woods or, if the hills slope gently enough, with farms. Usually, railroads cut right through the hills, then built embankments and bridges across the valleys, all of which makes for extremely interesting scenery that can easily fit on a 2-foot shelf. If you elevate the layout to near eye level, the horizon can be filled with rows of trees or even fences to disguise the point where you reach the end of your "world."

SCENIC CREDIBILITY

If you choose to re-create a real scene for a specific real railroad at a specific point in time, you will already have the basic research you need to make the scene realistic. Few model railroaders, however, care that much about re-creating reality. Still, you want your scenery to look like the real world—and there's no other place to research how it should look than in the real world. Find photographs of real-world areas that are similar to what you want to model and keep them available, even when you are planning your railroad, so you know how much table space the scenery will require. Use color photos, so you can match the colors with the scenic materials you buy. It does take a bit more effort than sprinkling green sawdust on plywood, but the results are worth the effort.

2 Jim Nelson's 10x22-foot N scale layout re-creates a typical midsize Midwestern town on the Milwaukee Road. The yard occupies the center of the room on a peninsula, while the mainline is built on foot-wide shelves around all four walls of the room.

3 Robert Mohr's N scale city scene occupies just 2x4 feet of space and is a portable NTRAK module as described in Project 3. Most of the buildings are plastic kits.

4 Lee Nicholas' 30x33-foot Utah, Colorado & Western HO scale layout features a mountain section with virtually floor-to-ceiling scenery. For a scene like this, you must design the benchwork as carefully as you design the track plan.

SECTION TWO
BENCHWORK

A model railroad really begins with the tables that support the track. Modelers call this the "benchwork." It's most often configured to match the flow of the tracks, with little consideration to retaining conventional table sizes or shapes. The methods of constructing benchwork are as varied as the modelers themselves. Some simply use shelf brackets to hang 2-foot-wide shelves from the walls, while others build benchwork that could support an outside deck or sun porch. The rule is simple: there is no rule. Build what is comfortable for you. One word of advice, however: do consider placing the tracks as close to eye level as possible and build the benchwork accordingly. All model railroads look more like the real thing when viewed from angles closest to those we have when watching real trains in action

One of the NTRAK-style modules that are part of the Northern Virginia club layout.

PROJECT 5 • DESIGN AND CONSTRUCT A WOODEN TABLE

Time: 4 to 400 hours

Tools: Electric drill, bits and pilot bits, power screwdriver, square, power saw, measuring tape, pencil, spirit level, Crescent wrench, and hammer

Materials: Your choice of 1x2, 1x3, or 1x4 and 2x2 or 2x4 lumber; 1/2-inch plywood; and 2-inch extruded polystyrene insulation board

Cost: $$

Talent: Beginner

Scales: HO, N, S, O and G

Space: Between 2x4 and 60x100 feet

Tip: Build no table larger or heavier, even with plaster scenery, than two people can easily lift. That's usually between 2x4 and 3x6 feet.

WHY: To elevate the trains so you see them from the same vantage point you see real trains

COMPLEMENTARY PROJECTS: 1 through 4, 6 through 21, and 84 through 101

1 Ed Patrone built the open-grid benchwork (upper left) for his layout after he had perfected a track plan. The track itself is supported on 1/2-inch plywood just wide enough to provide roadbed shoulders. The plywood is elevated above the actual benchwork or tabletop on 1x4 risers to leave room for bridges and fills. Like many experienced modelers, he installed all the roadbed and all the track to be sure everything ran perfectly. He then started on the scenery and structures, completing a "doable" segment of the layout each year or so. The trestle shown in Project 1 and the waterfall scene in Project 92 are parts of this layout.

You *can* operate your model railroad on the floor. If you chose G scale, you can even operate it outdoors. Most model railroaders, however, operate their trains on indoor tabletops. If you are going to mount the track on a tabletop, try to support the tabletop so the tracks are somewhere near eye level and you can see the models from the same vantage point that you view the real railroads. You will, then, need some kind of legs to support the tabletop and something to support the legs. Model railroaders refer to the supporting structure as "benchwork," because they often cut away the tabletop from all the areas where there is no track or buildings to make it easier to build mountains and valleys.

REALISTIC RIGHTS-OF-WAY

Model railroad tracks look far more realistic if you support them with just enough flat area on either side of the ballast to re-create the shape of real railroad rights-of-way. Most real railroads provide about 10 feet of flat area extending out from the bottom edges of the ballast. Usually, there is then an embankment of 10 or more feet elevating the tracks and ballast above ground level, even on the "flat" floor of the desert. In fact, that slope on either side of the tracks is even used in places where the railroad cuts through hills and tunnels—the extra space is needed so the cars and locomotives won't rub the sides of the cut or tunnel walls.

BENCHWORK BY DESIGN

Plan the benchwork to support the track and, even more importantly, plan it so there is enough room for scenery on both sides of the track. On an around-the-wall layout, the benchwork can vary in width from as little as 1 foot to as much as 6 feet. You should also give some thought to places where you might want high bridges. The benchwork is really there to support the track, but, in many cases, it

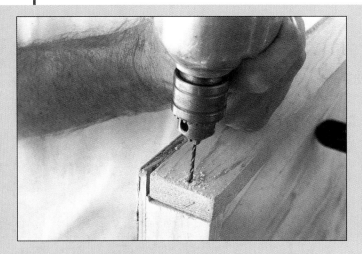

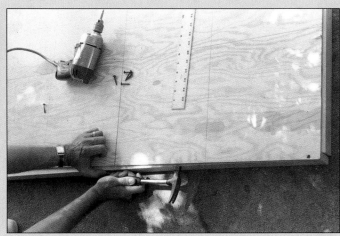

2 Use a piece of plywood (or a perfectly flat floor) when aligning each joint and predrill pilot holes for the screws. Secure each corner joint with number 8x1 1/2-inch Phillips flathead screws and a power screwdriver.

3 Use a carpenter's square or the tabletop itself (shown) to align each corner. Tap the framework to get it into perfect alignment before adding the cross braces that divide the area into 2x2-foot or smaller rectangles, making up the "egg crate" design.

needs to support the scenery as well. If you are planning a mountain railroad, decide now where you want the scenery to reach all the way to the floor.

OPEN-GRID BENCHWORK

The proven design for benchwork is simply to create a framework for the table from 1x2 boards for a layout 2x4 feet or smaller, 1x3 boards for a layout 2x6 feet or smaller, or 1x4 boards for anything larger. Place the boards on edge to create a frame. Add a grid inside to divide it into boxes no smaller than 2x2 feet. The finished product is called "open-grid" benchwork for obvious reasons. The boxes certainly do not have to have square corners anywhere but in the actual corners of the room. In fact, you may, for example, want the benchwork to angle inward or outward to more or less match the path of the track.

LAYOUTS IN SEGMENTS

What if you want to make a peninsula-style model railroad that's 8x18 feet to fill a single-car garage? No one is going to be able to lift anything that large with anything smaller than a crane and flatbed trailer. When you build the benchwork, spend some time designing it so it can be built in egg-crate style boxes no larger than 3x6 feet. You might build six 3x6-foot boxes and join them together side-by-side to make a 6x18-foot table.

Then build three more boxes, each 2x6 feet, and join them end-to-end to make a 2x18-foot table. Finally, join the 6x18 table and the 2x18 table along the 18-foot edge. Use stove bolts with nuts and flat washers to join the tables.

BUILDING THE BENCHWORK

I've spent some time explaining why you need to plan the benchwork; now it's time to build. Use a power table saw to make the cuts or, if you must, use a hand-held power saw or even just a handsaw, carefully marking the cuts with a square and pencil so the joints will be square and true. Decide which edge of each open grid will be the front and cut the front and back pieces full-length. Deduct twice the thickness of the wood from the crosspieces to make the egg-crate style 2x2-foot or smaller openings, and cut them to size.

Always use wood screws to assemble benchwork so you can remove them without disturbing the rest of the layout. I find number 8x1 1/4-inch Phillips flathead screws work well, but you may have your own favorite. Buy a pilot bit for an electric drill, and use it to drill a pilot hole for each screw to minimize the chances of splitting the wood. You may find that an electric screwdriver has the power you need to drive these screws, but I find a push-style Yankee screwdriver to work as quickly as an electric screw-

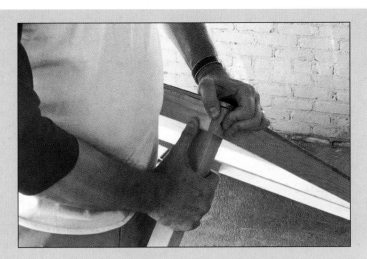

4 Legs made from 2x2 stock are strong enough, especially if you add 1x2 diagonal braces. Attach the legs to the benchwork with 3 1/2-inch carriage bolts, flat washers, and nuts.

driver and with far more torque and power. Try to find a perfectly flat and level portion of a garage or patio floor on which to assemble each segment of the benchwork so that you know it is square.

You can use this open grid to support the tabletop that, in turn, will support the track. The tabletop itself can be 1/2-inch plywood, but I do not recommend particle board or even MDF board, both of which can sag if you don't support it every foot or so. If you are using plywood, elevate it at least 2 inches, and preferably 6 or more inches, from the tabletop, using 1/2-inch-thick risers the width of the right-of-way. You can cut all the plywood from the tabletop except where it is beneath the tracks and where you will want flat surfaces to support buildings. An alternative to the plywood and risers is to use two or three layers of 2-inch blue extruded Styrofoam insulation board placed on top of the open-grid benchwork for both scenery and roadbed. This approach is described in Projects 6 and 11.

The legs can be 2x2 or 2x4 lumber attached to the 1x2, 1x3, or 1x4 with 3 1/2-inch carriage bolts, flat washers, and nuts. Use a Crescent wrench to turn the carriage bolts in or out to raise or lower the legs. Lock the bolts in place with the nuts. If you are building a shelf layout, you may be able to attach the layout to the wall with angled supports made of 1x2 boards. The back edges of the benchwork and the 1x2 angled support legs can be fastened to the wooden wall joists with screws or to a concrete wall with bolts and anchors.

PROJECT 6 • BUILD A STYROFOAM LAYOUT BASE

 Time: 4 to 400 hours

 Tools: A Woodland Scenics hot-wire foam cutter, Premium Concepts Tippi hot foam cutter, or a hacksaw blade and holder; Liquid Nails "Projects and Foamboard" cement or Chem Rex PL300 Foam Board Adhesive; and a caulking gun

 Materials: 2-inch extruded polystyrene insulation board

 Cost: $$

 Talent: Beginner

 Scales: HO, N, S, O and G

 Space: Between 2x4 and 60x100 feet

 Tip: Keep a vacuum cleaner and hose handy to remove the nearly weightless foam dust and scraps. Be sure to use extruded, not expanded, polystyrene insulation board.

? **WHY:** To provide the lightest possible tabletop for a portable model railroad

COMPLEMENTARY PROJECTS: 1 through 5, 7 through 21, and 84 through 101

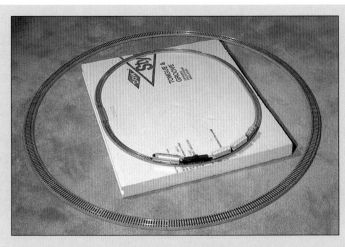

1 A 2-inch-thick piece of 24x30-inch extruded polystyrene insulation board makes a self-contained layout for an oval of N scale track. Protect the edges with strips of 2-inch wooden baseboard cemented to the insulation board.

The benchwork provides the structure to elevate a model railroad from the floor to near eye level. There is, however, a lot more to building a realistic model railroad than simply slapping a piece of 1/2-inch plywood on top of the benchwork. That plywood really should be elevated at least 2 inches above the top of the benchwork to leave room for fills and bridges. That means you have to add 1/2-inch plywood or 1x4 vertical "risers" to prop the plywood 2 inches or more above the benchwork. You can, however, skip right from the benchwork to the track by covering the open-grid benchwork from Project 5 with one, two, or three layers of 2-inch-thick extruded polystyrene.

SELECTING THE RIGHT INSULATION BOARD

The most common types of extruded polystyrene are the blue boards sold under Dow Corning's Styrofoam label, but there are other brands and other colors. Do not use the white "expanded polystyrene" or "beadboard" because it has virtually no strength. Extruded polystyrene boards are usually sold in 2x8- and 2x10-foot sizes in 1- or 2-inch thicknesses. If you need more than 2 inches, you can laminate two or more layers. Be warned, however, that some cement will melt insulation board. I use Liquid Nails "Projects and Foamboard" cement or Chem Rex PL300 Foam Board Adhesive, applied with a caulking gun, both to cement Styrofoam to Styrofoam and track or ballast strips to Styrofoam.

A STYROFOAM LAYOUT

Styrofoam is strong enough to be self-supporting up to about 2x4 feet. The edges are easily chipped, however, and should be protected with 2-inch-wide baseboard molding, which can be

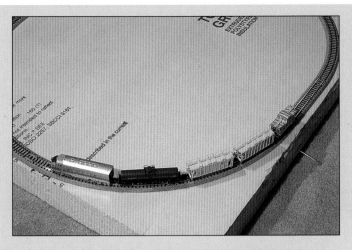

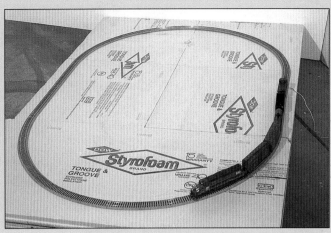

2 This N scale train is running on Bachmann's E-Z Track with built-in ballast. You can cement simple ties-and-rails sectional track directly to the insulation board and carve your own ballast shoulders as shown in Project 7. This track is really too close to the edge of the "table" to leave much room for scenery, but it makes one of the easiest imaginable "starter" layouts, because you can carve the insulation board to create scenery, as shown in Project 85.

3 This 4x6-foot HO scale model railroad is built on two 2-inch-thick layers of Dow Corning Styrofoam extruded polystyrene insulation board. The bottom layer is two 2x6-foot pieces cemented side-by-side, and the top layer is three 2x4-foot pieces with two of the pieces placed at right angles to the bottom layer to provide extra strength. Although the edges are fragile and should be protected with thin strips of wood, the tabletop itself is strong enough to be self-supporting. It can be placed on a bed, a couple of a card tables, sawhorses, or a lightweight open-grid benchwork, as described in Project 5.

cemented to the Styrofoam. You can also lay track with built-in ballast (described in Projects 9 and 10) directly onto the surface of the insulation board. You can even cement plain ties-and-rails sectional track, flex track, and turnouts directly to the surface of the insulation board. You can then carve your own ballast shoulders and roadbed shelves with a hot knife as shown in Project 11.

Cut the Styrofoam insulation board with a hacksaw blade in a handle or wrapped with tape to protect your hand, and use a steel ruler or straight piece of wood to guide the saw. Cutting will produce a dust that is virtually weightless and electrostatically charged, so it clings to everything. Have a vacuum cleaner with a hose attachment handy to remove the dust as quickly as you make it. You can also use a hot-wire cutter made by Woodland Scenics or Premium Concepts to make dust-free cuts.

STYROFOAM SCENERY

If you place enough Styrofoam on top of the benchwork, you can use it to carve the roadbed shoulders and any scenery that slopes below track level. This is the time to plan for that below-track-level scenery, so you can cover the benchwork with as many layers of the Styrofoam as you need to allow you to cut the fills and valleys later. If you need more than 4 to 6 inches of Styrofoam, you should modify the benchwork in those areas to provide support for the lowest edges of the scenery, like the floor-level scenery on Lee Nicholas' layout, illustrated in Project 4.

BENCHWORK

PROJECT 7 • MAKE A TRAMMEL FOR TRUE CURVES

Time: 30 minutes

Tools: Hammer

Materials: 1/4x1-inch lath or yardstick, finishing nail, and pencil

Cost: $

Talent: Beginner

Scales: HO, N, S, O and G

Space: None

Tip: Hold the pencil firmly so it transcribes a smooth arc.

WHY: To be certain that all curves, even those assembled for sectional track, are smooth and kinkless

COMPLEMENTARY PROJECTS: 1 through 6, 8 through 21, and 84 through 101

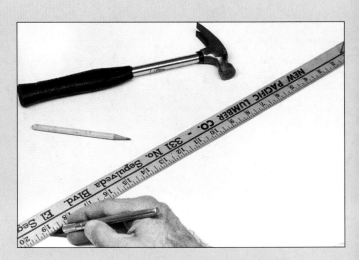

1 Pound a finishing nail through the center of the lath or yardstick, exactly 1 inch from the end. That's it. You've made a trammel.

One of the more delightful sights you see when watching a real railroad and its miniature in action is that of a train rolling smoothly from a straight into a large, sweeping curve. Conversely, one of the things that makes even the best-detailed model railroad look like a toy is a train that lurches and staggers through a curve.

If you use flexible track, it is absolutely necessary to provide a pencil line to locate at least the centerline of the track before you cement it (or the ballast support) to the subroadbed or tabletop. It's easy enough to make a tool for marking accurate curves; it is really just a large drafting compass, but it is generally referred to as a trammel.

Make the trammel from a piece of 1/4x1-inch lath or one of the giveaway yardsticks available at some lumberyards and fabric stores. The trammel must be long enough to include your largest radius curve, so the yardstick will really only be useful for 35-inch and smaller radius curves, allowing for the fact that the finishing nail is pounded through the yardstick at the 1-inch mark. If you need larger radii, buy a piece of lath long enough for those curves.

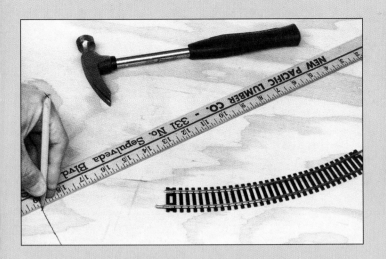

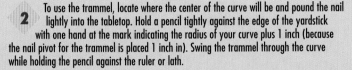

2 To use the trammel, locate where the center of the curve will be and pound the nail lightly into the tabletop. Hold a pencil tightly against the edge of the yardstick with one hand at the mark indicating the radius of your curve plus 1 inch (because the nail pivot for the trammel is placed 1 inch in). Swing the trammel through the curve while holding the pencil against the ruler or lath.

3 If you use simple ties-and-rails sectional track or flex track, you can mark the centerline of the track. But if you use track with built-in ballast, like that shown in Projects 9 and 10, you may want to mark the outside of the ballast shoulder rather than the centerline. Measure the width of the ballast and divide by two, then add that to the "nominal" radius of the curve. Use that dimension as the actual radius you mark on the tabletop with the trammel.

PROJECT 8 • BUILD GRADES WITH WOODLAND SCENICS SYSTEMS

Time: 4 to 400 hours

Tools: A Woodland Scenics Low Temp Foam Glue Gun, Liquid Nails "Projects and Foamboard" cement, or Chem Rex PL300 Foam Board Adhesive

Materials: Woodland Scenics Risers and Inclines

Cost: $$$

Talent: Novice

Scales: HO, N, S, O and G

Space: Between 2x4 and 60x100 feet

Tip: Be sure the track locations are accurately marked on the tabletop.

WHY: To make upgrades and downgrades as easily as possible on a flat tabletop

COMPLEMENTARY PROJECTS: 1 through 7, 9 through 21, and 84 through 101

1 Begin construction by positioning all of the track carefully on a flat tabletop. Next, mark both edges of the track so you can position the Risers and Inclines with the track centered on them. This step is critical because you can't move the Risers and Inclines to correct track alignment; all you can do is move the track slightly from side to side on top of the Riser and Inclines. Hold the Risers and Inclines in place with T-pins from a fabric store or with Woodland Scenics pins. Cement them to the tabletop or to each other with either a Styrofoam-friendly cement like Liquid Nails "Projects and Foamboard" cement or Chem Rex PL300 Foam Board Adhesive.

One of the more complex aspects of building a model railroad is including what railroads call "grades"—the uphills and downhills. With the open-grid style benchwork described in Project 5, it is possible to tilt the roadbed up on the vertical risers that are recommended with this type of construction. If you are using a flat tabletop, particularly one made of extruded polystyrene insulation board like that described in Project 11, upgrades and downgrades can be difficult to use.

THE SUB-TERRAIN SYSTEM

Woodland Scenics sells a vast array of supplies, from ground foam for textures to complete trees and rock molds. They have developed a scenery system that utilizes a traditional model railroad material, Hydrocal plaster–soaked gauze, to make a thin shell and relatively lightweight surfaces for hills, mountains, and valleys. They have also adapted this material to a layout construction system that starts with a flat tabletop—and that's where we started. Woodland Scenics Risers and Inclines are 2 1/2 inches wide, just enough to support the ballast shoulders *and* leave a few scale feet of flat surface on either side of the ballast for the roadbed profiles preferred by real railroads. For passing sidings or double-track line, simply use two Risers and Inclines side-by-side.

The Risers and Inclines are both made of expanded polystyrene (the "beadboard" material), but the material used by Woodland Scenics is somewhat stronger than typical beadboard. The Risers and Inclines are zigzag shaped when viewed from

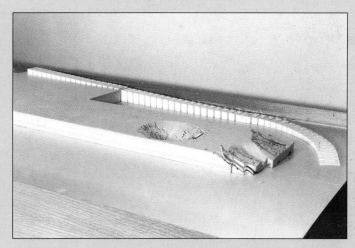

2 If you prefer a quicker joint, you can use the Woodland Scenics special Low Temp Glue Gun and Woodland Scenics glue sticks to cement the Risers and Inclines to the tabletop and to each other.

3 If you want to use the Woodland Scenics Inclines in combination with 2-inch-thick pieces of extruded polystyrene, you can start with the track on the tabletop and use the Inclines to elevate the track 2 inches. Add another piece of 2-inch-thick polystyrene and start with zero-elevation Risers and Inclines to resume the uphill climb.

the top down, so they can be positioned to match any curve or straight.

The Risers are intended to raise level track above the tabletop to an elevation that provides the necessary room for fills and bridges over streams and rivers. There's a choice of 1/2-, 1-, 2-, and 4-inch Risers and Inclines; I recommend starting with the 4-inch variety and going up from there.

The Inclines are tapered to produce uphill grades. You have a choice of 2, 3, and 4 percent grades. Unless you are modeling an industrial railroad, like a logging road, I recommend the 2 percent inclines.

When the layout is complete, including scenery, it will weigh much less than a layout built with conventional plywood roadbed and wooden risers. The layout can be even lighter if you use a thin 1/4-inch

plywood top for the table and 1x2 boards to frame the tabletop. Since this tabletop assembly will not be disturbed, you can both glue and screw it together for extra strength.

You can also use one or two 2-inch-thick layers of extruded polystyrene insulation board like the blue Styrofoam panels for the tabletop. You need to protect the outer edges of the layout anyway, so you can protect the outer edges of the blue Styrofoam while you protect the Woodland Scenics scenery, using 1/8-inch plywood for an outer facing or fascia around the edges of the layout. This fascia should extend to the bottom of the tabletop with top edges cut to match the scenery profiles at the edges of the table. The system can be used on shelf-style layouts, but it is most effective on small portable layouts where weight is a factor worth considering.

5 Use either conventional cork roadbed with sectional track or flex track. Just cement the cork to the tops of the Risers or Inclines, then use the same material to attach the track.

4 Woodland Scenics offers 1x2-foot pieces of white expanded polystyrene sheets in 1/4-, 1/2-, 1-, 2-, 3-, and 4-inch thicknesses. You can use this material to create elevated platforms for industrial sights (lower left) or as the tops of tunnels (upper, right). Shape the mountains and valleys with wadded-up newspapers.

6 The Sub-Terrain system is even easier to use if you opt for the sectional track with built-in ballast described in Project 9. Woodland Scenics recommends that you use its Plaster Cloth, a gauze impregnated with dry Hydrocal plaster. You can apply the material with the track in place, but Woodland Scenics recommends that you remove the track, so you can wrap the plaster over the tops of the Risers and Inclines. This method produces a much stronger system, and there's no chance of dribbling plaster onto the tracks.

7 When the plaster has dried, block-sand the roadbed so it is perfectly flat. Use a piece of 2x4 as a sanding block and start with coarse sandpaper. Be prepared for lots of dust—you'll be removing up to 1/4 inch of plaster in places. Use a ruler to determine if the tops of the Riser and Inclines are flat and, when you are satisfied, cement the roadbed in place and finish the scenery as described in Projects 85 through 97.

SECTION THREE
LAYING TRACK

In the 1950s and 1960s, the "expert" model railroaders used individual scale-size spikes and wooden ties to lay track just about the same way the real railroads still do. Few modelers have the patience for hand-spiked track today—in any case, most of the of flexible track with plastic ties available today is far more realistic than anything you could lay yourself. Most modelers use some type of sectional track that is assembled, domino-style, into the finished layout by simply snapping one piece of track into the next. That's the easy way. It's even easier if you use the track with built-in ballast like that used in Projects 9 and 10. For really smooth-flowing curves, however, consider using flexible track in 3-foot lengths, cutting the track as needed and bending it into smooth curves with transitions or spirals from straight into the actual curve radius.

James Schall and Phil Brooks' 3x12-foot NTRAK module set.

PROJECT 9 • SELECT TRACK YOU CAN TRUST

Time: 5 minutes or more

Tools: Your hands

Materials: Bachmann E-Z Track, Life-Like Power-Loc Track, Kato Uni-Track, Märklin C-Track, or Atlas True-Track

Cost: $$

Talent: Beginner

Scales: HO, N, S, O and G

Space: Between 1x2 and 60x100 feet

Tip: As you assemble the track, inspect every rail-to-rail joint to ensure alignment.

? **WHY:** To lay track in minutes instead of weeks

COMPLEMENTARY PROJECTS: 5 through 8 and 10 through 16

1 Track with built-in ballast makes it easy to assemble a model railroad. These are the N scale track sections from (left to right) Kato, Bachmann, and Life-Like, along with a piece of standard ties-and-rails sectional track.

The hobby of HO scale model railroading changed drastically in 1995 when Bachmann introduced its E-Z Track with built-in plastic ballast. Prior to that, nearly every train set and most model railroads were assembled from plastic track that consisted of nothing more than plastic ties and two rails. That track found its way into millions of HO scale train sets—sets that were destined to be operated on the floor.

FLOOR OR TABLETOP?

The tie-and-rail sectional track that used to be included in HO scale train sets was never designed to be used on the floor—it was designed, in the 1960s, to be used on tabletops. Unfortunately, mil-lions of frustrated moms, dads, and kids simply chucked their HO train sets in the trash because the track was so frustrating to use. That curse is no more. The E-Z Track is only a bit more costly than the older track and it snaps together firmly enough so you can use it on a hardwood or tile floor, or on short-pile carpeting.

Kato Uni-Track is similar to E-Z Track and has been available for decades, but is more costly (and much more realistic); Märklin's C-Track is even more costly, and even more realistic. Life-Like produces Power-Loc Track, which matches the quality and price of E-Z Track, but is offered in a more limited choice of track sections. Life-Like does, however, make an adapter track so you can adapt its track to E-Z Track, or even to conventional ties-and-rails plastic sectional track. Atlas offers True-Track with snap-in ballast, but the interlocking system is not strong enough to hold the track much better than rail joiners. The Atlas True-Track system is, however, a quick and clean way to have ballast beneath the rails, plus it's the most realistic of the sectional tracks.

ASSEMBLING SNAP-TOGETHER TRACK

You wouldn't think you'd need instructions to snap track sections together. Unfortunately, none of

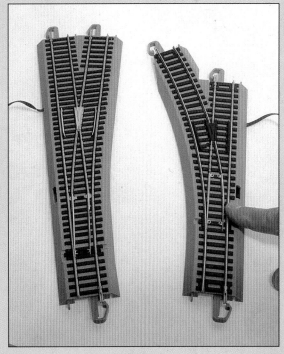

2 HO scale track with built-in ballast includes (left to right) Atlas True-Track, Kato Uni-Track, Märklin C-Track, Bachmann E-Z Track with nickel silver rail and gray ballast, Bachmann E-Z Track with plated-steel rail and black ballast, and Life-Like Power-Loc track.

3 The "toy" turnouts (right) from E-Z Track and Power-Loc can be used to replace either a standard train set's 18-inch-radius curve or 9-inch straight, but they cause large locomotives and longer cars to derail through the curved route. The E-Z Track number 5 turnout (left) allows just about any size locomotive or car to operate without derailing, but it is more complex to include in a layout.

the brands really fit tightly unless you are extremely careful with the assembly process. Kato's Uni-Track and Märklin's C-Track are the easiest to assemble—just be sure they click tightly at each joint. Uni-Track and C-Track joints are not, however, as strong as those on E-Z Track and Power-Loc Track, so be careful if you try to shift the track around, especially on carpet.

Life-Like's Power-Loc Track has a very tight locking system and is, perhaps, the strongest of the lot. It takes more force than you might realize, however, to get the Power-Loc Track snapped completely tight—there's a "feeling" that you've got the track snapped together when there's still a tiny fraction to go. You can check the alignment by holding the rails to your eye and sighting down the track to see if the joint is perfectly smooth.

Atlas True-Track features a removable ballast strip with interlocking tabs. The ballast provides the same insulation from dust and lint as the other brands of track with built-in ballast, but the True-Track joints are only slightly stronger than those with bare track and ties. True-Track works best on a tabletop, not the floor.

Bachmann's E-Z Track relies on rail joiners to connect the rails (as does True-Track), but has a firm snap system to hold the ballast together. In addition, the track is bonded to the ballast. As a result, you must assemble the track with the same care with which you would assemble the older ties-and-rails track, carefully aligning both rail joiners and each joint as you push the track together. It is very easy to get a rail joiner to slip beneath a rail rather than grabbing the edges of the rail. In some cases, you might need to pry the rail joiner apart slightly with needle-nose pliers to get it to slide onto the rail. I recommend using the needle-nose pliers to squeeze every rail joint tight after the layout is assembled.

MORE REALISTIC TRACK

Initially, Bachmann offered only E-Z Track with solid-black ballast in 18- and 22-inch radii with right or left "toy" turnouts. Later, they introduced a slightly more expensive series with nickel silver instead of plated-steel rail, and gray ballast with black ties. More recently, E-Z Track has become available with number 5 turnouts and 33 1/4 -and 35 1/2-inch-radius curves. The new sections make it practical to use E-Z Track for permanent layouts in which the large-radius curves are more realistic. In addition, Kato and Märklin offer an even wider range of track sections and turnouts, making these brands excellent choices for tabletop layouts.

LAYING TRACK

PROJECT 10 • TRICKS WITH E-Z TRACK TURNOUTS

Time: 5 minutes or more

Tools: Needle-nose pliers to tighten rail joints

Materials: Bachmann E-Z Track number 5 right-hand and left-hand turnouts

Cost: $$

Talent: Novice

Scales: HO

Space: Between 1x2 and 60x100 feet

Tip: Sight down the tracks, with the side of your head laying on the rails, to be sure each joint is smooth.

WHY: To allow larger diesel and steam locomotives to operate on a layout built with Bachmann's E-Z Track

COMPLEMENTARY PROJECTS: 5 through 8 and 10 through 16

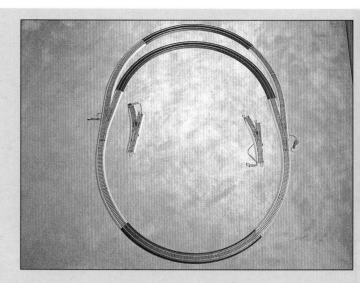

1 You can add a passing siding to an oval layout made with 18-inch curves by installing a right and left pair of E-Z Track number 5 turnouts with just five pieces of 18-inch curve on the inside. On the outside track, use two pieces of 22-inch curve on the right and left with three pieces of 18-inch curve in the center. The curves must be installed as shown to avoid kinks between the rail joints that will cause derailments. The 18-inch curves have black ballast to make it easier to see where they are located. This oval is about 2 1/2 inches wider than an oval made from just 18-inch-radius curves.

There's a major problem with the "toy" turnouts from just about any HO scale track manufacturer: they're designed to replace a single piece of 18-inch-radius curved track and/or a piece of 9-inch straight track. Toy turnouts make it simple to add a turnout to any layout assembled with those 18-inch curves that are standard in nearly every train set. Toy turnouts also work fine with short diesels that have no more than eight wheels, or with short steam locomotives, but larger diesels (with 12 wheels) and larger steam locomotives will derail while traveling through the curved route of a toy turnout.

Bachmann's E-Z Track number 5 turnouts solve that problem, allowing you to run just about anything but those massive imported brass articulated steam locomotives like the Union Pacific 4-8-8-4. You can also operate plastic-bodied ready-to-run articulateds, including Märklin's 4-8-8-4 "Big Boy," the Proto 2000 2-8-8-2, and any of the Rivarossi articulateds, through the number 5 turnouts.

REVISING THE HISTORY OF TRACK PLANS

I designed a number of layouts for volumes I and II of *Model Railroading Made "E-Z" with Bachmann's E-Z Track System* (both published by Bachmann) and for the *HO Scale Model Railroading Handbook*. No number 5 turnout was available at the time any of these books were printed, so the only solution was to limit the locomotives to eight-wheeled diesels and short steam locomotives that would not derail passing through the curved route of the "toy" turnouts.

It is possible to revise many of the plans in the three books I listed (as well as similar plans from Atlas and Life-Like) to incorporate number 5 turnouts. The number 5 turnout has the same connecting ends as all other E-Z Track, but its geometry does not match that

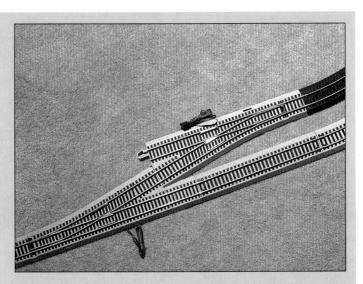

2 Bachmann E-Z Track number 5 turnouts are available as individual turnouts as well as in one-piece crossovers. The crossovers can be used to connect an inner oval of 18-inch-radius curved track with an outer oval of 22-inch-radius curved track. However, a short piece of straight track may be needed in the 18-inch curve to get the track to align perfectly.

the curve) are needed to compensate for the different geometry of the number 5 turnouts.

CROSSOVERS FROM INNER TO OUTER OVALS

The Burlington Northern layout also uses an unusual arrangement of two turnouts to make the crossover from the inner to the outer oval. You can use the crossover configuration shown in the photograph (again the 18-inch curves have black ballast, and the 22-inch curves have gray ballast) to assemble a similar inner and outer oval with E-Z Track number 5 turnouts. Note that the outer oval is assembled from only 22-inch-radius curves.

Things get a lot more complicated if you insist on replacing a piece of curved track with a number 5 turnout, because the geometry of the curved path through the number 5 really doesn't match the 18-inch curves. The curved path through the E-Z Track number 5 turnout is close to half the length of an E-Z Track 22-inch-radius curve. Fortunately, Bachmann offers short sections of 22-inch-radius curved track to fill the gaps. To replace an 18-inch curve, cut two 1/3-length pieces of 22-inch-radius curve (about 2 7/8 inches measured across the centerline of the track at the chord of the curve) to adjust for the difference between the 22 1/2 degrees of a 22-inch-radius curved track section and the 30 degrees of an 18-inch-radius curve track section. Insert a single piece of 22-inch curve and one of the 1/3-length 22-inch curves in the oval directly opposite the place where you install the number 5 turnout. The second 1/3 curve is needed at the curve of the number 5 turnout.

NUMBER 5 TURNOUTS ON STRAIGHT TRACK

If all this sounds too complicated, don't do it. Locate the number 5 turnouts along straight segments of the layout where you can simply replace a piece of straight track with the number 5 turnout. Actually, the number 5 turnout is 11 1/2 inches long, so it replaces about 1 3/4 track sections—you can remove two standard straights and install a number 5 turnout plus a 2 1/4-inch quarter-length straight and a 4 1/2-inch half-length straight. (Bachmann offers both quarter-length and half-length straights.) The resulting 18 1/4 inches is usually close enough to the length of two 9-inch straights.

of the "standard" train set's 9-inch straights and 18-inch curves with turnouts to match. There will, then, be some very slight rail misalignment when you incorporate number 5 turnouts into a layout made with E-Z Track 18- and 22-inch-radius curves, but you can push that misalignment into the joints between the 22-inch curves to minimize the chance of derailment.

The most complex layout in any of these books is the Burlington Northern layout in the *HO Scale Model Railroading Handbook*. That layout utilizes 14 toy turnouts. You can replace most of the turnouts that provide passing sidings on the inner and outer loops using a combination of 18- and 22-inch-radius curves as shown in this project. (The black curved track sections are 18-inch radius, and the gray ones are 22-inch radius to make them easier to see; both sizes are available with gray ballast.) Note that a combination of four 22-inch curves (two on each side of the curve) and three 18-inch-radius curves (all in the middle of

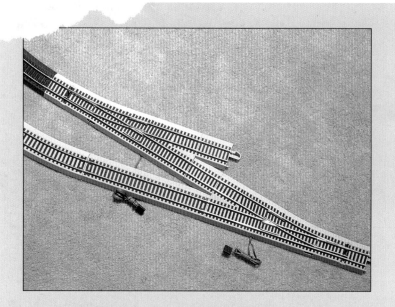

3 You can install a pair of crossovers between an inner oval with 18-inch radius as shown. Note that the crossover utilizes a right and a left rather than two right-hand turnouts—the curved route of the turnout is used to lead into the inner oval. Use five 18-inch-radius curves on the end of the inner oval and eight 22-inch-radius curves for the outer oval.

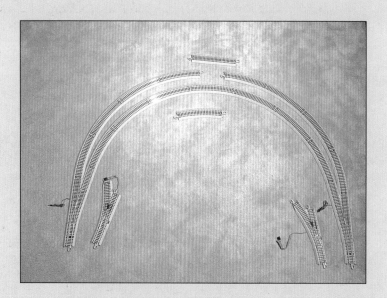

4 The number 5 turnouts are a bit easier to use with 22-inch-radius curved track sections than with 18-inch-radius curves. You need a half-length straight (4 1/2 inches) to fill in the gap in the outer oval. Bachmann does offer these half-length straights.

PROJECT 11 • LAY TRACK ON STYROFOAM

Time: 30 minutes or more

Tools: Pencil and razor saw

Materials: Track with plastic ties and rails or with built-in plastic ballast; Liquid Nails "Projects and Foamboard" cement, or Chem Rex PL300 Foam Board Adhesive; and a caulking gun

Cost: $$

Talent: Beginner and Novice

Scales: HO, N, S and O

Space: Between 1x2 and 60x100 feet

Tip: Test-run the entire layout for a month or more to be sure the track really is where you want it.

WHY: To create a model railroad right-of-way that is realistic with a minimum of mess or effort

COMPLEMENTARY PROJECTS: 5 through 10, 12 through 16, and 85

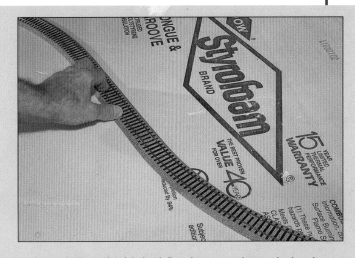

1 Use either track with built-in ballast (shown) or simple ties-and-rails track. Position the track carefully and hold it in place with a few nails so you can test-run the system to be certain the track is precisely where you want it.

The lightweight construction methods described in Project 6 provide a layout base that is soft enough to be carved with a knife. The obvious advantage of a tabletop that you can carve into is that it makes it easy to create streams and lakes that are below track level. You can also use the Styrofoam tabletop in Project 6 to provide a surface you can carve to create ballast shoulders if your ballast shoulders are not already built into the track. You can also carve into the surface of the Styrofoam to re-create the drainage ditches found near real railroad rights-of-way.

REAL RAILROAD RIGHTS-OF-WAY

Crushed-rock ballast holds railroad ties in place and provides a place for water to drain so it won't rot the wooden ties. But the water needs somewhere to drain after it seeps through the ballast. Real railroads, therefore, almost always provide drainage ditches along with the ballast, ties, and rails. Those drainage ditches are seldom modeled, but they are prominent features of virtually all real railroad rights-of-way. The exceptions might be yards or industrial tracks, but even yards have drainage systems surrounding the track complex, while industrial tracks see relatively light use.

MODELING RIGHTS-OF-WAY

If you choose, you can lay simple ties-and-rails track directly onto the Styrofoam tabletop using Liquid Nails "Projects and Foamboard" cement or Chem Rex PL300 Foam Board Adhesive, applied with a caulking gun. If you cement ties-and-rails sectional or flex-track, experiment to determine the minimum amount of cement you need to hold the ties to avoid cement squeezing over the tops of the ties. Be especially careful around the working parts of turnouts—keep the cement at least an inch away from the moving parts! If you simply cement the edges of built-in ballast to the tabletop as shown in Project 9, just run a small bead of cement down the edges of the ballast.

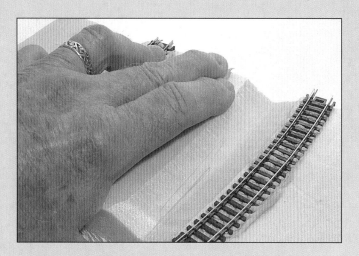

2 If you choose to cement the track directly to the Styrofoam, experiment to determine just the amount of cement to use so it does not squeeze up through the ties in sufficient quantity to cover the tops of the ties. This sample section of N scale right-of-way illustrates how you can cut both drainage channels and steep fills (embankments) directly into the Styrofoam tabletop.

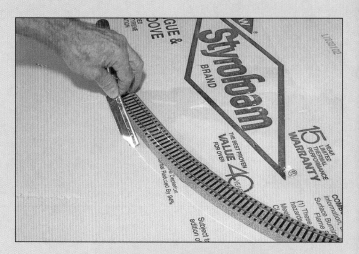

3 You can use a hot knife from Premium Concepts, a hacksaw blade, or a hobby razor saw like the one shown to cut into the Styrofoam. The track can remain in place, simply mark the edges of the drainage ditches, and push the blade into the Styrofoam as deeply as is necessary. Make the first cut about 6 scale feet from the ends of the ties and at about a 30-degree angle.

5 After the two cuts are made, the vee-shaped piece of Styrofoam can be pulled away from the tabletop to reveal the drainage ditch. When cutting a drainage ditch or fill, do not cut any deeper than about 1/2 inch with any single cut. If you need deeper cuts, make them 1/2 inch at a time, removing the cut material and cutting again. The styrofoam can also be cut to produce even more dramatic scenery as described in Project 85.

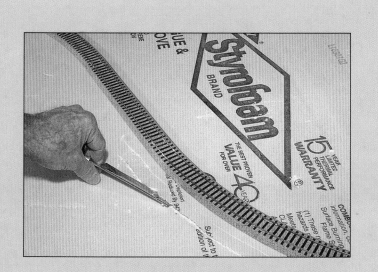

4 Make the second cut as far from the first cut as necessary to create the drainage ditch to the depth you desire. If the cut is too shallow, simply make a second cut and remove more material.

LAYING TRACK

PROJECT 12 • BALLAST TRACK

Time: 30 minutes or more

Tools: Pump-style hair spray atomizer, glass jar, 1/4-inch soft paintbrush, and a hard rubber eraser or track-cleaning eraser

Materials: Plastic-compatible oil; HO, N, S or O scale ballast; artist's matte medium and artist's gel medium; masking tape; aerosol gray paint; and mild liquid detergent

Cost: $$

Talent: Novice

Scales: HO, N, S and O

Space: Between 1x2 and 60x100 feet

Tip: Be certain the layout operates perfectly so you won't need to move the track. Also, apply a liberal amount of plastic-compatible oil around the moving parts of every turnout (switch) so you don't cement the switch solid.

WHY: To duplicate the effect of loose-crushed rock ballast holding down ties on a real railroad

COMPLEMENTARY PROJECTS: 5 through 11, 13 and 16

1 Ballast makes any track, even ties-and-rails track on a bare plywood tabletop, look more realistic.

Real railroads hold their track in place by burying the ties in crushed rock called "ballast." Ballast is as essential to a realistic model railroad as the track itself. Try to model real railroad track without ballast, and your model will look toylike.

BALLAST THE EASY WAY

The easiest way to install ballast on your model railroad is to buy track that already has the ballast molded in place. The most common brands of HO and N scale track with built-in ballast are illustrated in Project 9. The ballast on many of these brands has the correct shape and color, but it lacks the

"loose gravel" effect. You can increase the realism somewhat by simply brushing on a "wash" consisting of about three parts black paint to one part thinner. The paint will accumulate in the crevices to make the ballast look more realistic.

REAL ROCK BALLAST

The best way to simulate loose ballast is to use loose ballast. Your hobby dealer can supply ballast in several colors for HO, N, or O scale. Before you apply any loose ballast, liberally oil all the moving and sliding parts of the switches (turnouts) with plastic-compatible oil so the matte medium won't stick to these areas. Also apply a strip of masking tape along the bottom edge of the ballast where you want the ballast to end.

The black ties and shiny rail should be colored with a very light spray of gray paint to tone down the shiny black plastic so it looks like weathered wooden ties. You can use an aerosol can, but move the spray quickly so you only get a hint of gray. If you get too much, use a paintbrush and thinner to brush away the excess paint.

Pour the ballast over the track and brush it away from the tops of the ties and the sides of the rail with a soft-bristle 1/4-inch-wide brush.

2 Spray the track—rails, ties, and all—with a very light coat of gray paint to create a weathered appearance on the ties.

3 Sprinkle the ballast onto the track from a glass jar, then brush the individual grains from the tops of the ties, spreading the ballast so it matches the appearance of real railroad ballast. Hold the ballast in place with diluted artist's matte medium.

When you are satisfied with the shape and position of every grain of ballast, spray the ballast with water to wet it. You may need to move a few grains away from the rails and apply a few more that have washed away. Next, flood the ballast with a mixture of equal parts artist's matte medium and water, with a drop or two of liquid detergent added to break the surface tension of the water. You may want to add a few more ballast grains, to cover any areas that are washed away. The entire area will look milky until the matte medium dries to a clear, flat finish. You can blend the ballast with the colors of the ties, if you wish, with another very light misting of gray paint.

Remove the masking tape from the edges of the ballast to produce an even edge. Use a hard rubber eraser or a model railroad track cleaner eraser to remove any traces of paint or matte medium from the tops of the rails and the contact areas of the switch points.

Loose ballast can even be used on track with built-in ballast. First, apply a thick coat of artist's matte gel (it has a honey like consistency) to the sides of the ballast to hold the loose grains to the sloping sides. Then sprinkle on the loose ballast, brush it away from the ties, and apply the diluted artist's matte medium.

PROJECT 13 • WEATHER TRACK WITH A BRUSH

Time: 30 minutes or more

Tools: Number 1 paintbrush and a hard rubber eraser or track-cleaning eraser

Materials: Materials: HO, N, S or O scale ballast, artist's matte medium, masking tape, aerosol gray paint, and Box Car Red bottled paint

Cost: $$

Talent: Novice

Scales: HO, N, S and O

Space: Between 1x2 and 60x100 feet

Tip: Use the lightest possible coat of "weathering" gray; once you've used too much, it's hard to remove—plus, you can always apply more.

? **WHY:** To re-create the effects of sun and rain on railroad tracks, so your model right-of-way looks precisely like the real thing

COMPLEMENTARY PROJECTS: 5 through 12, 14, 15 and 16

1 Use a number 1 brush to paint the sides of the rails with Box Car Red to simulate rusted steel.

This is the first of many projects that will show you how to paint your railroad models to duplicate the colors that really are there in the real world. All real railroad equipment operates outdoors on track and rights-of-way and near structures that are also outdoors. All of these objects are subject to the fading effects of the elements and the general wear and tear that "weather" afflicts on everything outdoors. Most model railroads, however, are indoors, so we have to apply paint to duplicate the effects of weather—that's why modelers refer to the process as "weathering."

WEATHERING AS AN ART FORM

One of the better model railroad painters, Mike Budde, refers to a shiny new model railroad freight car as his "bare canvas," on which he applies various types of paint to precisely reproduce the effects of weather. It takes practice, patience, and learned skills, but you can do it.

Track is a good place to start when learning about weathering, because it's hard to make a serious mistake. If you have ballasted the track as described in Project 12, you already have produced one weathering effect by spraying a very light coat of gray paint over the ties to help tone down the black plastic color. You can carry that a step further by brushing the lengths of a few random ties with thinner to partially dissolve and streak the gray, duplicating the grain of the wood and the random effect of weathering on real railroad ties. Now try brushing on a "wash" of dark brown (equal parts paint and thinner) on some random ties and even adding another coat of the gray paint to other random ties.

THE WEATHERING TUTOR

How will you know when you get the weathering effect just right? When it looks exactly the way it does out there in the real world. You cannot, however, rely on your memory alone to duplicate what's really out there—you should take a color photograph of typical track (or buildings or a specific locomotive or car you want to duplicate) so you

2 Tone down the Box Car Red and blend in the ballast and ties with a very light "dust on" coat of gray paint.

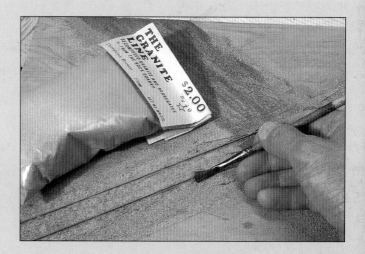

3 To simulate well-used ballast and track, sift some real dirt through a tea strainer and apply a bit of it to the track and ballast, brushing it in with a soft number 1 paintbrush.

4 Finish the model by applying loose sifted dirt, finely ground foam, and flocking to simulate the weeds that grow along nearly every railroad right-of-way.

have a "pattern." Remember, you are not trying to create something, you are trying to re-create what something really looks like. The process is almost exactly like making an oil painting, except you don't have to worry about replicating shapes or shadows.

Some real railroad track has about as much dirt as ballast. It often depends on how often the railroad "cleans" the ballast. (Yes, they really do have machines that dig out, clean, and replace the old ballast.) If the track is old, you can simulate the "dirty" ballast with real dirt sifted through a tea strainer, or you can buy already sifted dirt at your model railroad supply store. Brush the dirt around the sides of the rails and into the ballast until you achieve the effect you desire. Again, take a close look at the photograph of the real railroad's track to see what color dirt you should use.

Simulate rust on rails by painting the sides of the rails with Box Car Red paint. Try not to slather the paint onto the ties, but don't worry if it hits the simulated spike heads. Finally, dust on another coat of gray to blend the ballast and to soften the harsh effect of the brown rails. When you're satisfied, clean the tops of the rails with a hard rubber eraser or a track-cleaning eraser sold by hobby stores.

5 This is simple ties-and-rails track from an HO scale train set, but it has been weathered to match a specific stretch of real railroad right-of-way.

45

PROJECT 14 • WEATHER TRACK WITH AN AIRBRUSH

Time: 30 minutes or more

Tools: Airbrush, air compressor, and respirator

Materials: HO, N, S or O scale ballast, artist's matte medium, masking tape, gray and Box Car Red paint, and thinner

Cost: $$ to $$$

Talent: Novice

Scales: HO, N, S and O

Space: Between 1x2 and 60x100 feet

Tip: Practice, practice, practice. Experiment with paint-to-thinner ratios, airbrush adjustments, and air compressor pressures.

WHY: To re-create the effects of sun and rain on railroad tracks so your model right-of-way looks precisely like the real thing

COMPLEMENTARY PROJECTS: 5 through 13, 15 and 16

An airbrush is one of the most useful tools a modeler can purchase. Ask your hobby dealer to recommend an airbrush and an air compressor; if your hobby dealer doesn't know what you're asking for, search the Yellow Pages for an art supply store that carries airbrushes. (Also see Project 44 in this book for advice on purchasing an airbrush.)

An airbrush is really just a miniature version of the spray guns used to paint automobiles. Their spray patterns can be made so fine that you can literally paint the periods on this page or a line as thin as this line: _____. Be prepared to spend $200 to $300 for a quality airbrush and compressor. It's probably the largest expenditure you'll make for

a tool, but it will also be one of the wisest investments you make in the hobby. Also, buy a respirator and wear it any time you spray paint.

ONE THIN LINE

Weathering track with an airbrush is far simpler than weathering it with a paintbrush and an aerosol can. For starters, you can adjust the airbrush to apply a line of Box Car Red paint about 1/16-inch thick to weather the sides of a rail in a single pass. Practice first to learn how much thinner to use, how close you should hold the airbrush to the work, how to adjust the airbrush and the compressor to achieve that thin line, and how fast to move the airbrush. For rusty rails, thin the paint the minimum amount suggested by the paint manufacturer. Some paints are ready for the airbrush right out of the bottle, so read all labels first.

SUN-BLEACHING EFFECTS AND MORE

The gray paint used to weather track is one of the simplest examples of applying a "wash" with an airbrush, and it's fundamental to most weathering. The goal, here, is to use the least amount of paint possible so that the gray tones down the harsh black plastic rails, making them look sun-bleached and faded. Pick a light gray paint and mix it with an equal amount of thinner. With some paints, you might even want to use two parts thinner to one part paint. Adjust the airbrush to deliver about a 1-inch circle of paint when you hold the airbrush about 9 inches from the track. Adjust the air pressure to about 30 pounds per square inch (psi), but try it at 15, 20, and 25 psi, too. Again, practice on old cardboard or a scrap piece of track to get the feel of it. Also, test the spray on something dark—you want the paint to be thin enough so you can spray for about a second while still rendering the gray barely visible. When you're satisfied, spray the track, rails, and ballast.

The paint will probably dry a bit lighter than it appears when wet, so wait a few minutes before you decide to apply more gray. With practice, you'll be able to get the fading effect you desire in three or four passes, gently working the gray into the track to achieve that sun-bleached look. Some modelers prefer to apply this kind of "fading" effect in a sweeping motion, pressing the paint button down so the paint pattern begins at the start of the work (one edge of the ballast) and releasing it as soon as it reaches the other edge of the ballast.

1 Simulate rust on the sides of the rails with an airbrush adjusted to produce a 1/16-inch-wide line. Simply run the spray pattern down each side of the rail as shown.

2 Blend the bright colors of the rails, the ballast, and the black plastic ties with a wash of two parts thinner to one part paint. Use light gray paint to simulate the fading effects of sunlight and rain.

PROJECT 15 • DERAIL-PROOF TRACK

Time: 30 minutes or more

Tools: NMRA Standards Gauge, needle-nose pliers, flat jeweler's file, and a hacksaw blade

Materials: Cyanoacrylate cement, 5-minute epoxy

Cost: $

Talent: Beginner and Novice

Scales: HO, N, S and O

Space: Between 1x2 and 60x100 feet

Tip: Check every inch of track and every turnout for proper dimensions.

WHY: To avoid persistent derailments

COMPLEMENTARY PROJECTS: 5 through 14, 16 and 39

1 NMRA Standards Gauges are stamped-steel pieces that you can use to check track width and wheelsets to eliminate derailments. These gauges are for (left to right) Sn3, HO, HOn3, N, and (upper right) On3 track and wheelsets.

Virtually all model railroad track sold in the United States is assembled to a set of dimensional standards developed by the National Model Railroad Association (NMRA). These standards ensure that any brand of car or locomotive will operate on any brand of track. The NMRA also produces a stamped metal "Standards Gauge," effectively a "go/no go" gauge to check track, turnouts, and wheels. The gauge can also be used to check wheels on freight cars, passenger cars, and locomotives, as you'll learn in Project 39.

DERAIL-PROOFING BY THE GAUGE

NMRA Standards Gauges are available from the NMRA and through some hobby dealers. For price, send a stamped, self-addressed envelope to the NMRA (4121 Cromwell Road, Chattanooga, TN 37421). They'll provide you information on membership, the cost of the standards book, and other useful information. Currently, the NMRA offers stamped-steel Standards Gauges for HO and N scales, as well as for the 3-foot, narrow-gauge track used for HO scale (HOn3), S scale (Sn3), and O scale (On3). All but the On3 Gauges also include clearance-gauge profiles for tunnels on straight track and for side-loading ramps.

To use the gauge, study the illustrated instructions furnished with the tool. Briefly, the tabs are used to measure the minimum clearance between closely spaced rails like the frogs of turnouts (where the rails cross) and the guard rails that keep the wheels from derailing at the frog. The tabs also provide the maximum gap between the moving switch points and the adjacent rail.

You will discover that most turnouts need at least a bit of adjustment. If the rails are too close, you can sometimes bend them farther apart with needle-nose pliers. If the rails are too far apart, you can sometimes bend them in or cement strips of .010x.015-inch styrene beside the rails to narrow the gap. Strip styrene is available at hobby shops.

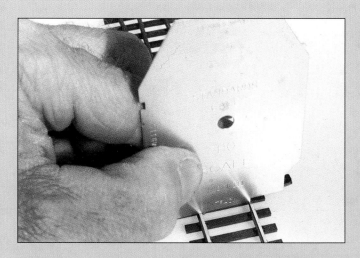

2 The two tabs at the bottom of the gauge are used to check the rail spacing. To correct track gauge that is too wide, force the rail in with needle-nose pliers and hold it in place with a drop of cyanoacrylate cement (like Super Glue).

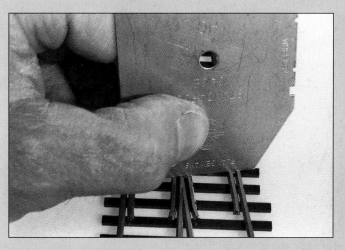

3 The two tabs on the top of the gauge are used to check the track and flangeway widths at the frog and guardrail areas of turnouts (shown) and crossings. If the gauge won't fit, you may need to use a jeweler's file to increase the width of the flangeways. If you need to decrease the width of the flangeway, you can cement strips of .010x.015-inch styrene plastic to the sides of the rail with cyanoacrylate cement.

4 The fat tab in the center at the top of the gauge is used to check the depth and the width of the flangeways at both the frog (shown) and the guardrails (the two closely spaced rails at the far right). If the tab goes in but does not allow the gauge to hit the tops of the rails, the flangeway may be too shallow. It can be made deeper by making several fine cuts with a hacksaw blade. If the flangeway is too deep, fill the bottom with 5-minute epoxy, recheck the depth when the epoxy cures and, if necessary, file or saw the epoxy to obtain the perfect depth.

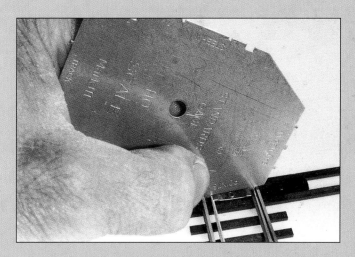

5 The tabs on the angled edge of the NMRA Standards Gauge are used to check the clearance between the open switch points (the moving parts of the turnout) and the stock (outer) rails. If the gauge doesn't fit, bend the point slightly to provide proper clearance so the tabs will drop in place. If the points have sharp corners they may pick at the wheels and cause derailments; use a jeweler's file to remove a radius of about 1/16 inch from the corners of each of the points.

PROJECT 16 • ASSEMBLE BRIDGES FOR CURVED TRACK

 Time: 3 to 4 hours

 Tools: Hobby knife, razor saw, cabinetmaker's file, and a number 0 paintbrush

 Materials: Plastic stone-arch bridge kit, plastic cement (in a tube), stone-color paint, dark gray paint, black paint, and thinner

 Cost: $$

 Talent: Novice and Expert

 Scales: HO and N

 Space: Between 4x12 inches and 4x100 inches

 Tip: Check every inch of track and every turnout for proper dimensions.

 WHY: To simulate curved track on bridges as exhibited by prototypes

COMPLEMENTARY PROJECTS: 9 through 15

1 This N scale curved stone-arch bridge is assembled from two out-of-the-box twin stone-arch pieces on both the inside and outside of the curve. The extra length needed for the bridge face on the outside of the curve is made with a wider central abutment. The base of that central abutment is somewhat triangular or keystone-shaped to fit.

Model railroaders need bridges on curved tracks far more often than real railroads do, for the simple reason that model railroads have far more curves than real railroads. As obvious as this may seem, there are very few bridge kits that address the problem. There are some kits for curved-truss bridges, but such bridges do not exist in the real world. Some straight bridge kits, like Micro Engineering's steel-deck truss and steel-trestle kits, provide suggestions on how to position the bridges so they support track on a curve in a manner similar to that used by prototype railroads.

SUPPORTING CURVES WITH STRAIGHT BRIDGES

Imagine looking down on a curved track as it passes over a straight bridge. You'll notice that the inside of the track is much closer to the outside edge of the bridge at the points where the track enters and leaves the bridge. Conversely, the outside of the curved track is closer to the outside edge of the bridge near the center of the bridge. What you are seeing is that a bridge must be wider if it is to support a curved track than if it is to support a similar length of straight track. In fact, the sharper the curve, the wider the bridge must be to adequately support the track. Real railroads have curves that are about 10 times larger than the broadest curve typically seen on a model railroad. Even so, it's rare for a real railroad to use a bridge longer than about 50 feet—that's about 7 inches in HO scale or 3 5/8 inches in N scale. If the bridge needs to be longer than that, the real railroads simply use more short bridges, each supported by an abutment or sturdy trestle. To make a bridge on a curve as realistic as possible, then, its length should be no longer than 50 scale feet.

One other element comes into play on a model railroad: the lengths of the opposite sides of the bridge will be different if you use more than one bridge to span the area. Imagine, again, looking down on a bridge supporting a curved track. You have two choices. The ends of the bridge can be square with its sides so it is a perfect rectangle, like a similar bridge on straight track. If the curve is tight, however, it is difficult to make the ends square with the sides; it's much more efficient to make the ends parallel to the ties in the center of the bridge, which will make the bridge shorter on the inside than on the outside of the curve. Virtually all model railroad curves are sharp enough to require that the ends of the bridge to be parallel to the ties, and the

2 Paint the bridge to match the color of the stone in the area you are modeling. Accent the mortar with a wash of light gray paint. Accent the shadows of the bricks by "dry brushing" dark gray onto the surfaces of the stones, using paint applied from the side of the brush.

sides adjusted in length to fit. Consider the 50 scale feet to be the maximum length for the bridge on the outside of the curve.

BUILDING THE BRIDGE

Bridges similar to those in the photographs are available in HO scale from Faller as the 477 Straight Viaduct or the 478 Curved Viaduct with either 479 Tall Piers or 480 Short Piers, or from Kibri as the 9640 Straight Stone-Arch Bridge or 9642 Curved Stone Viaduct with 9646 Stone Viaduct Piers. Stone-arch bridges are available in N scale from Faller as the 2586 Curved Viaduct and 2585 Straight Viaduct, or from Kibri as the 7640 Straight Stone Viaduct and the 7646 Straight Viaduct Piers for taller bridges. The curved bridges are designed for really tight 14-inch-radius curves in HO scale and 9-inch curves in N scale; you can build a far more realistic bridge, however, by starting with the "straight" kits and cutting the pieces to fit.

Each bridge must be custom-fitted to your model railroad. I'll show you what I did, and you can modify the work to fit your needs. For this bridge I elected to use out-of-the-box two-span arches for the inside faces of the bridge. I placed these on the inside of the curve. When I positioned the two matching pairs of arches on the outside of the bridges, I aligned the extreme ends with the ties in the center of each pair of arches. The right and left pairs of arches were about an inch short of meeting, so I simply cut a piece of one of the piers to fill the gap. Thus, the inside of the bridge is merely two pieces of plastic, each with two arches. The outside face of the bridge is three pieces of plastic: two

arches just like the inside, plus the third solid piece in the center. The abutments, or arch supports, are standard kit parts except for the slightly triangular-shaped central pier. I cut the abutment pieces to fit and filed the edges for a perfect joint before cementing them together.

When real railroads lay track on an arch bridge like this, and even on some steel bridges, the track is held in place by ballast. On these bridges, then, you want to have the same flat support for the ballast or track with built-in ballast as you have everywhere else on your layout. Be sure to make the bridge wide enough to accommodate the curved inner and outer edges of the ballast. Usually, that means you must make the bridge abutments wider than those in the kits. Cut two of the abutment pieces that go across the bridge (including the curved pieces that make the inside of the arch) and join them to create the extra width. To preserve the beveled joint edges on the outside of the pieces, make the extra width by cutting one edge from two pieces. If, for example, you need the abutment to be 1 1/2 times as wide, cut two pieces, each 3/4 of their width, and join them together to make the piece that is 1 1/2 times wider.

Use a razor saw to cut the pieces, but first mark a straight line so you can use it to help guide the saw. Try to find a cabinetmaker's file (as shown in Project 63) at a shop that specializes in cabinetmaker's supplies. The file makes perfectly straight cuts easier, and you can use it to file a bevel in the cut parts so they can be assembled just like the parts in the kit. Before cementing the pieces together, test fit each part to be sure it is correct. For projects with larger pieces of plastic, I use plastic cement in a tube.

SIMULATING STONE WITH PAINT

When the bridge is assembled, you can spray it the color of stones in the area you are modeling. To simulate the mortar joints, mix equal parts thinner and gray paint, then brush the mixture over the stones. The gray paint will settle into the deeper cracks and wash off the raised surfaces. If too much paint sticks to the surfaces, apply a bit more thinner to wash the excess into the simulated mortar joints. Finally, accent the roughness of the stones with some flat dark gray paint right out of the bottle. Squeeze most of the paint off the brush and back into the bottle, then use the side, not the tip, of the brush to lightly rub traces of black over the surfaces of the stones. This is called "dry brushing" because you try to leave so little paint that it is almost dry as soon as it touches the model. If the black seems too dark, apply another wash of diluted light gray.

SECTION FOUR
WIRING

All of the model locomotives in this book run on 12 to 18 volts of direct electrical current (DC) that is carried through the rails to each locomotive. If you look at a track plan for a model railroad and consider that each line represents not only two rails, but two wires, you can see how complex the circuit really is. There are several books available on wiring model railroads and, if you like working with electrical hobbies, I recommend that you buy one or two and tailor that side of your hobby to whatever level you desire. Conversely, if you want to keep the wiring to a minimum, there's no easier way of wiring than to use the digital command control or DCC systems described in Projects 17 and 18. DCC sounds exotic, but it has developed to the point where it is virtually "plug-and-play." In fact, I never hesitate to recommend it to any beginner who wants to run more than one train.

WIRING

PROJECT 17 • WIRE A DIGITAL COMMAND CONTROL (DCC) TO RUN TWO TRAINS

 Time: 2 to 4 hours

 Tools: Small screwdriver

 Materials: Digital command control (DCC) power supply and one or more DCC decoder-equipped locomotives

 Cost: $$$

 Talent: Beginner, Novice and Expert

 Scales: HO, N, S and O

 Space: Between 1x2 and 60x100 feet

 Tip: Before you buy a second power pack, or even a second locomotive, investigate DCC as an option.

 WHY: To make it easier to wire a model railroad and for more realistic operation

COMPLEMENTARY PROJECTS: 17 through 21 and 101

When you build a model railroad, you will want to be able to operate two or more trains. Even if you just want to park one while you operate the other, you will still want two or more trains.

Model railroad locomotives receive their power through the rails. To control two trains, then, you need to provide some type of electrical insulation in at least one rail so you can turn off the second locomotive while you operate the first. If you have more locomotives or want to be able to actually run two locomotives at the same time, the number of electrical insulation gaps in the rails, the number of wires, and the number of on-off switches can become massive.

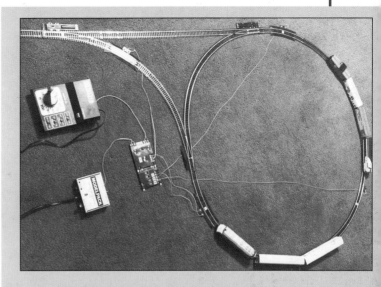

1 With conventional wiring, this segment of a model railroad requires two on-off switches and five wire connections, in addition to the power pack and the two wires to the rest of the layout. With DCC, you can control each locomotive independently with just the controls on the DCC power pack and two wires to the track, plus another two to the reversing section.

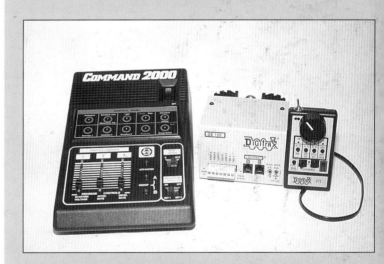

2 MRC's Command 2000 (left) and Digitrax system (right) are two of the more popular DCC power packs. The Command 2000 has built-in controls to operate two or more trains at once and is available with an optional plug-in walk-around throttle. Digitrax has a walk-around throttle (the small black box). Either system can be expanded to operate dozens of locomotives.

WIRING FOR TWO OR MORE TRAINS

There are dozens of books on how to wire a model railroad. In fact, basic two-rail wiring is included in virtually every beginner book. Essentially, you must install an insulated rail joiner to isolate segments of the layout and provide on-off switches to control these electrically isolated segments. You can avoid all of those gaps and virtually all but two wires by using a digital command control, or DCC, power pack. The DCC system feeds a constant 18 volts (give or take) through the rails. The rails are then used to carry a signal to each locomotive, telling it to start, stop, speed up, slow down, coast to a stop, or accelerate, as though it was really pulling 100 tons, and at what rate.

Each locomotive must have a DCC decoder installed (an example is shown in Project 16) to receive the signal that "tells" the motor what to do. Most DCC systems also provide control for one locomotive that is not equipped with a decoder. You can operate just one non-DCC locomotive at a time, however, so you must provide an electrically isolated siding on which to park each of the other locomotives. The option, of course, is to simply remove all but one of the non-DCC locomotives for the layout.

LOCOMOTIVE DECODERS

A few manufacturers offer their locomotives with DCC decoders already installed. Most HO and N scale locomotives produced in the last five years or so are prewired for DCC decoders so you can simply remove the body and plug a decoder in. Decoders sell for between $30 and $100, depending on how many features they include—some even offer a full range of sounds. Model Rectifier Corporation (MRC), Atlas, Digitrax, Wangrow, PSI, Lenz, North Coast, and Soundtraxx are some of the more popular brands of DCC power packs and decoders.

WIRING REVERSE LOOPS

One disadvantage of two-rail track (as opposed to three-rail like Lionel's) is that a short circuit is created every time you include a reverse loop or wye so you can reverse the direction of the trains without removing them from the track. With a conventional power pack, the reverse loop must be wired to a second on-off and reversing switch and, when the train leaves the reverse loop, the power pack switch must be flicked to accept the train's new direction of travel. The manufacturers of DCC power packs offer an accessory called an "automatic reverse loop" that is simply connected to the two rails of the reverse loop with two wires. It is still necessary to provide two sets of insulation gaps (to produce a "reversing" section of track), but no extra switches are needed. When the train enters the reverse loop, the automatic reverse loop device automatically corrects the flow of power so the train travels forward without a pause. When the train leaves the reverse loop, the DCC system maintains that same direction of travel. Some systems even provide a circuit to automatically actuate the turnout (switch) in the track at the reverse loop.

OPERATIONS WITH DCC

Perhaps the best description of what it's like to run a model railroad equipped with DCC is this: "You are running trains, not controlling track." With a conventional wiring system, you must constantly flip switches on the control panel to be sure your train has power as it travels from one electrically isolated section of track (called a "block") to another. With DCC, you control the locomotive. The system is particularly fascinating to use when you want to use two locomotives to pull a single train. Simply park the train anywhere on the layout. Select the second locomotive on your DCC controller (throttle) and run it through the necessary track so it can couple onto the first locomotive. Select both locomotives and the train will pull away smoothly with the single throttle controlling both locomotives. On a real railroad, controlling two locomotives at once is standard and referred to as "multiple-unit" operation—with DCC you can duplicate it on any model railroad.

If you have a layout large enough to operate two separate trains, you can run them at the same time. If they are traveling in the same direction, you can set the first for a steady pace and put it in the "memory" of the controller while pushing the button to select the second train. You can then vary the second train's speed so it keeps up with or even passes the first train (at a siding, of course). You can also park the second train on a siding and hold it there until the first train passes. It only takes a few minutes of operation with DCC to realize that you control the locomotives in almost exactly the same manner as a real railroad engineer. You also run the same dangers of colliding with other trains. Your focus shifts, then, from worrying about turning switches on and off at a control panel to paying attention to where your train is headed.

PROJECT 18 • INSTALL DCC DECODER

 Time: 30 to 59 minutes

 Tools: Small screwdriver and two thin metal rulers

 Materials: Digital command control (DCC) power supply, a DCC decoder, and double-stick tape

 Cost: $$

 Talent: Beginner, Novice and Expert

 Scales: HO, N, S and O

 Space: 9x9 inches

 Tip: Inspect the locomotive before you buy it to be sure it is "DCC plug-in ready" to accept a DCC decoder.

 WHY: To make it easier and more realistic to operate two or more locomotives

COMPLEMENTARY PROJECTS: 17, 19 through 21, and 101

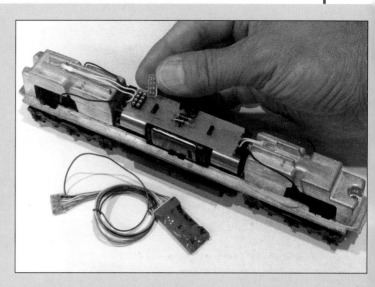

1 Most HO scale locomotives are prewired to accept a standard DCC decoder. Remove the body then remove the eight-prong plug as shown and replace it with the plug on the bundle of wires from the DCC decoder (bottom). Tuck the decoder into the chassis, test-run the locomotive, and reattach the body.

Virtually all scale-model steam and diesel locomotives produced over the past five years are prewired to accept a digital command control (DCC) decoder. The exceptions are the very low-cost "toy" train locomotives and some of the very expensive imported brass locomotives. It is possible to install a DCC decoder in nearly any model locomotive, even one as small as an N scale diesel switcher, but a few will require that you solder the connections.

REMOVING THE LOCOMOTIVE'S BODY

The most difficult part of installing a DCC decoder is getting the locomotive's body off its chassis. Nearly all diesel locomotive bodies and most plastic steam locomotive tender superstructures are held in place with invisible clips inside the body. If

you can spot a screw head or clip, try loosening it to see if it frees the body. Those obvious sources of attachment are rare, however. Spread the sides of the body apart with your fingers while you simultaneously pull downward on the fuel tank. Do not try to pull downward on the trucks or you may damage them or partially disengage the drive gears.

If you still have a problem, try pulling one side of the body far enough out from the side of the chassis so you can insert a thin metal ruler between the body and the chassis. Pry the opposite side out enough so you can insert another thin metal ruler. You should then be able to wiggle the chassis out from beneath the body.

INSTALLING THE DCC DECODER

Most HO scale locomotives have a simple eight-hole socket to accept a similar eight-prong plug that is wired to the DCC decoder. To install the decoder, just remove the existing plug from the stock locomotive and replace it with the plug from the DCC decoder. Be careful to position the decoder so it does not interfere with anything inside the body. If the decoder won't stay in place, stick it in position with a piece of double-stick tape. Always check the locomotive's operation before you install the body.

For most N scale locomotives, decoder installation is only slightly more complex. First, make sure

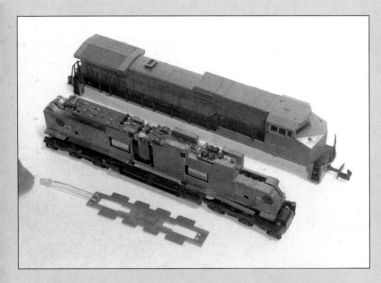

2 Most N scale locomotives are designed so the printed circuit board in the standard locomotive can be easily removed. Remove the body. The DCC decoder circuit board (bottom) is designed as a snap-in replacement for the stock circuit board.

3 Loosen the screws that hold the right and left halves of most N scale diesel chassis together, so you can snap out the standard circuit board. Snap the circuit board with the built-in DCC decoder in place, tighten the screws, test-run the chassis, and reattach the body.

you buy a decoder for your specific brand of model locomotive. Then, remove the body using the same techniques described for an HO model. Most N scale (and a few HO scale) decoders are complete circuit boards designed to replace the circuit board already in the locomotive. Carefully loosen the screws that are on the sides of the chassis. With the screws loose (but NOT removed) you should be able to gently pry the right and left halves of the chassis just far enough apart to free the standard circuit board. Snap the new DCC decoder board into exactly the same position and tighten the screws. Check the trucks to be sure they are free to swivel. Also check the locomotive's operation before you install the body.

If you wish to install a DCC decoder in a locomotive that is not prewired for DCC, you must cut the existing wires and solder the connections with the decoder's wires. You should leave these more complicated locomotives alone until you have installed a few plug-in DCC decoders and understand basic DCC operating concepts. Most systems provide a channel to operate one locomotive that is not equipped with a decoder anyway, so you may not even have to bother installing a decoder in that "problem" locomotive.

WIRING

PROJECT 19 • SOLDER WIRES TO RAILS

 Time: 30 minutes

 Tools: Soldering gun, wire strippers (or diagonal cutters), hobby knife, flat jeweler's file, needle-nose pliers, electric drill, 1/16-inch drill bit, and eye protection

 Materials: Rosin core solder (preferably a 60/40 tin-to-lead ratio), and acid flux (optional)

 Cost: $$

 Talent: Beginner, Novice and Expert

 Scales: HO, N, S and O

 Space: 9x9 inches

 Tip: Be certain the metal is absolutely clean. Allow the metal, not the soldering iron, to melt the solder.

 WHY: To make trouble-free wiring connections

COMPLEMENTARY PROJECTS: 17, 18, 19 and 21

1 Before soldering wire directly to a rail, use a hobby knife or the tip of a jeweler's file to completely scrape the outside of the rail until it shines.

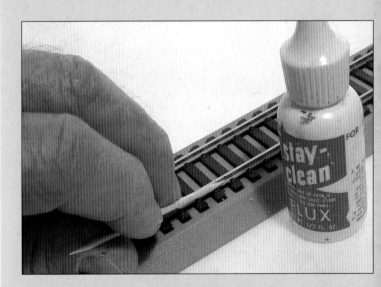

2 This step is optional but it can make the soldering a bit quicker. Apply a single drop of acid flux to the wire and the rail. Be sure to wear gloves and eye protection.

It is possible to build a model railroad without ever learning to solder. Sectional track with presoldered terminals for attaching wires with screws or rail joiners with wires can be ordered from any hobby store. However, neither is as reliable as soldering your own wire connections to the track.

I recommend a 100-watt soldering gun because it's much easier to work with than the other options. I've know folks who solder with a wood burning-pencil and others who prefer a 200-watt soldering iron, but the soldering gun works best for me.

I am able to use diagonal cutters (dikes) to strip insulation from wire without breaking or nicking a single strand, but it takes practice—better to buy a pair of wire strippers. Strip only about 1/4 inch or less of the insulation from the end of the wire.

If you are soldering a wire to a model railroad rail, I recommend making the connections on the outsides of the rails. Yes, it will be more obvious, but there's also no chance the solder or wire will hit the wheels of the locomotives and cars. If you are weathering the track for maximum realism (Project 13), the paint will make the solder joint virtually disappear.

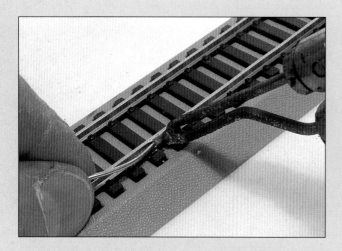

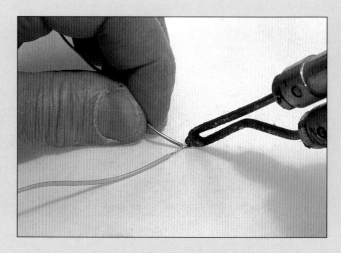

3 Soldering is easier if you first "tin" the rail. Preheat the soldering gun, then, while holding the rosin core solder against the rail, touch the already-hot tip of the gun to the joint just long enough for the solder to begin to melt to avoid melting the plastic ties.

4 Next, touch the already-hot tip of the solder to the bare end of the wire. Remove the soldering gun before it melts too much of the plastic insulation.

Use the tip of a jeweler's file or a hobby knife to scrape away all oxide and grime from the 1/4 inch where you will attach the bare wire.

I also apply a single drop of acid flux to the wire and the clean portion of the rail. This is not absolutely necessary but it makes the solder flow just a bit quicker. Be sure to wear eye protection and gloves because the acid can splatter. And, when you're done, wash the area with water to remove any traces of the acid.

Soldering will be quicker if you "tin" the rail and the wire before joining the two: heat the rail just long enough for the solder to flow, then immediately remove the iron. Repeat the process to "tin" the bare wire.

Hold the now-solder-coated bare wire tightly against the now-solder-coated side of the rail with your fingers or needle-nose pliers. Hold the hot soldering iron tip against the wire and push the wire solder against the rail so the rail itself, not the tip of the soldering iron, melts the solder. The instant the solder moves (it's melting) remove the soldering iron. Be sure to retain the pressure of the wire against the rail until the solder cools. The solder will change from a wet and shiny sheen to a dull appearance as it hardens.

Practice on some old sections of track to learn the technique. After three or four tries, you should be able to get the solder to melt and cool before it melts the tiny plastic spikes that hold the rail to the ties.

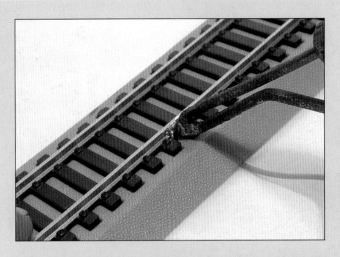

5 Drill a 1/16-inch hole in the tabletop (or, in this case, between two ties at the edge of the plastic ballast) so the wire will be barely visible. Bend the solder-coated end of the wire so it rests tightly against the solder-coated portion of the rail.

6 With the already-heated soldering gun, touch the tip to the wire just long enough to melt the solder, then remove the iron. With the hot tip of the soldering gun, push the wire against the rail so the rail itself, not the tip of the gun, melts the solder. The instant the solder moves, remove the soldering iron. Using your fingers or needle-nose pliers, retain the pressure of the wire against the rail until the solder cools.

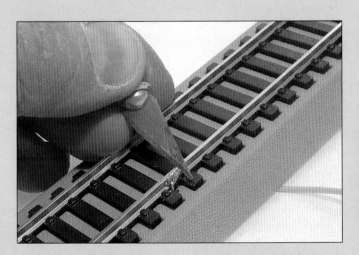

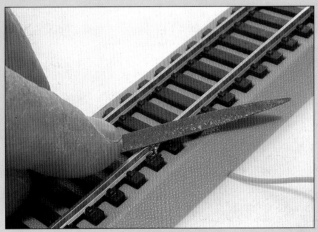

7 If the solder touches the top of the rail, slice it away with a hobby knife. You can also use the knife to whittle away any excess solder on the outside of the rail.

8 Use a jeweler's file to smooth the top and, if necessary, the inside of the rail so no trace of solder touches the wheels of passing cars and locomotives.

WIRING

PROJECT 20 • CUT ELECTRICAL INSULATION GAPS

Time: 30 minutes

Tools: Motor tool, cutoff disc, eye protection, tweezers, and a hobby knife

Materials: .010x.020-inch styrene strips and cyanoacrylate cement

Cost: $$

Talent: Beginner and Novice

Scales: HO, N, S and O

Space: 9x9 inches

Tip: Trim the plastic strip when the cement has dried so there's no chance it will hit a wheel and cause a derailment.

? WHY: To make trouble-free electrical insulation joints in the track

COMPLEMENTARY PROJECTS: 17, 18, 19 and 21

1 Try to locate any electrical insulation gaps at least 2 inches from any metal-to-metal rail joint. Use a cutoff disc in a motor tool or a razor saw to slice through the rail to the ties. Wear eye protection whenever using a motor tool.

If you intend to operate more than one locomotive with a conventional power pack, or if you have a track arrangement like a reverse loop or wye that allows you to turn the trains, you need some electrical insulation gaps in the rails. Insulated gaps effectively "cut" the rail, which serves as one of the two wires (the second "wire" being the other rail) that carry electrical current to and from the locomotive's motor. You can buy plastic rail joiners that can serve this function, but they are bulky and compromise the strength of the rail joint. Use these techniques to create virtually invisible insulation gaps.

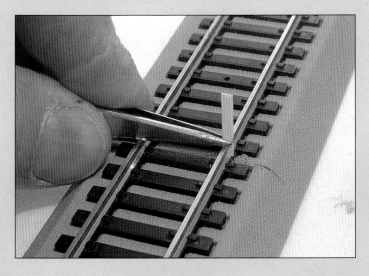

2 Cut a half-inch-long piece of .010x020-inch styrene plastic strip. Use tweezers to push the strip into the gap you cut in the rails. Leave the end protruding above the rails for now.

3 Use a toothpick to apply cyanoacrylate cement to hold the styrene strip in the gap. Allow the cement to harden for an hour.

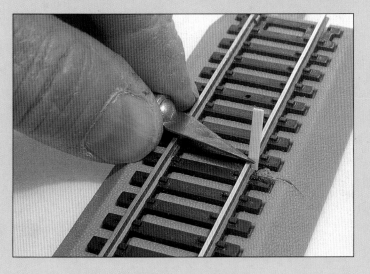

4 With a hobby knife, slice the styrene flush with the tops and both sides of the rails. If you weather the rails with Box Car Red (Project 13), the joint will be invisible. If you want to know where the joint is, install a scale-model whistle post sign or a scale-model electrical cabinet at the edge of the right-of-way to mark the spot.

PROJECT 21 • WIRE A CONTROL PANEL

Time: 1 to 40 hours

Tools: Wire strippers, small screwdrivers, saw, electric drill, and a 3/8-inch drill bit

Materials: Double-pole double-throw (DPDT) (reversing and center-off block-selection) toggle switches, single-pole single-throw (SPST) (quick-contact) push buttons, 22-gauge wire, terminal strips, 1/8-inch or PVC plastic sheet, 1x2-foot boards, number 10x1/2 round-head wood screws

Cost: $$ and up

Talent: Beginner, Novice and Expert

Scales: HO, N, S and O

Space: 6x24 inches or more

Tip: Check each circuit for perfect operation before proceeding to the next.

WHY: To make it easier to locate remote-controlled switches and insulated electrical blocks

COMPLEMENTARY PROJECTS: 17 through 20

1 This 6x24-inch panel is used to control all of the tracks in a small town. The track positions are indicated on the schematic diagram on the face of the panel. On this panel, the yellow strips represent visible tracks and the white strips indicate hidden tracks. The small red push buttons are made by Kadee to actuate remote-controlled turnouts. The toggle switches with rubber covers are DPDT switches that reverse a hidden wye. The other toggle switches are DPDT switches that select either "Throttle A" or "Throttle B" or turn a block off. The throttle itself is a tethered walk-around control that plugs into a socket near the control panel.

M ost real railroads are operated through a control panel similar to the one you see in the photos, but about 100 times larger. On a real railroad, these control panels are used to control turnouts and actuate signals seen by engineers in the cab of the locomotive—they are not really used to control trains.

On traditional model railroads, entire layouts were controlled from a panel like this. Even if it had the capacity for a dozen trains, all 12 engineers sat side-by-side running their trains. Later, model railroaders devised walk-around controls, so the throttle could be connected to the layout on a long tether of electrical cable. This allowed the engineer to walk along beside his or her train, but the control panel still controlled the flow of electricity to the "block," or section, where the train was operating. Sometimes blocks were controlled by on-off switches next to the layout and within a few feet of the track they controlled, while others were controlled from the master panel.

THE DISPATCHER'S TOWER

Today, most model railroaders build new layouts or rebuild older ones to include digital command control or DCC (see Project 17). With this technology, the control panel needs to include only a schematic diagram of the track and switches or push buttons to actuate the turnouts. Again, these controls can be placed on the edge of the benchwork near the turnouts. Really, only massive layouts that might run 20 or more trains need a control panel. For the same reasons, a real railroad needs a control panel of some kind: to locate the positions of the trains on the system. Prototype panels usually have indicator lights that show where the trains are located. Often the positions and colors of the signals that are located beside the track are

2 All of the wires from the control panel are connected to one side of four terminal strips like this. The wires from the opposite side of the terminal strip lead to the layout. The terminal strips make it easier to trace any short circuits or faults and to remove the control panel if necessary.

3 Each DPDT switch is wired before installing it in the control panel. If you decide to use DCC (Project 17) for your layout, about 90 percent of these switches—and the wiring that connects them—can be eliminated.

replicated on the master panel. Generally, these panels are operated by a professional railroader called a "dispatcher." Larger model railroads often have a dispatcher and a control panel that are located in a room apart from the model railroad to better simulate the action of real railroad dispatchers. Usually a real railroad dispatcher is located in a tower where he or she can see at least part of the railroad.

CONTROL PANELS FOR MODEL RAILROADS

So, you have a choice of a variety of control panels or of simply locating the block and turnout controls on the edge of the benchwork. If you choose to build a control panel, you can construct a simple box frame of 1x2 lumber placed on edge and nailed and glued together. Cut a control panel face from 1/8-inch or similar hardboard or from 1/8-inch PVC sheet plastic or Plexiglas. Attach the sheet to the 1x2 framework with four or more number 10x1/2-inch screws. Draw a schematic diagram of the track that the panel controls on the face of the panel and mark the tracks with color striping tape sold at art and drafting supply stores. Position the push buttons that will actuate the turnouts at the junctions of the turnouts on the

diagram. Drill a hole to match the size of the push button's case in the panel and install the button. You can also install a reversing DPDT (double-pole double-throw) switch on the panel, if you need one to control a reversing loop or wye. If you use conventional-block control rather than DCC, you can use DPDT center-off switches to control each block. In addition, Atlas offers a system of slide switches to perform all of these functions, as well as books to explain the system.

If you do elect to group all the controls for at least a segment of your layout into a control panel, it's wise to connect one circuit at a time, then test that circuit to be sure it operates before moving on to the next. It's also wise to buy enough terminal strips so you can connect the wires from the control panel to the screw connectors on the terminal strip, then run the wires from the opposite side of the terminal strip to the layout itself. This gives you the option of removing the control panel without cutting any wires—just remove the necessary wires from the terminal strips. The terminal strip also provides a convenient place to collect wires that will operate similar devices, like switch machine control wires for remote-control turnouts.

SECTION FIVE
COUPLERS

Some model railroaders assemble two or three or more trains and just run them, never uncoupling to drop off cars and never adding cars. In fact, that's what you see most real railroads doing most of the time—just running trains. For the modeler, however, making up and breaking down trains one car at a time, or moving cars in and out of industrial sidings, can be even more enjoyable than just watching the trains roll by.

Kadee pioneered the magnetic knuckle-style coupler. Its couplers and more recent products from other makers feature "real railroad" knuckles that are actually hinged much like real railroad couplers. The knuckle on Kadee and similar style couplers, however, are actuated by a thin wire that hangs below it. The wire is repelled by magnets placed between the rails. When the modeler stops the train with a pair of couplers centered over one of the magnets (called uncoupling ramps), the couplers move apart. To actually uncouple, however, the modeler needs to push the train backward a fraction of an inch and then pull forward.

Kadee offers books and instructions on where to place magnets and how to operate with them. I recommend purchasing the Kadee material and studying it, if only to determine if it is the system you prefer. Some modelers use these operating knuckle-style couplers, but uncouple the cars and locomotives by simply prying the pivoting knuckles apart with a small screwdriver; that way, the couplers can couple and uncouple anywhere.

Dennis Blunt's 18x28-foot HO scale Omaha Road.

COUPLERS

PROJECT 22 • MAGNETIC COUPLERS FOR ATHEARN HO DIESELS

Time: 1 hour

Tools: Small screwdrivers, pin vise, 2-56 tap, electric drill, number 50 drill bit, needle-nose pliers, and a Kadee number 205 coupler height gauge

Materials: Kadee number 5 couplers

Cost: S

Talent: Novice and Expert

Scales: HO

Space: 6x9 inches

Tip: Check every coupler installation with your Kadee number 205 gauge.

WHY: For realistic and reliable coupling and uncoupling

COMPLEMENTARY PROJECTS: 23 and 29 through 38

1 Tim Fornstrom mounted a Kadee number 5 on this older Athearn SD40-2 diesel by cutting the metal mounting pad from the chassis and mounting the coupler on the body. Newer Athearn SD40-2 diesels have a mounting pad built into the body. Fornstrom added a Details West 140 snowplow and Detail Associates 2212 coupler lift bars, 1508 MU hoses, 1505 MU stands, 1404 drop steps, and 6206 air hoses to his model.

Magnetically operated knuckle-style couplers have become the standard fitting on virtually all HO cars and locomotives, except for lower-priced toys and some kits. Kadee pioneered the design back in the 1940s, and, when their patent expired in the late 1990s, a host of others, including Bachmann, Accurail, InterMountain, Life-Like, and McHenry, began producing similar couplers. Kadee, however, has by far the greatest variety of coupler mounting shanks, so you can get shorter, longer, higher, or lower couplers, even couplers with a second swivel for tight curves, and both metal and plastic couplers.

KADEES FOR ATHEARN LOCOMOTIVES

Athearn has produced several different chassis for their diesel locomotives. Their current HO scale models are designed to accept Kadee number 5 couplers on the plastic body of the locomotive. Older Athearn diesel designs, however, provide a metal coupler-mounting pad as part of the chassis. Many locomotives currently in the Athearn series still utilize this style. Follow the steps depicted in the photographs to install Athearn couplers on most older Athearn diesels.

I strongly recommend that you buy the Kadee catalog so you understand the wide choice you have in couplers. I find it most useful in selecting special couplers that mount closer to the body for a more realistic appearance, and for finding lower or higher couplers that correct the height without using a lot of shims or requiring filing of the chassis.

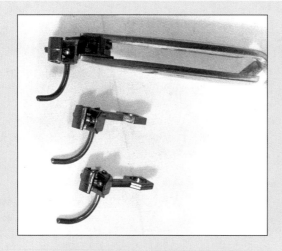

2 The most common Kadee coupler is the number 5 which, along with the numbers 3 and 9, has the coupler centered vertically on the shank. You can use the following offset Kadee couplers to raise or lower the coupler position to replace the number 5: The two Kadee number 27 (and numbers 37 and 47) couplers shown at left have the knuckle offset upward to "raise" the coupler height by about 3/32 inch. The numbers 22 (and 32 and 42) shown at far right have the knuckle offset upward to "lower" the coupler height by about 1/8 inch. For smaller adjustment of the coupler height, you can use .010x.250-inch styrene plastic shims between the coupler box (called a "draft gear box") and the floor of the car or the mounting pad on the locomotive.

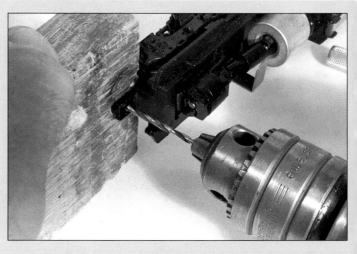

3 The older style Athearn metal diesel frames have metal mounting pads for couplers. Use a number 50 drill bit to drill through the dimple that's cast into each pad.

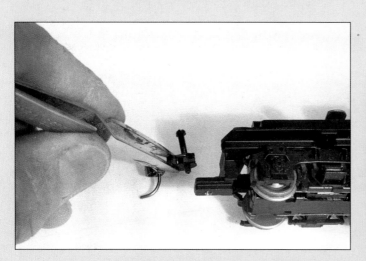

6 Assemble the coupler, the hairpin spring, and the draft gearbox, and hold the unit with tweezers while you insert the 2-56 screw to mount the assembly on the model.

7 When I checked the coupler mounting with the Kadee number 205 Coupler Height Gauge (right), I discovered that the coupler was about 1/8 inch too high. Because it would not be possible to file that much metal from the mounting pad, I opted for the Kadee number 35 coupler with the knuckle offset downward. All of the 30-series couplers are designed to be mounted in two different positions in the coupler pocket. Read the instructions carefully when you assemble the coupler and the draft gearbox to be sure you get the height you need.

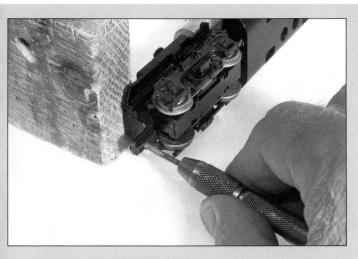

4 Hold a 2-56 tap in a pin vise and thread the hole to accept a 2-56 screw.

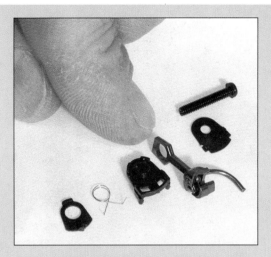

5 I wanted the shortest possible coupler for this particular Athearn diesel so I selected the Kadee number 33. The 30 Series Kadee couplers have this compact draft gearbox with a hairpin-style centering spring.

8 When you are satisfied with coupler installation, cut the nylon screw flush with the metal mounting pad.

COUPLERS

PROJECT 23 • BODY-MOUNTED MAGNETIC COUPLERS FOR ATHEARN HO DIESELS

 Time: 1 hour

 Tools: Hacksaw or razor saw, small screwdrivers, pin vise, 2-56 tap, number 50 drill bit, needle-nose pliers, hobby knife, and a Kadee number 205 coupler height gauge

 Materials: Kadee number 5 couplers, .100x.188-inch styrene strip, and liquid cement for plastics

 Cost: $

 Talent: Novice

 Scales: HO

 Space: 6x9 inches

 Tip: Check every coupler installation with your Kadee number 205 gauge.

WHY: For realistic and reliable coupling and uncoupling

COMPLEMENTARY PROJECTS: 22 and 29 through 38

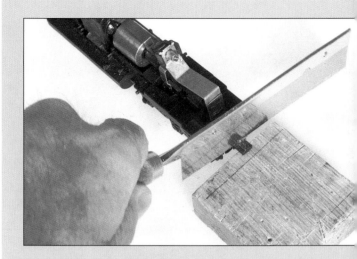

1 Use a razor saw or hacksaw to cut metal coupler mounting pads off older-style Athearn chassis. Support the pad on a block of wood so you don't break the chassis with the pressure of the saw.

The older Athearn diesel designs provide a metal tab on the chassis to mount the coupler. The tab makes it difficult to install a well-detailed pilot or snowplow because the coupler has to be removed before the body can be removed. It's relatively easy to mount couplers on the bodies of these older Athearn diesels. The first step is to remove the stock coupler-mounting pad from the chassis with a hacksaw. Cut as close to the end of the frame as possible to leave as much room as you can for the new coupler pocket. You want to leave at least three-fourths of the thickness of the curved end-piece on the chassis. With the original coupler mounting pad removed, there is just enough space to mount the coupler on the body.

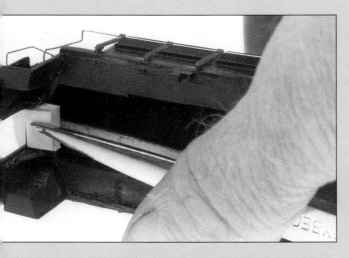

2 Next, you need to install mounting pads underneath the end platforms of the Athearn diesel bodies. Use two 3/8-inch-long pieces of .100x.188 styrene strip to lower the coupler to the proper height. Test-fit the assembled coupler and draft gearbox with two pieces of the styrene strip to see where it places the coupler height. Check that height with the Kadee number 205 gauge. You can buy the strip in a variety of thicknesses, so it's easy enough to add more or use less at this stage. When you are satisfied, use liquid cement for plastics (the tube type can take months to dry) to cement the shims to the body.

3 Let the cement dry for at least 24 hours, then hold the coupler and draft gear in place and mark the location of the mounting hole. Drill the hole with a number 50 drill bit and thread it with a 2-56 tap.

4 I used a number 8 coupler to get the shortest shank possible. Since I made this model, Kadee has introduced the number 33 coupler, which is somewhat shorter and has an easier-to-install hairpin-style centering spring. Either coupler will work

5 Install the coupler with a 2-56 screw and cut the screw thread so it's flush with the top of the end platform. Double-check the coupler height with the number 205 gauge and add whatever details you wish (see Project 22) to the front and rear pilots.

COUPLERS

PROJECT 24 • BODY-MOUNTED MAGNETIC COUPLERS FOR KATO AND ATLAS HO DIESELS

 Time: 1 hour

 Tools: Small screwdriver, pin vise, 2-56 tap, number 50 drill bit, needle-nose pliers, hobby knife, and a Kadee number 205 coupler height gauge

 Materials: Kadee number 5 couplers, .100x.188-inch styrene strip, and liquid cement for plastics

 Cost: $

 Talent: Novice

 Scales: HO

 Space: 6x9 inches

 Tip: Check every coupler installation with your Kadee number 205 gauge.

 WHY: For realistic and reliable coupling and uncoupling

COMPLEMENTARY PROJECTS: 22, 23, and 29 through 38

Most HO scale diesels sold for the hobby market, as opposed to toys, are now equipped with some kind of magnetic knuckle coupler. There are, however, thousands of older models that were fitted with the strange "horn hook"–style coupler that is still used on most HO toy trains. It's relatively simple to replace these older couplers. Kato and Atlas feature similar mounting platforms for their couplers. To mount a Kadee or similar coupler, it's only necessary to thread the holes needed to attach the new coupler. Virtually all of the firms who now produce Kadee-style couplers use the size of the Kadee number 5 as their standard, so you can fit almost any Accurail, Bachmann, Life-Like, InterMountain, or McHenry coupler to an older Atlas or Kato diesel with these techniques.

1 Remove the body from the locomotive as described in Project 22. Most Atlas and Kato diesels already have a mounting hole for the coupler-retaining pin. If not, use an electric drill and a number 50 drill bit to drill a hole. Thread the hole with a 2-56 tap held in a pin vise as shown.

2 Kadee number 5 couplers, as well as most other brands, have small tabs on each side of the draft gearbox. Use a hobby knife to remove these tabs so they look like those on the right.

3 Use the 2-56 screw provided with the Kadee number 5 couplers to mount the assembled draft gear, spring, and coupler. Check the height of the coupler with a Kadee number 205 coupler height gauge. If the coupler is too high, remove it and install shims cut from .100x.188-inch styrene strip. If the coupler is too low, consider replacing it and the draft gear with one described in Project 23.

COUPLERS

PROJECT 25 • MAGNETIC COUPLERS FOR HO STEAM LOCOMOTIVES

Time: 1 hour

Tools: Hobby knife, small screwdriver, and Kadee number 205 coupler height gauge

Materials: Kadee number 362 couplers

Cost: $

Talent: Novice

Scales: HO

Space: 6x9 inches

Tip: Check every coupler installation with your Kadee number 205 gauge

? WHY: For realistic and reliable coupling and uncoupling

COMPLEMENTARY PROJECTS: 22 and 29 through 38

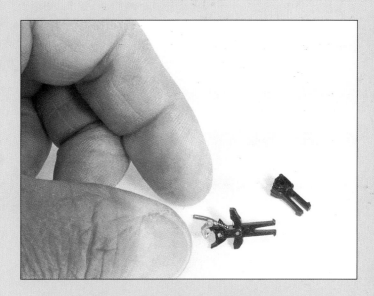

1 The number 362 coupler (bottom) is designed to replace the snap-in couplers on many European-made steam locomotives, like the dummy coupler (top) from an IHC steam locomotive by Mehanotenika.

Most HO scale steam locomotives are fitted with nonoperating "dummy" front couplers to match the appearance of prototype couplers. There's seldom enough room around the pilot of the locomotive to use a conventional Kadee or similar magnetic coupler. Kadee's number 362 coupler, however, has a swivel built into its shank to eliminate the need for a bulky draft gearbox. The coupler is actually designed for use in European prototype models, so it has a rather unusual shank. The shank is plastic, however, and easy enough to trim to length with a hobby knife.

The 362 coupler can be installed in place of nearly any dummy coupler. There is no way, however, to adjust the height of the coupler and no offset versions are available. If the coupler height

does not match the number 205 gauge, you can remove it and file the coupler pocket itself to raise or lower the coupler.

You may also discover that there is no room beneath the pilot for the steel uncoupling pin (the simulated air hose) of a car that will be coupled to the front of the locomotive. You have three choices:

1. Cut off all the coupler hoses on all your cars and use a small screwdriver or Accurail's uncoupling pick to operate the couplers manually (many modelers prefer this system to the use of Kadee's magnetic uncoupling ramps);

2. Extend the coupler on the pilot far enough so the hoses on coupled cars will clear the pilot; or

3. Remove enough material from the bottom of the pilot to clear the air hoses of coupled cars.

The tender on most HO scale steam locomotives can be fitted with either a standard Kadee number 5 coupler or one of the special couplers listed in Kadee's catalog.

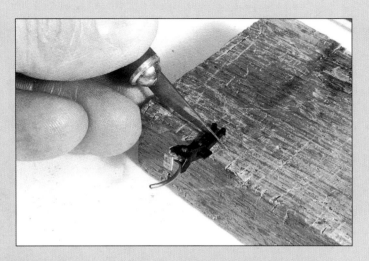

2 Test-fit the coupler in the pilot and check its height with the Kadee 205 coupler gauge. Also check to see if the uncoupling pins (simulated air hoses) for coupled cars will clear the bottom of the pilot — you may need to extend the new coupler farther from the pilot so the air hoses do clear. When you are sure the length of shank needed, cut off the excess with a hobby knife.

3 The coupler mounting area on this IHC 0-4-0T was not large enough to clear the T-shaped shank of the number 362 coupler until the area was trimmed to fit with hobby knife. Check the coupler height with the Kadee number 205 gauge. The only way to raise or lower the height is to file the top or bottom of the coupler-mounting hole.

4 The coupler shank can be installed with a tough, rubbery cement like Walthers Goo or Goodyear Pliobond. These cements should make it possible to pry the coupler free with a screwdriver or needle-nose pliers if it ever needs to be replaced.

COUPLERS

PROJECT 26 • MAGNETIC COUPLERS FOR HO FREIGHT CARS

 Time: 1 hour

 Tools: Hobby knife, small screwdriver, and Kadee number 205 coupler height gauge

 Materials: Kadee number 5 couplers or their equivalent and Kadee number 209 washers

 Cost: $

 Talent: Novice

 Scales: HO

 Space: 6x9 inches

 Tip: Check every coupler installation with your Kadee number 205 gauge.

 WHY: For realistic and reliable coupling and uncoupling

COMPLEMENTARY PROJECTS: 22 and 29 through 38

1 Test-fit any magnetic coupler installation with the Kadee number 205 coupler gauge to be sure that both the coupler and the steel wire uncoupling pin (air hose) are the correct height. This coupler is drooping so much that the wire hose fouls the gauge. The coupler must be raised.

Nearly every HO scale freight car is equipped with a standard draft gearbox (the box where the coupler mounts). Kadee number 5 couplers and similar couplers from Accurail, Bachmann, InterMountain, Life-Like, and McHenry are designed to fit this draft gearbox. In theory, you should be able to just drop any one of these couplers into the draft gearbox and replace the mounting pin or screw. In practice, however, the installation may require a few more steps.

Try to install the coupler as it comes from the package. Test the coupler height with the Kadee number 205 gauge. On many cars, you may find that the coupler is so loose that it droops far enough for the wire uncoupling pin (the simulated air hose) hanging below the coupler to foul the gauge. (It will also hit some of the switch and crossing frogs and cause derailments.) The drooping coupler problem can usually be solved by simply inserting one or more Kadee number 209 fiber washers between the coupler and the draft gearbox. You may need to experiment to determine if the washer should be placed below or above the coupler so the coupler matches the number 205 gauge.

2 Kadee makes a .010-inch-thick washer (number 209) that can be used to take up any excess clearance inside the draft gear box.

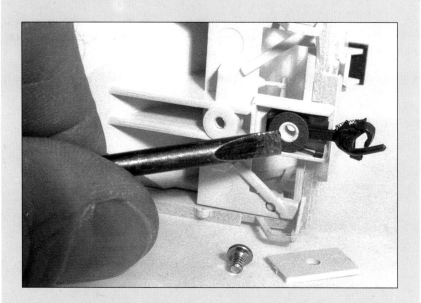

3 For this coupler, the number 209 washer was installed between the coupler and the lid of the draft gearbox to raise the coupler slightly. To lower the coupler, place the washer between the car and the coupler.

COUPLERS

PROJECT 27 • MAGNETIC COUPLERS FOR N SCALE FREIGHT AND PASSENGER CARS

 Time: 1 hour

 Tools: Hobby knife, small screwdriver, pin vise, number 62 drill bit, and Micro-Trains 1055 coupler height gauge

 Materials: Micro-Trains 1023 (assembled) or 1025 (kit) couplers and thickened cyanoacrylate cement or 5-minute epoxy

 Cost: $

 Talent: Novice

 Scales: N

 Space: 6x9 inches

 Tip: Check every coupler installation with the Micro-Trains number 1055 gauge.

 WHY: For realistic and reliable coupling and uncoupling

COMPLEMENTARY PROJECTS: 22, 28, 34 and 35

1 Use a small screwdriver to gently pry the trucks from the bolsters. Insert the screwdriver as close to the mounting pin as possible so you do not break off the pin. Pry the floor from inside the body.

More expensive N scale freight and passenger cars are now furnished with knuckle-style couplers. Older models and less-expensive cars, however, are usually fitted with a large black chunk of plastic that serves as a coupler. The design dates back to the early 1960s, when Arnold-Rapido pioneered mass-produced N scale equipment and made this their standard coupler. The industry adopted the design in spite of the fact that it made it almost impossible to couple two cars without derailing both. The newer knuckle-style couplers were designed by Micro-Trains, and when their patents ran out in the 1990s, as happened when Kadee's HO knuckle coupler patent expired, several other manufacturers produced similar couplers. Some of these couple with the Micro-Trains coupler. Micro-Trains offers a variety of couplers that snap right into the coupler pockets of cars equipped with the Arnold-Rapido–style couplers, as well as conversion pilots for virtually every N scale steam and diesel locomotive, making it easy to fit the couplers to these locomotives.

BODY-MOUNTED COUPLERS

Nearly all N scale freight and passenger cars (even Micro-Trains' own rolling stock) are fitted with trucks that include couplers. They are essentially the same type of truck-mounted couplers found on toy trains from Lionel and other manufacturers of O scale, and were designed in N scale to allow equipment to run around 7-inch-radius turns. If you use 12-inch or larger curves on your layout, you will find that the trains run smoother and derail less frequently (especially when reversing) if the couplers are mounted on the bodies of the cars as they are on nearly all HO scale models. Micro-Trains' 1023 assembled couplers are designed to be mounted on N scale bodies and are also offered in kit form as number 1025 couplers. The 1025 couplers can be tricky to assemble, but you can learn the technique with a bit of practice.

To body-mount the couplers, remove the trucks and cut off the original couplers and draft gearboxes. The procedure is virtually the same for any brand of N scale freight car. If you body-mount the couplers you cut from a Micro-Trains model, you can use the techniques shown in Project 28, and you won't have to purchase another set of couplers.

2 Use a hobby knife to make a deep cut across the bottom of the coupler pocket. Slice across the top of the coupler pocket, along the molded-in ridge. Hold the bolster in needle-nose pliers and pry up and down on the coupler pocket. The pocket should snap off cleanly along the lines you cut.

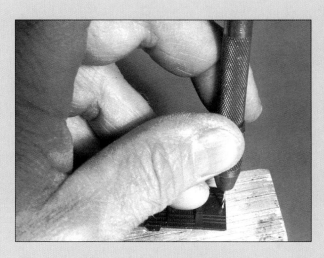

3 Use a number 62 drill bit mounted in a pin vise to drill mounting holes for the 00-90 screws furnished with the Micro-Trains 1023 (assembled) or 1025 (kit) couplers.

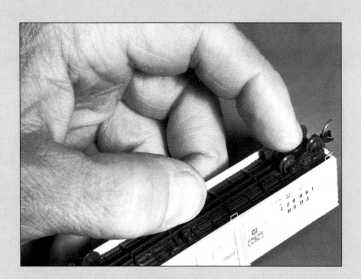

5 Use the original mounting pins to reinstall the trucks. Mount the trucks with the cut-off pocket toward the center of the car. If a truck interferes with the rear of the coupler pocket, remove it and slice more material from the edge of the truck bolster. Use the Micro-Trains 1055 coupler height gauge to check the height of the coupler and the brake hose.

6 Gold Medal Models produces etched-brass components to upgrade virtually any N scale freight car. Their 160-47 Modern Boxcar Details set includes enough stirrup steps, brake wheels, and end platforms (shown) for seven cars. Paint the end platforms and the brake wheel aluminum and let them dry overnight. Use the thickened cyanoacrylate cement or 5-minute epoxy to attach the end platforms.

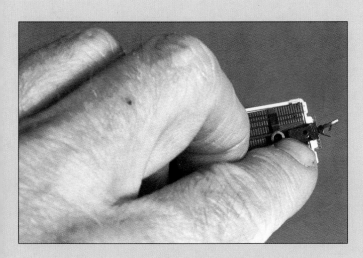

4 Use either thickened cyanoacrylate cement or 5-minute epoxy to hold the coupler pocket firmly to the car. Use only a small drop, placed so it cannot flow inside the coupler pocket and seize the coupler. Install the 00-90 Micro-Trains mounting screw. The mounting screw serves to reinforce the cement or epoxy.

COUPLERS

PROJECT 28 • BODY-MOUNTED COUPLERS FOR N SCALE FREIGHT CARS

 Time: 1 hour

 Tools: Hobby knife, small screwdriver, pin vise, 00-90 tap, diagonal cutters, and Micro-Trains 1055 coupler height gauge

 Materials: Micro-Trains 1028 adapter and thickened cyanoacrylate cement

 Cost: $

 Talent: Expert

 Scales: N

 Space: 6x9 inches

 Tip: Check every coupler installation with the Micro-Trains number 1055 gauge.

 WHY: For realistic and reliable coupling and uncoupling

COMPLEMENTARY PROJECTS: 22, 27, 34 and 35

Body-mounted couplers are a major step in improving both the appearance and operation of N scale freight cars. Nearly all N scale manufacturers equip their models with truck-mounted couplers, so the couplers swivel with trucks. Even Micro-Trains, the pioneer of realistic N scale rolling stock, uses truck-mounted couplers. If you convert your roster of N scale rolling stock to body-mounted couplers, you will certainly want to convert your Micro-Trains cars as well. You can use the Micro-Trains number 1025 couplers as described in Project 27 and simply throw away the Micro-Trains couplers that came with the model. If you'd rather not waste a pair of couplers, however, it is possible to remove the couplers from the Micro-Trains trucks and mount them on the floors of the cars.

1 Body-mounted couplers fit closer to the floor of the car than truck-mounted couplers. Check the height of the finished installation with the Micro-Trains 1055 coupler height gauge.

4 When you reinstall the trucks, rotate them 180 degrees, so the ends that used to hold the couplers face the centers of the cars.

2 Gently pry the metal underframe from the Micro-Trains plastic body. This is Micro-Trains' flat car, but nearly all the cars share a similar frame. Note how the plastic end steps are mounted so you can replace them in their proper positions. Now, pry the trucks and couplers from the metal frame.

3 Use a hobby knife to trim each coupler from its truck. Work carefully so you do not damage the edges of the truck-mounting holes. Make a deep cut from the top of the truck with the coupler supported on a scrap of wood, then turn the truck over, as shown here, and slice through to the first cut from the bottom side of the truck.

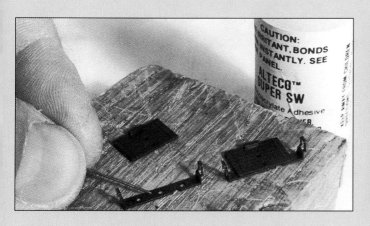

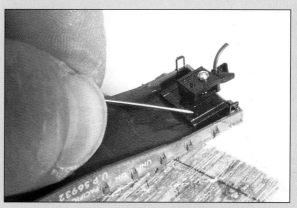

5 Use thickened cyanoacrylate cement to mount the steps to the Micro-Trains 1028 adapters. Thread the adapter with a 00-90 tap held in a pin vise.

6 Carefully trim the cut edges of the original couplers so they sit firmly on the 1028 adapter. Attach the couplers to the adapters with the screws provided and cut off the excess lengths of screw with heavy diagonal cutters.

7 Test-fit the couplers and, when you are satisfied, use thickened cyanoacrylate cement to hold the adapter to the floor of the car. Reinstall the metal underframe and the trucks, using the original mounting pins.

SECTION SIX
LOCOMOTIVES

For most model railroaders, the locomotive is the most fascinating part of the entire railroad scene. Part of the fascination with model railroading is that, however small the models, the locomotives perform exactly like the real ones, pulling long strings of cars over what can be a maze of trackwork. Like real locomotives, you can couple two or more locomotives to double or triple their pulling power, allowing them to pull really long trains or just simulate the multiple units that the real railroads so often run. For multiple locomotive operations, I suggest flipping back to Projects 17 and 18. But to keep your locomotives running smoothly and to superdetail them to precisely match the appearance of any real locomotive, read on.

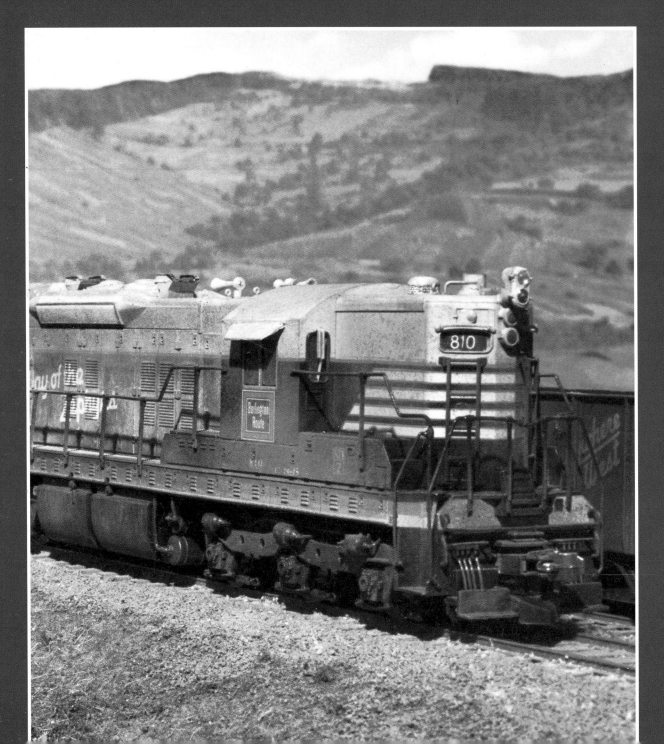

LOCOMOTIVES

PROJECT 29 • DIESEL TUNE-UP

Time: 1 hour

Tools: Hobby knife, small screwdriver, needle-nose pliers, small screwdriver, and NMRA Standard 5 Gauge

Materials: Pipe cleaners, toothpicks, plastic-compatible oil, plastic-compatible grease, and cyanoacrylate cement

Cost: $

Talent: Expert

Scales: HO and N

Space: 6x9 inches

Tip: Wipe away any trace of excess oil and grease so it cannot reach the wheels or motor brushes.

WHY: For smoother and more reliable locomotive operation

COMPLEMENTARY PROJECTS: 22, 24, and 30 through 38

Model railroad locomotives are machines that are in many ways similar to the real locomotives they represent. And like all machines, they occasionally need maintenance. Most of today's HO and N scale diesel locomotives have very similar chassis and drive trains. (You can see a photo of the chassis of a typical N scale diesel in Project 18.) It should only be necessary to clean and lubricate a model locomotive after several hundred hours of operation or if it has been out of use for several years.

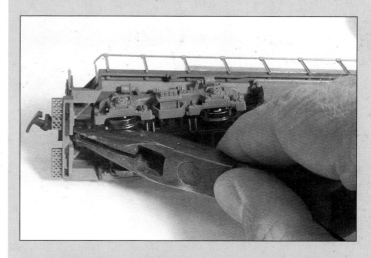

1 Some HO scale diesels are designed so you must remove the coupler before you can remove the body. If the coupler is held in place with a pin, use needle-nose pliers to remove the pin. On brands that use screws to retain the coupler, remove the retaining screw with a screwdriver.

2 The superstructure is usually held in place with invisible clips inside the body. If you can spot a screw head or clip, try loosening it to see if frees the body. Such obvious sources of attachment are rare, however. Spread the sides of the body apart with your fingers while simultaneously pulling downward on the fuel tank. Do not try to pull downward on the trucks or you may damage them or partially disengage the drive gears. If this doesn't help, try pulling one side of the body far enough out from the side of the chassis so you can insert a thin metal ruler between the body and the chassis. Then pry the opposite side from the chassis by inserting another thin metal ruler. You should then be able to wiggle the chassis free from the body.

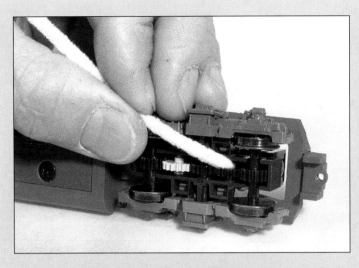 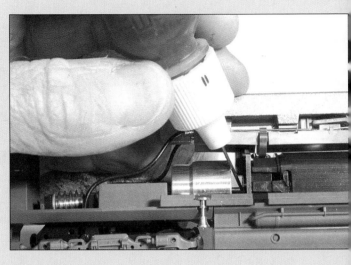

3 Use a small screwdriver to remove the plastic caps from the bottoms of the trucks. Dip a pipe cleaner in model railroad track–cleaning fluid. Work outdoors away from flames and don't get the solvent anywhere near the painted parts. Clean any excess grease from around the gears and from the treads of the wheels. If the wheels are encrusted with grime, use a toothpick or a sharpened ice cream stick to scrape the treads. Do not use a metal tool such as a screwdriver or hobby knife—you'll scratch the treads, and the scratches will attract even more grime.

4 Apply a single drop of plastic-compatible oil to each of the two motor bearings.

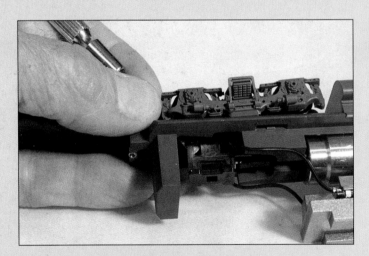 

6 The worm gear in most HO scale locomotives is covered with a removable plastic cap. It's difficult to pry the cap off from the top of the chassis, but you can reach up beside the trucks with a small screwdriver as shown to push the cap off.

5 Use an NMRA Standards Gauge, as described in Tip 39, to check the spacing of each wheelset. If the spacing is too wide or too narrow, remove the wheelsets and gently twist the opposite wheels to move them in or out on the axles. Once the wheels are in the correct position, apply a single drop of cyanoacrylate cement (like Super Glue) to each wheel to cement it tightly to the axle.

7 Use a toothpick to apply plastic-compatible grease to the hollows between the worm gear's teeth. With the cap removed, it is also easier to apply a single drop of oil to each of the bearings on the ends of the worm.

8 Apply just a trace of plastic-compatible grease to the gear teeth underneath the locomotive. Use a fresh pipe cleaner to wipe any grease from the sides and tops of the teeth—it should only rest in the hollows of each gear tooth.

PROJECT 30 • SUPERDETAILS: CAB SUNSHADES FOR HO DIESELS

Time: 1 hour

Tools: Tweezers and a hobby knife with a number 17 blade

Materials: Thickened cyanoacrylate cement and Cal Scale 437, Detail Associates 1304, or Precision Scale 29087 cab sunshades for HO scale

Cost: $

Talent: Novice

Scales: HO

Space: 6x9 inches

Tip: Double-check the alignment and fit before applying cement.

WHY: To match a specific prototype diesel

COMPLEMENTARY PROJECTS: 22, 29, 32, 37, and 52 through 55

1 These diesels started as out-of-the-box Proto 2000 SD7s by Life-Like. Extra details were added in this project, as well as in Projects 32, 33, 52, and 53. In addition, the locomotives underwent simple powdered pastel chalk weathering, as described in Project 54. I upgraded three Proto 2000 SD7 diesels because the real railroad often ran them in sets of three.

When you start with a locomotive that is already as highly detailed as the Life-Like Proto 2000 SD7, for example, the extra details that are needed are often only those that identify the locomotive as belonging to a particular railroad. You can easily add those details to any model diesel and make it a closer match to a particular prototype.

Life-Like includes some extra detail parts with each of their Proto 2000 diesels so that you can make them a closer match for specific real railroads. The SD7 models include all-weather cab windows, cab awnings, rerail frogs, a winterization hatch, and a three-piece steam generator set. Life-Like molds holes on the inside of their bodies to accept the mounting pegs for the winterization hatch and for two of the three pieces of the steam generator set. The rerail frogs plug into holes in the sides of the trucks, and the cab awnings or all-weather cab windows must be attached to the sides of the cab with thickened cyanoacrylate cement.

You can easily upgrade an Athearn SD9 or a Rail Power Products SD9 body with additional parts that are specific to Chicago, Burlington & Quincy SD7s and available from several sources. EMD SD7 diesels, when purchased by the CB&Q (and the subsidiary Colorado & Southern and Fort Worth & Denver) had cab awnings, an extra pair of high-mounted headlights on each hood, steam generators, winterization hatches over the forward exhaust fans, and spark arrestors on each of the exhaust stacks. Later, the upper headlights were removed, some of the locomotives received all-weather cab windows, and all were fitted with rotating beacons on the roofs.

2 Remove the lower lips of the rain gutter from the sides of the cab. Use the X-Acto number 17 blade to slice into the gutter to the face of the cab wall and to chisel the ends from the gutters.

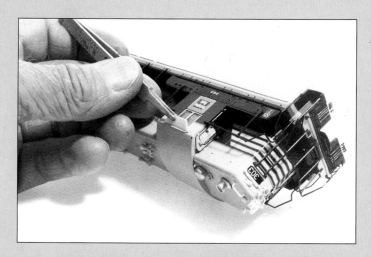

3 Affix the Proto 2000 cab sunshades (awnings) with thickened cyanoacrylate cement.

LOCOMOTIVES

PROJECT 31 • SUPERDETAILS: CAB SUNSHADES FOR N DIESELS

Time: 1 hour

Tools: Tweezers, hobby knife with number 11 blade, pin vise, and number 52 drill bit

Materials: Thickened cyanoacrylate cement and JnJ Trains 84 or Gold Medal Models 160-7 N scale cab sunshades

Cost: $

Talent: Novice

Scales: N and HO

Space: 6x9 inches

Tip: Double-check alignment and fit before adding cement.

WHY: To match a specific prototype diesel

COMPLEMENTARY PROJECTS: 22, 29, 31 through 33, and 52 through 55

These N scale cab shades are etched from brass. (Similar cab sunshades are available in HO scale from A-Line as number 29210.) Metal cab sunshades are designed to be mounted in two holes that you must drill above the cab windows. The two tabs on each sunshade are then inserted into the holes and held in place with a drop of thickened cyanoacrylate cement. Scale-model cab sunshades are very vulnerable because it's easy to grab them accidentally when picking up the locomotive. While some modelers prefer the cement-on style shown in Project 30, the metal replicas in this project are far stronger. If you do accidentally grab the model by the sunshades, they will bend rather than break off, and you can rebend them back to the proper shape.

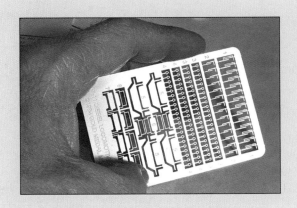

1 Gold Medal Models offers several sheets of etched-brass details for specific locomotives. Their number 160-40 set includes (left to right): mirrors, windscreens, cab sunshades, four rows of lift rings, single-blade windshield wipers, and double-blade windshield wipers.

3 Using a pin vise to hold a number 52 drill bit, drill gently into each of the two holes you marked. Position the holes as close as possible to the top of the window without breaking through the window frame.

86

2 Hold a straight pin in the jaws of a pin vise or use the tip of a dart as a scribe to mark the locations of the tabs on the cab sunshade. Hold the cab awning itself with tweezers, an essential tool for any N scale modeling project.

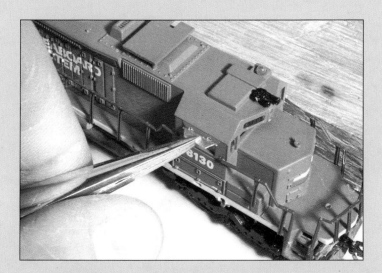

4 Test-fit the cab sunshade and, if necessary, use a hobby knife to enlarge the holes to fit the tabs. Dip each of the tabs in thickened cynoacrylate cement and push the tabs into the holes.

LOCOMOTIVES

PROJECT 32 • SUPERDETAILS: HEADLIGHTS FOR DIESELS

 Time: 1 hour

 Tools: Tweezers and a hobby knife with a number 11 blade

 Materials: Thickened cyanoacrylate cement and Details West 116, Detail Associates 1008, or Custom Finishing 256 headlights for HO scale or JnJ Trains 232 for N scale

 Cost: $

 Talent: Novice

 Scales: HO and N

 Space: 6x9 inches

 Tip: Double-check alignment and fit before adding cement.

 WHY: To match a specific prototype diesel

COMPLEMENTARY PROJECTS: 22, 29, 30, 32 through 38, and 52 through 55

If you look closely, you'll discover that nearly every real railroad has a "signature" detail that makes its locomotives unique. Examine a variety of photographs of locomotives that were operated by your favorite real railroad. The Burlington, for example, fitted most of their 1950s-era diesels with an extra set of headlights that protruded above the high nose. The Southern Pacific had a similar array, but with different style lights. The firms that sell detail parts offer models of virtually all the headlights, as well as other details, which you can use to make your models match those of any specific prototype railroad.

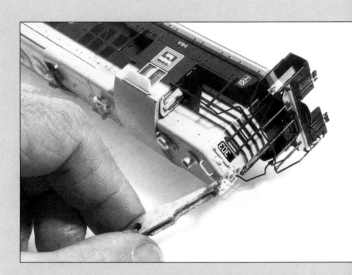

1 I used Details West 116 headlights on this Life-Like Proto 2000 HO scale SD7 dies but Detail Associates 1008 are similar. The Custom Finishing 256 headlight has realistic mounting brackets built in—with other brands, you have to build your own mounting brackets. Use thickened cyanoacrylate cement to mount the headlights.

2 Add fillet of thickened hobby-type cyanoacrylate cement to simulate the bracket th retains the top headlights and to add strength to the mounting. Allow to dry overnight.

PROJECT 33 • SUPERDETAILS: STEAM GENERATORS FOR DIESELS

Time: 1 hour

Tools: Tweezers, a hobby knife with a number 11 blade, pin vise, and number 40 and 55 drill bits

Materials: Thickened cyanoacrylate cement, Details West HO scale 118 or JnJ Trains N scale 135 steam generator set, and paint to match the model

Cost: $

Talent: Novice

Scales: HO and N

Space: 6x9 inches

Tip: Double-check locations before drilling holes.

WHY: To match a specific prototype diesel

COMPLEMENTARY PROJECTS: 22, 29, 30, 31, 33, 38, and 52 through 55

Every little lump on a real diesel locomotive has a specific purpose or it would not be there. Model manufacturers capture the more significant shapes in the body—in fact, today's diesel models are virtually perfect in replicating the real locomotive in miniature. However, every real railroad has always had its own ideas in regard to specific appliances. When you look closely at your favorite prototype railroad's locomotives, you will likely find that there are specific details like headlights, snowplows, cab window awnings, cab window windshields, radio antennae, flashing roof lights, and air horns unique to that railroad. Several railroads' locomotives may use the same air horns, but one road will have a different headlight than the other, or its locomotives will have cab sunshades while another's may not. In effect, each railroad "personalizes" its locomotives.

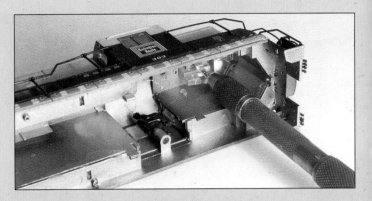

1 The Proto 2000 body has pilot holes for the steam generator parts and winterization hatch predrilled on the inside of the body. The holes must be drilled through, however. If you use the Details West number 118 parts, drill the holes in the Proto 2000 body with a number 55 drill bit held in a pin vise (use a number 40 bit if you use the Proto 2000 parts). I could not find a hole inside the Proto 2000 body for the exhaust, so I located it per Details West instructions just ahead of the intake filter. Drill the third hole with the number 55 (or number 40) drill bit.

If you want to capture the personalized look of your favorite real railroad, you have to include the appropriate small details.

SPOTTING PASSENGER DIESELS

In the 1950s, 1960s, and 1970s, many real railroads used their diesels for both freight and passenger service. Usually, the locomotives purchased exclusively for passenger service were wide-body units like the Santa Fe's famous silver, red, and yellow "warbonnet" F3 and F7 diesels that are the most popular model railroad locomotives in history. Two significant mechanical fittings made these passenger locomotives different from nearly identical F3s and F7s used for freight service: the passenger locomotives were usually fitted with gears inside the trucks to allow higher top speeds, as well as steam generators to supply the heat for the entire train.

You cannot see the differences in gearing, although you can adjust the DCC throttles shown in Projects 17 and 18 to provide different speeds for "freight" and "passenger" locomotives. You can, however, install the small roof details unique to EMD diesels (including SD7s and SD9s) that were fitted with steam generators. The fittings are offered in HO scale by Details West as their number 118, and in N scale by JnJ Trains as number 135. Do some research on your favorite prototype road to determine which locomotives, in which number series, were fitted with steam generators. Often, you can spot the steam generator fittings in photographs that were taken high enough above the rails for the roof to be visible.

2 Use a jeweler's file or sharp hobby knife to trim away the molding sprue from the bottom of the Details West exhaust stack.

3 The Details West number 118 steam generator set includes (top, left to right) an exhaust stack, engine exhaust, and air intake filter. The Proto 2000 parts are shown at the bottom. JnJ Trains offers steam generator detail sets in N scale. The steam generators were used when locomotives hauled passenger cars. Though this was a rare assignment for Burlington SD7s, all units had them.

4 Affix the Details West number 118 steam generator parts to the body with thickened cyanoacrylate cement.

PROJECT 34 • SUPERDETAILS: WIND DEFLECTORS FOR DIESELS

 Time: 1 hour

 Tools: Tweezers and a hobby knife with a number 11 blade

 Materials: Thickened cyanoacrylate cement and Gold Medal Models 160-7 or JnJ Trains 100 N scale wind deflectors, or Detail Associates 2304, Overland Models 39327, or Precision Scale 39150 HO scale wind deflectors

 Cost: S

 Talent: Novice

 Scales: HO and N

 Space: 6x9 inches

 Tip: Double-check locations before drilling holes.

 WHY: To match a specific prototype diesel

COMPLEMENTARY PROJECTS: 30, 34, and 52 through 55

Wind deflectors are one of several fittings that often identify a locomotive as belonging to a specific railroad, even if the locomotive is not lettered. N scale diesel locomotives are just large enough to show such identifying details. There's more information about real railroad locomotives in Projects 30 through 33. Briefly, each road has its own idea about specific details like headlights, snowplows, cab window sunshades, cab window windshields, radio antennae, flashing roof lights, and air horns. These details are well worth adding to your models to make them look even more realistic.

1 This Bachmann SD40-2 has had a Micro-Trains 1167 magnetic knuckle coupler conversion and a Detail Associates 8211 snowplow installed, as well as cab sunshade and wind deflector superdetails.

2 Whenever you add superdetails to a model locomotive it is essential to have a photograph of the prototype. You can use photographs from books or magazines, but an original photo will often reveal details that are not visible in published photos.

3 Gold Medal Models' number 160-7 Diesel Locomotive Detailing Set includes wind deflectors, cab sunshades, lift rings, and (not shown) windshield wipers etched from brass.

4 The wind deflectors and mirrors on full-size diesel locomotives are designed to fold flat against the sides of the cab. Usually, they are extended straight out, but that puts them in a very vulnerable position on a model locomotive. These tiny details will be less likely to break off when you handle the locomotive if you cement them flat against the sides of the cab with cyanoacrylate cement. Paint the wind deflectors to match the body.

LOCOMOTIVES

PROJECT 35 • SUPERDETAILS: LIFT RINGS, GRABIRONS, AND LIFT BARS

 Time: 1 to 2 hours

 Tools: Tweezers, a hobby knife with a number 11 blade, pin vise, number 78 drill bit, and needle-nose pliers

 Materials: Thickened cyanoacrylate cement; paint to match the model's color; Gold Medal Models 160-7 lift rings and 160-25 grabirons; JnJ Trains 16 N scale lift rings and 1543 grabirons; Detail Associates 2501 .006-inch wire for lift bars in N scale or 2206 lift rings, 2202 grabirons, and 2205 coupler lift bars; Overland Models 9150 coupler lift bars; or Precision Scale 48277-1 lift rings for HO scale models

 Cost: $$

 Talent: Novice

 Scales: HO and N

 Space: 6x9 inches

 Tip: Double-check locations before drilling holes.

 WHY: To match a specific prototype diesel

COMPLEMENTARY PROJECTS: 30, 34, 36, and 52 through 55

The superdetails that stand out most on a model are the replicas of the parts that are made from steel rods on the real locomotive, including the lift rings on the roof, the grabirons (ladder rungs), the handrails, and the coupler lift bars or levers that are used by switchmen to open and close the couplers from beside the loco-motive. Some of the higher-priced HO scale models are fitted with separate lift rings, grabirons, and lift bars, but many HO models lack these details. Imported brass models are the only N scale locomotives with separate lift rings, grabirons, and lift bars. These parts are avail-able as etched-metal components in N scale and as shaped-wire parts in HO scale. To install them, simply drill a hole for each lift ring or lift bar, or two holes for each grabiron, dip the ends of the parts in thickened cyanoacrylate cement, and install them on the model. Paint them with a brush and matching paint after the cement cures.

1 This N scale Atlas diesel was superdetailed with Gold Medal Models' etched-brass detail parts. Drill a number 78 hole for each of the lift rings, dip the lift ring into thickened cyanoacrylate cement, and press it into the hole with tweezers.

2 Gold Medal Models 160-25 ladders come with a drilling template so you can locate the holes for the rungs or grabirons. Most HO scale diesels have small dimples in the places where the grabirons are to be located—if not, use a ladder on a boxcar to determine the spacing between the grabirons. Use a number 78 drill bit in a pin vise to drill the holes, then dip the ends of the grabirons in thickened cyanoacrylate cement and push them into the holes with tweezers.

3 Preshaped coupler lift bars are available in HO scale from Detail Associates and Overland Models. Use tweezers to attach the lift bars. You can bend your own lift bars for an N scale model using the HO scale parts as patterns for the shape.

LOCOMOTIVES

PROJECT 36 • SUPERDETAILS: HANDMADE HANDRAILS

 Time: 1 hour

 Tools: Diagonal cutters, pin vise, number 78 drill bit, and needle-nose pliers

 Materials: Thickened cyanoacrylate cement, masking tape, and Detail Associates number 2501 .006-inch diameter wire for N scale or 2504 .012-inch diameter wire for HO scale

 Cost: $$

 Talent: Novice

 Scales: HO and N

 Space: 6x9 inches

 Tip: Double-check locations before drilling holes.

 WHY: To match a specific prototype diesel

COMPLEMENTARY PROJECTS: 30, 34, 36, and 52 through 55

Detail Associates offers a variety of preformed grabirons for HO scale diesels and freight cars. However, modelers want to include grabirons on models for which they cannot be bought. If you model in N scale, you may want to bend all your own grabirons and handrails from .006-inch-diameter wire rather than use etched-metal parts from Gold Medal Models or JnJ Trains.

If you need to make a dozen or more duplicate grabirons, bend one or two grabirons until you get the width exactly right. Then use a pair of needle-nose pliers and masking tape to make the "jig" and bend the rest of the grabirons to the same size.

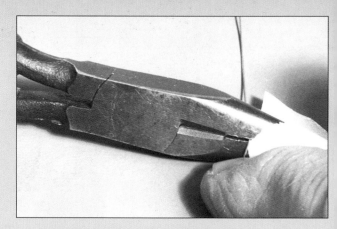

1 Hold the grabiron in needle-nose pliers with the grabiron shoved as far up into the tapered jaws of the pliers as necessary to achieve the width of grabiron you need. Mark the position on the pliers with a strip of masking tape. When it's time to bend the next grabiron, simply grip a piece of wire in the pliers (with about 1/8 inch or more protruding from each side) at the masking tape marker.

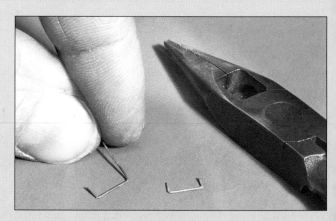

2 Grip the wire firmly in the needle-nose pliers while you bend each protruding end of the wire sharply downward by rotating the pliers on the workbench. The masking tape will help ensure that every grabiron is the same size.

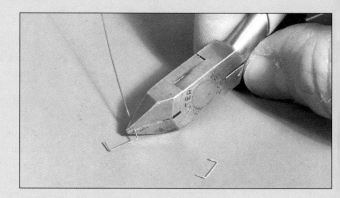

3 Use diagonal cutters to trim the ends of the grabirons to the correct length.

LOCOMOTIVES

PROJECT 37 • A WRECKED LOCOMOTIVE FLATCAR LOAD

 Time: 2 hours

 Tools: Hobby knife and razor saw

 Materials: Thickened cyanoacrylate cement, liquid cement for plastic, touch-up paint, and parts from the "bill of materials" below

 Cost: $$

 Talent: Novice

 Scales: HO

 Space: 6x9 inches

 Tip: Paint any cut edges.

 WHY: To create an eye-catching load for a flatcar

COMPLEMENTARY PROJECTS: 30, 31, 33 and 34

BILL OF MATERIALS:

ATHEARN:
10424 handrail stanchions
30510 GP9 diesel body
40007 GP35 cab roof

CAMPBELL SCALE MODELS:
256 chain

DETAIL ASSOCIATES:
1401 drop steps
1502 MU receptacles
1507 MU receptacles
2505 .015-inch wire

EVERGREEN SCALE MODELS:
.020-inch sheet styrene
.030-inch sheet styrene
.060x.060 styrene strip

K&S:
1/16-inch square brass tube

KADEE:
5 couplers

MODEL DIE CASTING:
1283 ATSF 60-foot flatcar kit

NORTHEASTERN SCALE MODELS:
1/8-inch square basswood

PRECISION SCALE COMPANY:
3996 diesel cab door

FLOQUIL:
11015 Flat Clear Finish
11031 Reefer Yellow

SCALECOAT:
24 ATSF Blue

MICROSCALE:
87-29 decals

Model railroaders find wrecked and derelict locomotives fascinating, in part because they're the only older locomotives we see in "real life." Bob Ernst elected to include a wrecked locomotive as a moving part of his railroad by building it as a flatcar load. He started with an Athearn superstructure, which meant he had to use a razor saw to cut the body from the running boards. (Some other brands have separate running boards.) He then used a styrene strip and sheet to build up the missing back walls of the cab. Included is a complete list of the materials he used, in case you want to make an exact duplicate. You have the option of starting with a decorated locomotive superstructure or applying your own paint and decals to an undecorated model. In either case, use touch-up paint to cover the saw cuts.

1 Real railroads often return the wrecked components of diesel locomotives to their own shops for repair or scrapping. These components are usually loaded onto flat cars for the trip back to the shops (or scrapyards).

2 You can simulate a wrecked locomotive by using portions of a superstructure, including the handrails and other details. In this instance, the "wreck" damaged the long hood and the salvageable portion of the locomotive is being returned to the shops.

LOCOMOTIVES

PROJECT 38 • DROP-IN NUMBERBOARDS AND MARKER LIGHT LENSES

Time: 1 hour

Tools: Hobby knife, scissors, tweezers, and a 00 paintbrush

Materials: Microscale Krystal Clear or clear white cement, and red and green paint

Cost: $$

Talent: Novice

Scales: HO

Space: 6x9 inches

Tip: Wipe any excess clear paint from the edges before it has a chance to dry.

WHY: To duplicate some very small but significant and highly visible prototype locomotive details

COMPLEMENTARY PROJECTS: 50 through 53

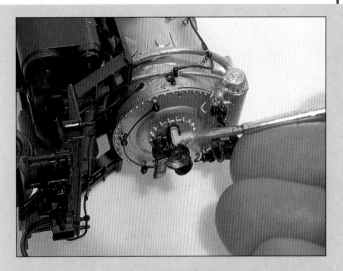

1 To add locomotive numbers to the tiny headlight number plates, use number decals but do not soak them from the paper. Position both decal and paper in place, then cover the area with Microscale's Krystal Klear. The fluid will protect the numbers, hold them in place and provide a clear, glasslike covering.

2 Use a sharpened toothpick to apply dots of green and red paint to the marker light lenses on the locomotive and tender. Let the paint dry completely, then apply a drop of Microscale Krystal Klear to each lens to simulate the prototype's glass lens. I used Badger Modelflex number 85 Reading Green and number 87 Signal Red for the colors.

Sometimes it's the more delicate details that stand out on a model—or that are most obvious in their absence. Steam locomotive and early diesels have 1-square-foot lights called "markers." The marker lights were usually used to indicate the train's class and if another part of the train (called a section) would follow the first. Many steam and early diesel locomotives also had small illuminated numberboards. The numbers in the boards varied from railroad to railroad; some repeated the locomotive's number, while others displayed the train's number.

97

SECTION SEVEN
FREIGHT CARS

Real railroads are in the transportation business. They don't just run trains for the sheer joy of it all, as you and I do. The companies that build real railroad freight cars have designed a variety of cars that are easily loaded and unloaded with whatever commodity they were designed to carry. Box cars, for example, have doors designed so that a forklift with a pallet can easily enter the car. Covered hoppers are designed to carry the specific cargo needed by specific shippers. Covered hoppers that carry powdered clay, for example, have different shapes, troughs, and discharge valves than cars that carry grain. You can buy a precise scale replica of virtually every freight car you see today and nearly every freight car that has seen major use in any era from 1900 to the present. You can buy superdetailed HO, N, S, O, and G scale cars with individual grabirons and ladder rungs, see-through roofwalks and walkways, and just about every other visible detail. For somewhat less money, you can also buy cars that have less detail and add the details that you feel are necessary.

FREIGHT CARS

PROJECT 39 • DERAIL-PROOF FREIGHT CARS

 Time: 30 minutes or more

 Tools: NMRA Standards Gauge and needle-nose pliers

 Materials: Cyanoacrylate cement

 Cost: $

 Talent: Beginner

 Scales: HO, N, S and O

 Space: 2x2 inches

 Tip: Check every wheel set for proper dimensions.

 WHY: To avoid persistent derailments

COMPLEMENTARY PROJECT: 14

1 The two shallow notches on the side of the NMRA Standards Gauge are used to check the spacing or back-to-back gauge of the wheelsets. If the flanges fit into both notches at once, the wheels are fine. If not, hold the center of the axle with needle-nose pliers and gently rotate and push or pull one of the wheels into the proper gauge. The same tabs can be used to check for the size of the flanges. The NMRA has a set of "Recommended Practices"—or RP designs— and RP-25 applies to wheel flanges for HO scale models. If the wheel flanges fit the notches, they should meet RP-25 design. If the wheel flanges are larger than the notches, you may find that they will cause derailments on some turnouts and on track with rail smaller than the HO scale train set-size code 100. (Some track uses smaller code 70 or code 83 rail to match smaller real railroad rail.)

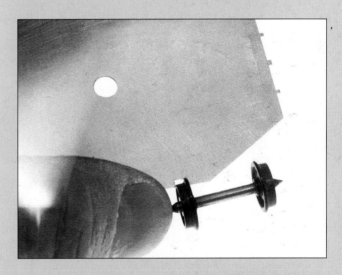

2 The gauges for all scales have similar checking notches. The larger notch on the side of the gauge is used to check the overall width of the wheel. If the wheel is narrower than the gauge, it may derail at switch frogs and crossings. You can buy replacement wheelsets with the correct wheel flanges for most HO, N, S, and O scale models.

The National Model Railroad Association (NMRA) Standards are used by virtually every manufacturer of model railroad equipment. The standards apply primarily to trackwork, coupler locations, and wheels and drivers, and when all the equipment is set to the same standard, you can operate any locomotive and freight or passenger car on any track without fear of accidental derailments. The NMRA even produces a stamped-metal "Standards Gauge" that is available directly from the NMRA (4121 Cromwell Road, Chattanooga, TN 37421) or from most hobby dealers. Use of the gauge for checking track and turnout dimensions is shown and explained in Project 14, but it also has tabs to check the width and depth of wheel flanges and the width of entire wheels. Check every wheel on every locomotive and every car to be certain they all meet the same standards. Even if a particular car or locomotive is not derailing, it will roll more smoothly if the wheels are correct.

PROJECT 40 • SEE-THROUGH METAL ROOFWALKS FOR HO SCALE CARS

Time: 1 hour

Tools: Hobby knife, small screwdriver, cabinetmaker's file, heavy steel ruler, tweezers, pin vise, number 78 drill bit, and a number 0 paintbrush

Materials: Plano Models or Detail Associates etched-metal roofwalks or Kadee plastic see-through roofwalks, Detail Associates 6224 boxcar roof plugs, Goodyear Pliobond or Walthers Goo cement, liquid cement for plastics, and paint to match car

Cost: $

Talent: Novice

Scales: HO

Space: 6x9 inches

Tip: Be sure the roofwalk is perfectly flat, with the end walks angled to match the roof, before cementing it in place.

WHY: To superdetail the highly visible roofs of steam and early diesel-era box cars, covered hoppers, and reefers

COMPLEMENTARY PROJECTS: 59 and 60

1 You really can see through these replacement roofwalks. If you use Plano or Detail Associates etched–stainless steel roofwalks, you also need to use a pin vise to drill number 78 holes to accept the corner grabirons furnished with the roofwalks. These components are molded into Kadee's plastic roofwalks.

Real railroads began to remove roofwalks from freight cars in the 1960s. If you are modeling an era earlier than that, however, virtually every freight car had some type of walkway so that a brakeman could walk the length of the train while it was in motion. Before World War II, roofwalks were made of wood and, even when treated with antiskid paint, were quite slippery when wet. In the 1940s, car-builders began installing metal roofwalks made of strips of metal placed on edge to provide a nonskid surface in all types of weather. Modelers generally refer to these roofwalks as "see-through."

The most visible roofwalks are, of course, those on the tops of boxcars, covered hoppers, and reefers. Some of the more expensive kits and ready-built models are fitted with see-through roofwalks.

If you wish to add this superdetail, you can buy from Plano a roofwalk made of etched–stainless steel to fit just about any HO scale freight car, and etched–stainless steel roofwalks from Detail Associates for 40-foot and 50-foot cars. Plano even offers several choices of patterns to match specific prototype roofwalks.

If you replace a roofwalk on a 40-foot boxcar or reefer, or on a 50-foot box car, you may be able to buy one of the see-through plastic roofwalks that Kadee fits to their ready-to-run freight cars. The Kadee roofwalks are even more realistic than most etched-metal roofwalks because they better capture the steel-on-edge appearance of the prototype. It is difficult to paint the Kadee plastic, however, so you should buy a roofwalk that closely matches the paint on the car. You should, of course, paint the stainless steel roofwalks from Plano and Detail Associates a color that matches the car as closely as possible. Don't worry if you don't exactly match the car's color because you really should weather the car as described in Projects 59 and 60—that process will effectively blend the roofwalk's color into the rest of the car.

2 Hold the roofwalk tightly against a scrap of wood with a steel ruler while you gently bend the end platforms down to match the slope of the roof. Look carefully before you bend to be sure the roofwalk is right-side up.

3 You can use the pegs that retained the original plastic roofwalk to fill the holes in the roof; simply cut the pins from the bottom of the roofwalk. Detail Associates also offers plugs with sloped surfaces that you can use to fill the holes. Cement them in place with liquid cement for plastic and paint to match the color of the car. You may need to drill additional holes to accept the mounting pins on the bottom of the Kadee roofwalks.

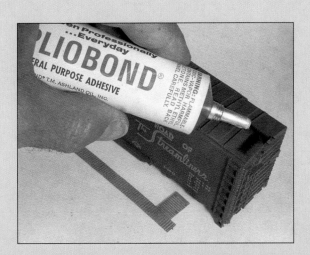

4 Use a single dab of Goodyear Pliobond or Walthers Goo to attach the roofwalks. These cements dry flexibly enough to allow the roofwalk to move slightly if it expands or contracts later. You can also use a drop of Pliobond or Goo to attach the Kadee plastic roofwalks. Let the cement dry overnight, then paint the metal roofwalk to match the color of the car. Finally, weather the car as described in Projects 59 and 60.

FREIGHT CARS

PROJECT 41 • SEE-THROUGH METAL ROOFWALKS FOR N SCALE CARS

 Time: 1 hour

 Tools: Hobby knife, small screwdriver, cabinetmaker's file, heavy steel ruler, tweezers, and a number 0 paintbrush

 Materials: Gold Medal Models 160-41 etched-metal roofwalks, Goodyear Pliobond or Walthers Goo cement, and paint to match car

 Cost: $

 Talent: Novice

 Scales: N

 Space: 6x9 inches

 Tip: Be sure that the roofwalk is perfectly flat, with the end walks angled to match the roof before cementing it in place.

 WHY: To superdetail the highly visible roofs of steam and early diesel-era box cars, covered hoppers, and reefers

COMPLEMENTARY PROJECTS: 27, 28 and 60

Most N scale cars lack some of the finer details of HO scale cars. These details, including smaller couplers from Micro-Trains (see Projects 27 and 28) bring the appearance of out-of-the-box N scale freight cars and locomotives up to the appearance standards of HO scale models. The older Atlas N scale, two-bay covered hopper model shown in this project has particularly fine steps and grabiron moldings, and Atlas even provides a molded-in dimple to locate body-mounted couplers like Micro-Trains' number 1025. These features make this one of the best one-piece N scale plastic freight car bodies. You can upgrade this realism further by installing a see-through roofwalk, one of the most visible details on these models.

1 Before . . .

4 Gold Medal Models produces etched-brass upgrade parts for most N scale freight cars. This 160-41 set includes enough parts for two cars. I opted to leave the Atlas stirrup steps and brake wheel and replaced only the roofwalk on this car. Use a sharp hobby knife or a pair of fingernail clippers to trim the parts from the sprue.

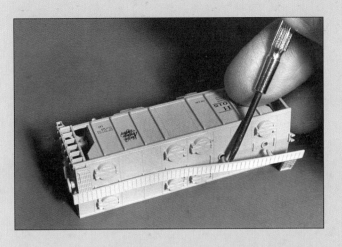

2 . . . and after. This Atlas N scale PS-2 was upgraded with a new Gold Medal Models roofwalk, body-mounted Micro-Trains couplers, and minimal (for a cement-carrying car) weathering.

3 Use a small screwdriver to pry the existing roofwalk from the top of the car by working each mounting peg out about 1/16 inch at a time. Slice the mounting pegs flush with the bottom of the roofwalk. It's wise to hold the peg with a pair of tweezers while you cut, so it does not go flying across the room. Push the pegs back firmly into their original holes and apply a drop of liquid cement for plastics. Let them dry overnight.

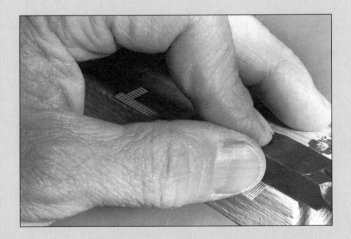

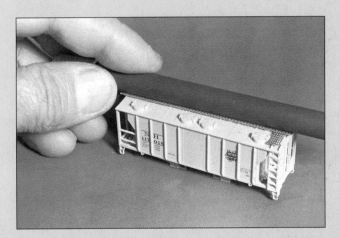

5 Gently bend the roofwalk end platforms to match the angle of the roof. Use Walthers Goo or Goodyear Pliobond to attach the roofwalk to the roofwalk supports on the car. Hold the walk in place with a knife or other tool until the glue hardens.

6 Use a flat medium-cut cabinetmaker's file to smooth the mounting pegs flush with the roof. (The teeth you see are the rough-cut side of the file; the medium-cut teeth are on the "down" side.) You may want to paint the pegs to match the car, but they can be disguised with simple weathering colors. Paint the roofwalk a light gray to match the model. The color can be a bit off, because the weathering will blend it into the color of the car body. Use the powdered pastel chalk weathering technique shown in Project 60.

PROJECT 42 • ETCHED-METAL DETAILS FOR TANK CARS

 Time: 2 hours

 Tools: Hobby knife, small screwdriver, needle-nose pliers, two blocks of wood, pin vise, number 78 drill bit, tweezers, and a number 0 paintbrush

 Materials: Plano 235 etched-brass details for MDC N scale tank cars or 305 for MDC HO scale tank cars, Micro-Trains 1064 hopper car stirrup steps for N scale models, Goodyear Pliobond or Walthers Goo cement, liquid cement for plastics, and paint to match car

 Cost: $$

 Talent: Expert

 Scales: HO and N

 Space: 6x9 inches

 Tip: Test-fit all of the etched-metal parts before cementing them in place.

? **WHY:** To superdetail lower cost N and HO scale tank cars

COMPLEMENTARY PROJECTS: 27, 28, 40, 41, 59 and 60

The handrails and walkways on a tank car are some of the more visible superdetails in model railroading. Unfortunately, virtually all N scale models and most HO scale models have grossly oversized handrails and far too-thick walkways. You can upgrade the appearance of most model tank cars by replacing the walkways with etched metal parts and the handrails with wire railings. Plano offers a series of etched–stainless steel walkways with handrails for most HO and N scale tank cars. The walkways have clever built-in handrails that are bent into position to avoid the complex fitting and soldering necessary to install wire handrails; be sure you order the proper set to match the model you are superdetailing. Also, if you are working on an N scale model, replace the couplers with Micro-Trains knuckle couplers (Projects 27 and 28).

1 Before . . .

4 Replace the heavy end platforms with Micro-Trains number 1064 hopper car stirrup steps and braces (left). File the bottom of the tank car's end platforms to clear the new Micro-Trains steps.

2 . . . and after. This MDC N scale tank car has been upgraded with new etched–stainless steel walkways and Micro-Trains couplers. The oversize components on the N scale car have been replaced and the finished model looks as realistic as the best HO cars.

3 To remove the oversize steps, use a hobby knife to slice them flush with the sides of the end walkways.

5 Use a hobby knife with a sharp blade to trim the Plano ladders, walkways, and handrails from the tree. Read the instructions carefully before you cut so you cut in all the right places.

6 Use two blocks of wood to bend the Plano walkways and handrails. Note that there is an etched notch indicating where to bend, and that the notch is supposed to be *inside* the bends.

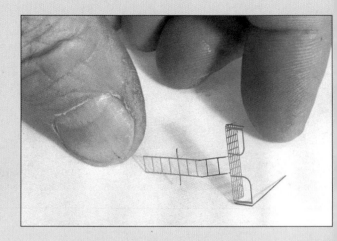

7 Test-fit the ladders and bend them at a shallow angle as shown on this finished part.

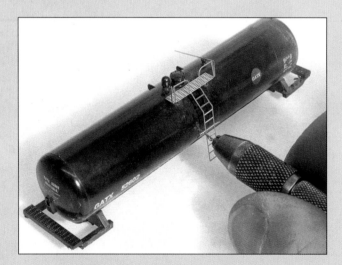

8 Cement the stock ladders to the car, then slice them flush with the sides of the car so their mounting pegs fill the holes. Test-fit the Plano ladder and walkway again to see where to drill the two holes to fit the mounting pegs on the sides of the ladders. Use a number 78 bit to drill the holes for the mounting pins. You can spray the ladders black with an aerosol can or an airbrush before installing them on the car. Use Goodyear Pliobond or Walthers Goo to install the metal parts. Install the trucks and couplers and weather the model using the techniques in Projects 59 and 60.

PROJECT 43 • HAY LOADS FOR STOCK CARS

 Time: 1 hour

 Tools: Scissors and tweezers

 Materials: Beige polypropylene twine, Woodland Scenics Field Grass in the Natural Straw color, or Static Grass Flock in Burnt Grass and Wild Honey colors, and artist's matte medium

 Cost: $

 Talent: Novice

 Scales: HO and N

 Space: 6x9 inches

 Tip: Try to keep the lengths of cut pieces within the 1/8- to 1/4-inch range.

WHY: To superdetail HO and N scale stock cars

COMPLEMENTARY PROJECTS: 59, 60 and 93

1 Cut the straight-fiber polypropylene twine into 1/8- to 1/4-inch lengths to simulate hay. You can mix in a small proportion of green to simulate fresher hay.

Generally, stock cars are considered enclosed rolling stock like boxcars or reefers. In truth, you can see right into them between the slats. Stock cars were almost always "loaded" with a layer of hay or straw on the floor to soak up animal droppings. The hay was removed shortly after the animals but not always at the unloading site. The hay was sometimes placed in the cars at a central point that might or might not be near the cattle pens where the cattle were loaded. So, even if you do not want to "load" your stock cars with cattle, then, you might want to superdetail the floors with a layer of hay

You can simulate hay with short, 1/8- to 1/4-inch pieces of fiber. Craft stores usually sell a beige-colored polypropylene twine that you can cut into the proper lengths. Buy the kind that has straight, rather than kinky, fibers. You can also substitute Woodland Scenics Field Grass in their Natural Straw color or, for finer fibers and N scale models, Woodland Scenics "Static Grass Flock," mixing about equal parts Burnt Grass and Wild Honey colors to match real hay.

2 It is far easier to install the hay if you can remove either the roof or the floor, but it is possible to work with a completed car as long as you can slide the doors open or temporarily remove them. Cover the floor with a thick layer of artist's matte medium.

3 Use tweezers to push the hay onto the still-wet matte medium. If you cannot remove the roof or the floor, stuff some pieces of hay between the slats on the bottom of the sides.

4 The hay-covered floor can be left as is (if so, do close the door), or you can load the car with scale-model cows. If you do, dip the hooves of each cow in the matte medium and press them firmly into the hay. It's better to add the cattle while the original matte medium that holds the hay is still wet, so you can force the hooves as close as possible to the floor of the car.

SECTION EIGHT
PAINTING AND DECALS

More and more model railroad locomotives, freight cars, passenger cars, and even structures are available ready to use. The vast majority of model railroad products, however, are still sold only as kits that you must assemble and, for maximum realism, paint and letter yourself. You can use aerosol cans or a small paintbrush and a bottle of paint to paint a model, but I do not recommend it. There is really no easy way to apply paint that will not hide the finely molded details on the model or result in runs and ugly blobs of paint. If you have any interest in painting models, purchase an airbrush to paint all of your models. The airbrush and its air supply can be as expensive as a half-dozen locomotives, but they are tools that you can use to make your models more realistic than anything you can buy. And, as mentioned previously, buy a respirator and wear it every time you use an airbrush or aerosol paint.

PROJECT 44 • PAINT WITH AN AIRBRUSH

 Time: 1 to 2 hours

 Tools: Airbrush, air compressor, and respirator

 Materials: Model paint and matching thinner, pipe cleaners, and clean rags

 Cost: $$$

 Talent: Novice

 Scales: HO, N, S, O and G

 Space: 2x10 inches

 Tip: Test each color or each adjustment on the airbrush before you spray the model.

 WHY: To apply colors under complete control, which is not possible with a paintbrush or aerosol cans

COMPLEMENTARY PROJECTS: 45 through 62

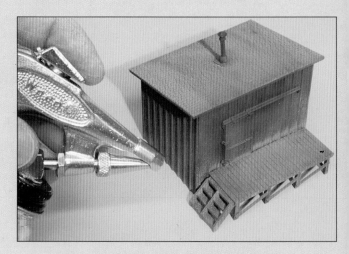

1 This is the least-expensive type of airbrush, an external-flow model. You cannot adjust the paint flow, but you can compensate a bit by adding more thinner or even some clear flat paint to the mix, two things you cannot do with a can of aerosol paint.

The airbrush is, perhaps, the most essential modeling tool for those who truly want to match their models to the real thing. It is also by far the largest investment you will likely make in the hobby (see Project 14). An airbrush is a miniature version of the spray guns used to paint automobiles. The airbrush was originally designed for artists who wanted to produce shadows and highlight effects in the easiest possible manner. Those same needs coincide with a modeler's desire to paint relatively small areas with complete control of color, intensity, and pattern. With the degree of adjustment an airbrush affords, you can also produce very light coats of paint for faded effects on weathered cars and locomotives.

AIRBRUSH ADVANTAGES

The airbrush offers some key advantages. First, many more colors are available in bottles than in aerosol cans. Second, you can mix clear coat or thinner with the paint in an airbrush, allowing you to spray just a haze of color if you desire. Finally, you can custom-mix colors that are not even available in bottles.

It is also far easier to accomplish a smooth and blemish-free finish with an airbrush because you can control the air pressure, the paint pattern, the amount of thinner, and the distance you hold the spray from the model. Yes, it does take practice, but it's not that difficult to learn—in fact it is much, much easier to spray with an airbrush than to use either an aerosol can or paint from a bottle with a bristle brush.

SELECTING AN AIRBRUSH

There are essentially three types of airbrushes: external mix, internal mix with paint-flow adjustment, and internal mix with paint-flow and air-flow

2 Sometimes, the color you want is only available in an aerosol can. There's nothing wrong with spraying the paint into the airbrush bottle and applying the paint with an airbrush. The airbrush will allow you to control the size of the paint pattern and, if necessary, even add thinner.

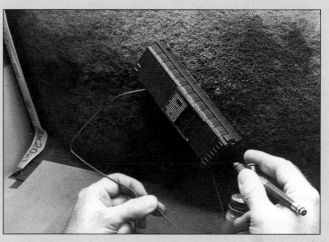

3 Bend a coat hanger into an ampersand (&) shape so the ends will grip inside the body of the model or into the trucks. You can then hold the coat hanger in one hand while you apply paint with the airbrush with your other hand. Always wear a respirator when using an airbrush or aerosol paint! In this case, the painting area is even vented to the outside. If you don't have a vent to the outside, you can attach a furnace filter, like the one shown, to a non-oscillating box-type fan. Face the fan so it blows *out* an open window. The filter will prevent paint particles from ruining the fan and your window screens.

adjustment. The costs range from about $30 to $150. If you only paint occasionally, you can try an external mix airbrush that uses throw away cans of propellant. If you really want to weather models and match prototypes, however, I recommend an internal-mix airbrush with paint-flow adjustment. Personally, I don't like the air-flow adjustment of the more expensive brushes, as it just confuses me. Most experienced modelers, however, recommend internal-mix airbrushes with both paint-flow and air-flow adjustments.

CHOOSING PAINT

Briefly, you have the choice between acrylic and lacquer-based paints. Lacquer-based paints are by far the easiest to apply, but long-term use can damage your health. With any spray, especially lacquers or solvents, work outdoors or buy a paint spray booth with a high-capacity fan to vent the fumes to the outdoors. Always work away from flames or sparks. It's also a good idea to wear a filter mask to keep both the fumes and airborne particles from

entering your respiratory tract. All that applies, of course, even when using bottled paints.

THE AIR COMPRESSOR

The air compressor is likely to cost twice as much as the airbrush itself. You want a compressor that includes an adjustable air flow and some type of tank or regulator to keep the air pressure at the setting you choose. You want to be able to adjust the air pressure from between about 15 and 40 psi. The least expensive compressors lack this adjustment and can, in fact, transfer the throbbing strokes of the air compressor's pump right into the spray pattern. Plan on spending at least $100, and I suggest as much as $200, for an adjustable compressor. If you also want it to be quiet, you'll have to spend more.

I do not recommend using aerosol cans with an airbrush because there's usually no way to adjust the air pressure so, in effect, all you are creating is a complex aerosol can outfit. Yes, you can pick colors and thin the paint, but as far as control is concerned you're really not much better off than you would be using just an aerosol can.

LIMITING THE VARIABLES

There is no specific formula for setting the adjustments on an airbrush or the compressor, or for mixing thinner and paint. You simply have to experiment until you get a balance that suits you. The settings can also vary with paint type and color, temperature, altitude, and humidity.

Some paints are designed to be sprayed right out of the bottle, but most must be thinned with 10 to 50 percent thinner. If you use a lacquer-based paint, you can use either the airbrush or paint manufacturer's thinner or lacquer thinner. If you use an acrylic paint, try the manufacturer's thinner first. If that doesn't give you the results you want, try the clear flat, semigloss, or gloss from the same paint maker. The clear paints are virtually as thin as thinner and they allow the acrylics to retain the grip and controllable flow that is sometimes lost with water or thinner.

Windex window cleaner is a third choice for thinning acrylics. A few modelers, however, have had to resort to isopropyl alcohol (never methyl alcohol—it is far too hazardous for modeling work). But, alcohol is extremely flammable and virtually negates the advantages of acrylic paints, so it's a poor choice. Experiment with other thinners and adjustments in air pressure, paint flow, and thinner-paint mixes first. After all, the major advantage of acrylic paint is that it cleans up with water or

relatively harmless thinner. First, adjust the paint and air flow on the airbrush to deliver a pattern about 2 inches in diameter when the airbrush is held about 9 inches from the work. Try about 25 psi of air pressure and thin the paint with about one part thinner to one part paint. If you don't get the results you wish, change one variable at a time: first try 20 psi, then 30 psi. If that doesn't do it, adjust the paint flow to deliver more paint. If that still doesn't work, add a bit more thinner or a bit less, depending on your initial results. If you use acrylic paints, try one of the special tips that most airbrush-makers offer specifically for spraying acrylics. For example, a single drop of glycerin like that sold in drugstores helps acrylic paints flow more smoothly. You will get it.

CLEANING AN AIRBRUSH

The only drawback of an airbrush is that you need to clean it after each use and between every color change. Even that is not difficult. Simply replace the paint bottle with a bottle of thinner. Next, spray into a clean cloth until there is no more color, then depress the trigger while holding a clean cloth lightly over the nozzle until bubbles appear in the thinner—this is called "back flushing" and it will usually clean all the internal passages. You also need to remove the cup or bottle from the airbrush and clean the threads and any other external places where paint accumulates. When you clean an airbrush that you have used for acrylic water-based paint, clean the airbrush with hot water while the paint is still wet.

PAINTING AND DECALS

PROJECT 45 • MASK FOR TWO-COLOR PAINTING

 Time: 1 to 2 hours

 Tools: Airbrush, air compressor, and respirator

 Materials: Model paint and matching thinner, Testors Dullcote, clean rags, automotive masking tape, masking tape, mild liquid detergent, and a coat hanger

 Cost: $$$

 Talent: Novice

 Scales: HO, N, S, O and G

 Space: 2x10 inches

 Tip: Paint the lightest color first.

 WHY: To re-create paint schemes you cannot buy on a ready-to-run model.

COMPLEMENTARY PROJECTS: 43, 46 through 62

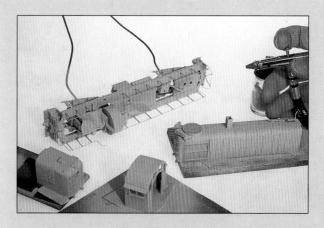

1 Hold the heavier parts with a bent wire coat hanger (upper left); smaller parts can be attached to scraps of wood with masking tape folded into loops to produce double-sided tape. These improvised handles make it easier to manipulate the parts to direct the paint spray pattern into every corner. Metal parts should be cleaned with alcohol or vinegar, either outdoors or in a ventilated area. After all parts (plastic and metal) are washed in detergent, rinsed, and allowed to dry, a coat of light gray primer can be applied. The entire project can be done without an airbrush. Start with an aerosol can of light gray primer and apply the remaining coats of paint with a paintbrush. The final clear coat, sprayed on to protect the decals, will hide most of the visible brush marks.

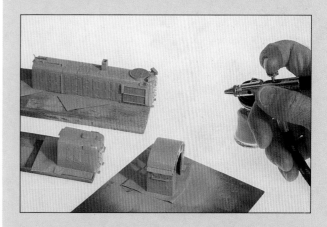

2 Apply the lightest color coat first and let it dry for at least 48 hours. I used Scalecoat number 22 Union Pacific Armour Yellow mixed 13 parts to 1 part Reefer Orange. Let this coat dry for another 48 hours.

You will discover that some paint schemes, particularly on diesels, require two colors. Before you decide you need to apply two different colors, buy the decals needed to finish the model; on some paint schemes, the second (or third or fourth) color is so small that it is included on the decal sheet. Before you begin, decide which color is the lightest and apply it first. If, by chance, one of the colors is a light gray, you can consider that to be the first paint color. On this particular model, I decided that the gray was far too dark to serve as a primer for the yellow.

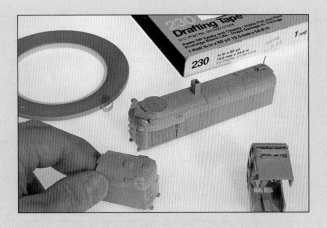

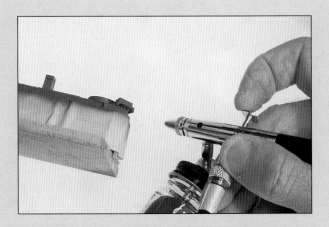

3   Automobile paint supply shops sell a thin masking tape in 1/8-inch widths. This tape is more flexible than regular masking tape and it can be bent into fairly tight curves. Apply a band of this tape at the point where the second color meets the first. To save time, finish the masking with drafting tape (it's wider than regular masking tape, less sticky, and less prone to lift the first coat) to completely cover the first coat of paint.

4   If you use an airbrush, adjust the paint and air flow so the pattern is only about the size of a dime. With this small pattern, it's easier to avoid building up a thick layer of paint along the tape's edge.

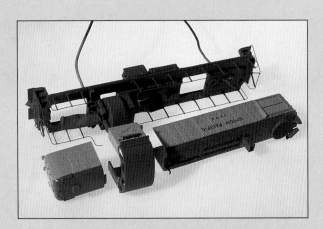

6   Apply the decals to the individual parts, then assemble the model. Finally, spray a thin coat of Testors Dullcote to protect the decals and to blend the shines of the different colors.

7   The completed model. This is an Alco RS2 that I converted to an RS3. Atlas has since introduced a ready-to-run RS3.

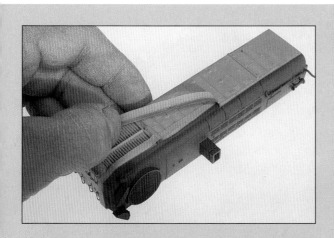

5 Peel the tape away as soon as the second coat is tacky. First, slice along the edge of the tape with a sharp hobby knife to literally cut the second coat of paint away from the edge of the tape. When you pull the tape, peel it back over itself as shown so there is less "pull" on the original paint.

PROJECT 46 • MASK AND PAINT A STEAM LOCOMOTIVE

 Time: 2 to 3 hours

 Tools: Airbrush, air compressor, and respirator

 Materials: Model paint and matching thinner, number 0 paintbrush, Testors Model Master Semi-Gloss clear, Scotch Magic Tape, and coat hangers

 Cost: $$$

 Talent: Novice

 Scales: HO, N, S, O and G

 Space: 2x10 inches

 Tip: Use flat paint, then finish with semigloss clear before applying any weathering.

 WHY: To duplicate the way steam locomotives really looked

COMPLEMENTARY PROJECTS: 43, 44, and 47 through 62

1 The steam locomotive featured in Projects 46 and 47, as well as 56, is a Rivarossi HO scale model of the USRA "Heavy" 2-8-2 Mikado. I fitted it with etched-brass superdetail parts, including an Elesco feedwater heater and oil tender tank. Use the Magic Tape to cover the drivers and valve gear.

Unlike their models, prototype steam locomotives were never solid black. These techniques can make it easier to match various shades of black and the metallic paints used on the smokeboxes (the portion of the boiler below the smokestack) and the firebox (the area of the boiler beneath the cab where the actual fire burned) of prototypes. The techniques are the same for both brass and plastic models.

When you paint, decal, and letter a locomotive or any other model, you are effectively creating a three-dimensional portrait. The shape and form are there, but you must add the color and, often, the shading. Since we are not really trying to create something, so much as to re-create it, we need the best possible examples of what we are re-creating.

In other words, you cannot hope to create a realistic model without color photographs of the real thing.

Fortunately, there are dozens of books that illustrate almost any prototype railroad in color. You can use these books, even if you are modeling an era of which only black-and-white photographs are available, as color resources. If, for example, you want to paint and weather a steam locomotive from 1935, you won't go wrong using a photo of the prototype taken in the 1950s.

You will notice that prototype steam locomotives were neither solid black nor the greenish gray known to modelers as Grimy Black. The prototypes for my model are typical of well-maintained steam locomotives that operated in the Midwest. In this region the fresh black paint retained its shine and most of the dulling effects of soot and smoke were confined to the areas along the roofs, with occasional dribbles of steam or boiler compound from various valves. The undercarriage received the usual degree of rain-splashed mud, oil drippings, and grime thrown up by the drivers and wheels. These stains usually add a brownish green tinge that can be (but is not always) very close to that popular Grimy Black. Locomotives that operated in the Sun Belt have markedly different

2 I removed the trailing truck so it could be painted as a separate piece. Mask the wheels, however, before painting the truck. Follow the paint manufacturer's instructions for applying paint with an airbrush; many paints can be used right out of the bottle, while others require the addition of thinner. I tried three different brands of paint on this model, and they all worked well.

3 Remove all of the tape. Apply the black paint to the side of a paintbrush and use it to just touch the tops of the pipes that cross in front of the firebox. This roof has already been painted Caboose Red, using the techniques described in Project 47.

shades of black that resulted from the effects of both the bleaching sun and wind blown sand and dirt. Similarly, locomotives from the Coal Belt were more likely to be black than Grimy Black, as coal dust was washed onto the drivers, the undercarriage, and the tender by the wheels and drivers.

SCALE COLOR THEORY

When you paint any model in any scale, it is important to consider the effect of the actual size of the model compared to the size of the prototype. You almost always view the prototype at effectively a much closer distance than the model. This affects the color. To prove it, paint two 8x10-inch rectangles of cardboard flat black. Place one rectangle in direct sunlight about 20 feet away. Hold the second rectangle just a foot away and compare the colors. You will see that the distant card appears somewhat more gray than the nearer card. This "Scale Color Theory" is common knowledge among military and aircraft modelers. It applies just as well to model railroads. To achieve the effect, add about I part white to every 20 parts of black. This will produce a black with just a slight tint of gray. Experiment with the mix until you match that slightly grayed-out card at 20 feet.

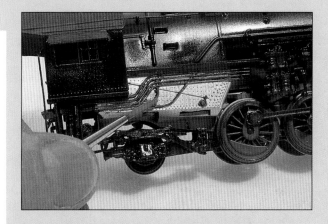

4 If you apply too much black, let it dry and apply Old Silver with a brush. I repeated these steps several times around some of the more complex areas of piping.

SCALE SHINE THEORY

Notice, also, that prototypes have a shine, particularly on the sides of the tender and on the lower sides of the boiler and cylinders. That shine often makes the rivets on tenders show prominently in photographs. The effect is seldom modeled successfully because it is difficult to get the right degree of reflection or shine. Our models are about 1/87 the size of the real thing, but neither light source nor our eyes are reduced to match that scale. The result is that any bright patch that reflects the light on our models appears much, much larger (about 87 times larger) than the prototype. To reduce the size of reflected light patches, reduce the shine with a semigloss after the paint is dry.

Listed are the materials I used for the model shown. Feel free to substitute your own favorites.

PAINT AND DECALS:

FLOQUIL:
110100 Old Silver

POLLYSCALE:
414110 Steam Power Black
414113 Reefer White
(Note: Above mixed 19 parts black to 1 part white for locomotive and tender.)
414128 Caboose Red
414275 Roof Brown

TESTORS MODEL MASTER:
Semi-Gloss clear aerosol paint

CHAMP:
EH-20 CB&Q Steam Locomotive decals

MICROSCALE:
87-126 Passenger Car Lettering decals (for head-light numberboards)
Micro Sol decal-softening fluid (see Project 50)

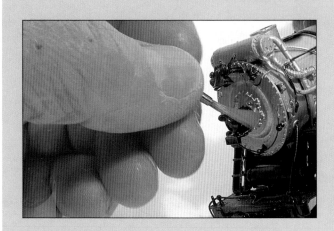

5 Use a brush to paint the headlight and marker lights black.

8 Let the paint dry for at least 24 hours. Cover the cab roof, smokebox, and firebox — and recover the drivers and valve gear — with Magic Tape, then apply the black to the remainder of the model. Apply the decals and protect them with Testors Model Master Semi-Gloss clear paint.

6 When the painting is complete, mask off the superstructure and paint the drivers and frame Grimy Black using a paintbrush. I thought the Rivarossi colors for those areas were fine as they were, but I did paint the side rods, main rods, and valve gear with a thin coat of Grimy Black — the plated parts remained visible through the single layer of paint, resulting in a metallic look that closely resembles the oily appearance of the prototype.

7 Fashion a coat hanger into a handle with hooks on each end to grip the axles of the tender when you paint it. To hold the locomotive, use a disposable rubber glove and grip the model by the drivers.

9 The semigloss sheen is most apparent on the model's tender — and it's precisely the sheen that appeared on the prototype, even after months of use.

PAINTING AND DECALS

PROJECT 47 • TWO-COLOR MASKING FOR STEAM LOCOMOTIVES

Time: 2 to 3 hours

Tools: Airbrush, air compressor, respirator, and a number 0 paintbrush

Materials: Model paint and matching thinner, Testors Model Master Semi-Gloss clear, automotive masking tape, Scotch Magic Tape, and coat hangers

Cost: $$$

Talent: Expert

Scales: HO, N, S, O and G

Space: 2x10 inches

Tip: On a steam locomotive, apply the lighter colors before applying the black.

WHY: To duplicate how steam locomotives really looked

COMPLEMENTARY PROJECTS: 43 through 46 and 48 through 62

When most people think of a steam locomotive, they think black. In truth, very few steam locomotives were all black—on most, the areas that were subjected to extreme heat were painted in special silver-colored compounds, the most common of which was a graphite mix applied to the smokebox and the firebox. In addition, many railroads painted the cab roofs another color, often red or dark green, to reflect the sun's heat.

Look carefully at photographs of prototypes to determine which areas are some color other than basic black. On the prototype for this model, the roof is red and the firebox and smokebox are silver.

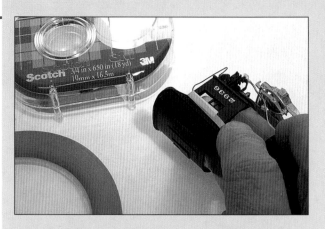

1 For complex areas, like the edges of the roof and around the firebox, use automotive masking tape like that described in Project 45. The tape is flexible and just sticky enough to hold without pulling up the previous layer of paint. The 1/4-inch variety seems most useful. After masking the edges, mask the remainder of the boiler with regular masking tape or Scotch Magic Tape. If you use the latter, press it onto a clean glass surface, then pull it free to remove some of its stickiness.

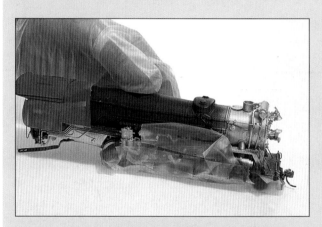

4 The second (silver) and third (red) colors are complete and the model is ready to be masked for the final coat of black.

7 The finished model, ready to accept the weathering in Project 56 that will make it look more like its prototype.

120

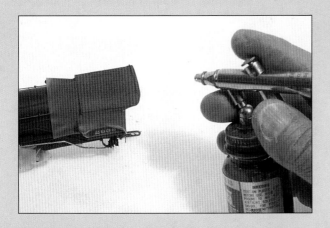

2 Mask off the cab roof, paint it Caboose Red, and remove the tape when the paint is dry.

3 If the prototype has an aluminum- or graphite-coated firebox and smokebox, spray those areas *before* the first overall coat of black is applied, as shown in Project 46. It might be possible to mask off some of the pipes and other details, but I find it easier to just paint it all Old Silver and touch up the parts with black paint and a brush.

5 Using the same techniques described for freight cars in Project 50, apply the decals with as much decal-softening fluid as necessary to get them to adhere around the rivets. Let the fluid dry overnight, then remove any residue with water and a cotton swab. Blow the locomotive and tender dry with the airbrush, then spray them with Testors Model Master Semi-Gloss clear paint.

6 Simulate the weathered canvas sunshade with a very thick coat of Roof Brown. Sprinkle some talcum powder over the still-wet paint, then apply another coat of Roof Brown.

PROJECT 48 • SPRAY PAINT "STAINLESS STEEL" PASSENGER CARS

Time: 1 hour

Tools: Wire coat hanger, filter mask, and a number 0 paintbrush

Materials: Testors 1290 Chrome Silver aerosol and Glosscote

Cost: $

Talent: Novice

Scales: HO, N, S, O and G

Space: 2x10 inches

Tip: Protect decals and preserve the metallic look with a brush-on coat of Glosscote.

WHY: To make painted cars look like stainless steel

COMPLEMENTARY PROJECT: 50

1 Using a wire coat hanger, fashion a handle with which to hold the body of the passenger car model. Spray the car with Testors 1290 Chrome Silver.

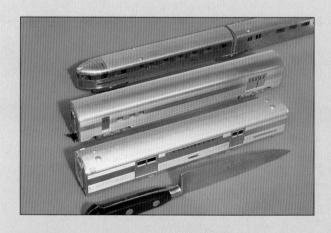

2 The knife is stainless steel, the baggage car has been painted with Testors Chrome Silver, the baggage-mail is a polished bare aluminum OK Engine Company HO scale kit, and the observation car is a typical plated-brass import. The painted car really does capture the effect of real stainless steel.

Prototype "silver" passenger cars are usually constructed of unpainted stainless steel. The most realistic models of these are plated-brass imports. In addition, OK Engine Company makes some HO scale passenger cars from extruded aluminum that certainly look metallic when polished. Because modelers who build plastic automobile kits have a need for a paint to simulate chrome, several firms offer "chrome" paint that can be used on railroad models. Testors Chrome Silver is about as close as you can get to simulating stainless steel on a model passenger car. The trick, with this paint, is to protect the decals with a clear finish without spraying the entire model and dulling the "bare metal" appearance. When applying the Glosscote, use either the bottled version or spray the aerosol into an empty bottle so you can brush the Glosscote over only the add decals.

PAINTING AND DECALS

PROJECT 49 • STRIP PAINT FROM PLASTIC MODELS

 Time: 1 hour

 Tools: Wire coat hanger, toothbrush, rubber gloves, respirator, and eye protection

 Materials: Scalecoat II Wash Away Paint Remover, 91 percent isopropyl alcohol or 3M Safest Stripper, and a glass jar or glass bread pan
Cost: $

 Talent: Expert

 Scales: HO, N, S, O and G

 Space: 2x10 inches

 Tip: Test any paint remover on a small sample of the material before covering the entire model.

 WHY: To custom-paint models without hiding the molded-in details beneath excessive amounts of paint.

COMPLEMENTARY PROJECT: 50

1 Stripping requires a container large enough to hold at least half of the model. It's better, of course, to have a container large enough to hold the entire model, but it can be done half at a time.

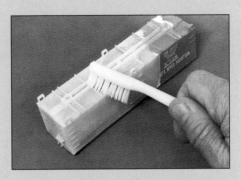

2 Do not wait for the paint to fall off of the model. As soon as the paint has softened, scrub it off with a brush. If necessary, submerge the model and scrub it again.

You can buy almost any car or locomotive you desire painted and ready-to-run. Sometimes, however, the model you desire is only available in paint schemes that are not suitable for your model railroad; or, you may find a bargain that is worth the trouble of stripping and repainting. With care and the proper materials, it's possible to remove the existing paint and lettering, leaving an undecorated car to support the new paint and lettering.

A variety of paints are used on model railroad equipment. Some will respond to one kind of paint remover while another has no visible effect on them. There are three different fluids you can try: Scalecoat II Wash Away Paint Remover, 91 percent isopropyl alcohol, and 3M Safest Stripper. The Scalecoat II Wash Away stripper is probably the least toxic of the three, but always wear rubber gloves, long sleeves, and eye protection when working with any paint stripper.

Before you ruin the model, try brushing some of the fluid on the inside or another part of the model to see if it damages the plastic. Because modern paints are usually easier to remove, you are likely to have more trouble removing paint from older models. You may also find that none of these three fluids will remove the paint. If that's the case, you may be able to sand the original lettering on the model with 400-grit sandpaper so the lettering does not show through the new paint.

Once you have tested the stripper on an inconspicuous area, disassemble the model so you can strip the body as a separate part. Use a jar or a glass bread pan large enough to submerge the entire body. Follow the instructions on the stripper, but do check the model every few minutes to be sure the paint is the only thing that is softening, not the plastic itself. With most strippers, the fluid merely softens the paint, so you need to scrub it to remove it from the model.

You can usually strain the stripper through an old pair of pantyhose and reuse it many times.

PROJECT 50 • LETTER A FREIGHT CAR WITH DECALS

Time: 1 hour

Tools: Scissors, tweezers, number 1 paintbrush, and cup

Materials: Decals, decal solvent, paper towel, facial tissue, and Testors Dullcote

Cost: $

Talent: Novice

Scales: HO, N, S, O and G

Space: 2x10 inches

Tip: Avoid touching the decal with your fingertips because it can stick to them—handle the decal only with tweezers or a paintbrush.

WHY: To re-create a specific car you cannot buy already painted and lettered

COMPLEMENTARY PROJECTS: 44 through 49 and 51 through 62

1 Cut each decal from the decal sheet. Hold the decal with tweezers while you dip it into a cup of warm water for about a count of 10. Place the wet decal on a piece of paper towel or facial tissue and let it sit for a minute or two while the water soaks through the paper and reaches the glue that will hold the decal. Try to gently push the decal on the paper with the tip of the tweezers to determine when it is ready to move.

If you are willing to paint a model railroad locomotive, freight car, or passenger car, you can likely find the lettering, logos, and stripes as a decal set, so you can match a specific prototype down to the last digit. The motivation to paint and decal a model is the desire to have something you cannot buy. You may, for example, have photos to prove that a railroad operated RS2, SD24, and E8 diesels, yet there are no prepainted models that duplicate those prototypes. What to do? Buy an undecorated model and paint and letter it.

There are two ways to letter and number a model railroad locomotive or car: with decals or with dry transfers. The selection of decals is immense—you have choices of thousands, with another 50 or more added each year. Microscale, Champion, Oddballs, and Walthers are four popular suppliers. The number of dry transfers available is but a fraction of that. Other than availability, the advantage of decals is that you can move them around as you apply them to get perfect position. The disadvantage is that you have to follow some specific techniques to disguise the clear film around each decal. The advantage to dry transfers is that there is no decal film. The disadvantage is that you must position them perfectly the first time because there is no second chance. You'll see how to apply dry transfers in Project 51.

You can minimize the amount of excess decal film by trimming the decal as close to the letters, numbers, or stripes as possible when you cut them from the sheet. Hold the decal near a light so the reflection on the surface shows where the decal film ends. Some of the more popular brands, like Microscale, already have the decal film trimmed about as close as you would want.

2 Position the model so the side you are going to letter with decals is perfectly flat and fluids cannot run off. Coat the side of the model where the first decal will be placed with decal-softening fluid like Microscale's Microsol or Walthers Solvaset.

3 Position the decal and its paper backing exactly where you want the decal to rest. If necessary, add a bit more decal-softening fluid to cover the area beneath the paper. Because the decal-softening fluids literally turn the decal to sticky paint, you cannot move the decal after it has soaked in the fluid for a few seconds. Hold the face of the decal firmly with the tip of a number 1 paintbrush while you slide the paper from beneath the decal film with tweezers.

Decals stick best to a smooth and glossy surface, so it sometimes helps to apply a single light spray of gloss and let it dry before applying the decals. The final spray of Dullcote blends the sheen of the decal to the sheen of the model to make the remaining portions of clear decal film all but invisible.

Try to find a photograph of the car or locomotive you're repainting so you do not have to rely on the decal sheet's instructions and lettering diagrams. In some cases, there are no instructions or lettering diagrams and, when there are, they may apply to a somewhat different car or locomotive. Sometimes you even need to buy three or more sets of decals just to get all the proper letters and numbers to match a specific prototype car or locomotive.

4 When the decal is precisely where you want it, apply another coat of decal-softening fluid over the top of the decal. Let the decal dry for at least 6 hours. If the decal has milky areas that indicate trapped particles or air bubbles, prick them with the tip of a hobby knife and apply another coat of decal-softening fluid. If the decal does not cling like paint to the rivets and ribs, apply another coat of decal-softening fluid and allow it to dry overnight. When you are satisfied, use a piece of wet facial tissue to scrub away any visible glue or other residue. Let the surface dry completely, then spray the entire model with a light coat of Testor's Dullcote.

PROJECT 51 • LETTER A FREIGHT CAR WITH DRY TRANSFERS

 Time: 1 hour

 Tools: Scissors, tweezers, and burnishing tool

 Materials: Dry transfers, drafting tape, and Testors Dullcote

 Cost: $

 Talent: Novice

 Scales: HO, N, S, O and G

 Space: 2x10 inches

 Tip: When you are certain the dry transfer is exactly where you want it, tape one edge to the model with drafting tape.

 WHY: To re-create a specific car you cannot buy

COMPLEMENTARY PROJECTS: 44 through 50 and 52 through 62

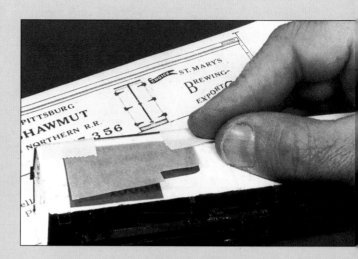

1 Position the dry transfer exactly where you want it, then tape one edge to the side of the model with drafting tape. The lettering diagrams furnished will help you position each dry transfer.

Dry transfers allow you to letter, number, and stripe a model locomotive or car by simply rubbing over the dry transfer's paper backing to transfer the characters or lines to the surface of the model. Kids' "rub-ons" use a similar process. You can buy dry transfers for lettering all types of model railroad equipment, as well as industrial and commercial signs and billboards. Woodland Scenics, C-D-S, Clover House, and Vintage Reproductions are four popular brands.

Dry transfers stick best to a glossy surface, so spray the model with a light coat of clear gloss if you have already painted it with the usual model railroad flat-finish paints. There is no clear decal film to worry about, but you should cut each dry transfer from the sheet. Do cut close to the letters, however, so you are able to position the dry transfer without running out of model. Because it takes some practice to learn how to apply dry transfers, I recommend buying two of the first set to have one set just for practice.

2 You can use a number 2 wooden pencil with a well-worn point to rub the dry transfer, but an artist's burnishing tool like this one works best. Rub up and down, left and right, and in a circular motion to force all of the dry transfer onto the model. You can see where the lettering transfers, because the dry transfer's film will become cloudy or opaque.

3 Gently lift the drafting paper to see if all of the dry transfer has stuck. If not, lower the dry transfer backing into position and burnish some more. You may need a sharper tool to gently force the transfer into panel lines or between boards.

4 When you are satisfied with the position of the numbers and lettering, place the backing paper that came with the dry transfers over the side of the model and burnish over the paper to "set" the dry transfer. Finally, spray the model with Testors Dullcote to seal and protect the dry transfer. Weather the model to match the prototype.

PROJECT 52 • RENUMBER A DIESEL

Time: 1 hour

Tools: Scissors, tweezers, number 00 paintbrush, cup, and paper towel

Materials: Decals and decal solvent

Cost: S

Talent: Novice

Scales: HO, N, S, O and G

Space: 2x10 inches

Tip: Avoid touching the decal with your fingertips because it can stick to them—handle the decal only with tweezers or a paintbrush.

WHY: To add that final detail, matching the model's number to that of the real locomotive

COMPLEMENTARY PROJECTS: 50, 51 and 53

You can make any ready-painted diesel belong to your particular railroad by simply changing the numbers in the numberboards and on the cab. The process is also useful when you want two or more of the same diesel (just like most real railroads). With this technique each diesel can have its own number.

1. Remove the painted-on numbers with a toothpick dipped in paint thinner. If you can stand the slivers, the fiberglass erasers also work well for this task. The side of the model must be level while you apply the cab decals; support the long hood portion of the body on a pencil. Cut each number from the decal sheet with scissors and di it in water. This time, though, place the decal directly on the model along with a drop of water that will likely come along. Use a hobby knife to push the decal off the paper and to push the paper out of the way.

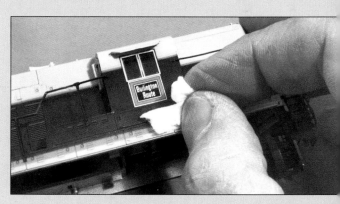

2. You want to work in a tiny puddle of water. Wick-up any excess water with a corner of a facial tissue.

3. If necessary, move the decal back in place. When the decal is in place and the excess water is removed, apply a drop of decal solvent and let it dry overnight. Clean the area with a damp cloth and spray the decal with Testors Dullcote to seal and protect it.

PAINTING AND DECALS

PROJECT 53 • RENUMBER NUMBERBOARDS

 Time: 1 hour

 Tools: Scissors, tweezers, burnishing tool, number 00 paintbrush, cup, and paper towel

 Materials: Dry transfers, decals, decal solvent, and artist's gloss medium

 Cost: $

 Talent: Novice

 Scales: HO, N, S, O and G

 Space: 2x10 inches

 Tip: Avoid touching the decal with your fingertips because it can stick to them—handle the decal only with tweezers or a paintbrush.

 WHY: To add that final detail, matching the model's number to that of the real locomotive

COMPLEMENTARY PROJECTS: 50, 51 and 52

Few model diesel have numbers in their numberboards, but they are essential to any real locomotive. Be careful, here, because some railroads simply repeat(ed) the number of the locomotive in the number board while other rail roads use(d) the number board for a train number. Like every other superdetail, it pays to find photographs of the specific locomotives you model to see exactly what you want to duplicate.

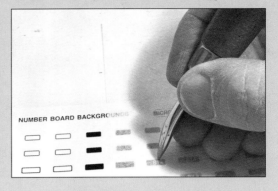

1 You can use decals on numberboards, but they float free when you soak the numberboards. Alternately, you can apply decal numbers directly to the numberboards on the model, one number at a time. It's far easier, I find, to use dry transfers and rub the numbers directly onto the white decal before soaking the decal numberboards. I use an artist's burnishing tool, but a blunt pencil tip also works. I burnished Woodland Scenics DT512 dry transfer letters to Microscale's 87-904 Number Board Backgrounds. The numbers' typeface, however, is not completely accurate for the Burlington. I later discovered that Clover House 9650-11 numbers had the correct typeface.

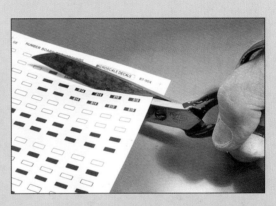

2 After applying the dry transfers to the numberboard decals, cut each number board from the decal sheet with scissors.

3 Dip each numberboard into warm water, then set it on a piece of facial tissue while the water soaks through the paper backing. Position the paper and decal and slide the paper from beneath the decal. Push the decal into perfect alignment and apply a drop of decal solvent. Let it dry and cover the numberboard with a coat of artist's gloss medium.

SECTION NINE
WEATHERING

The scale-model locomotives, cars, and structures you can buy as kits or ready-builts all look reasonably like the real thing, but you can improve their appearance so they look even more realistic. Perhaps the most important superdetail is the color of the car. Real freight cars and locomotives begin to change color almost as soon as they leave the paint shop. Modelers call this process of change "weathering," and it will do more than any other single technique to make those models look like replicas of real railroad equipment. Weathering requires some special techniques, most of which you'll find in this section. Try them all, and use those that work best for you. This is one area of the hobby where you really can develop and apply the skills of an artist, using materials and techniques that are simple and easy to learn.

WEATHERING

PROJECT 54 • WEATHER A DIESEL WITH PASTEL CHALKS

Time: 1 to 2 hours

Tools: Fine sandpaper, number 1 paintbrush, and cotton swabs

Materials: Artist's pastel chalks in black, light gray, burnt umber, burnt sienna, ochre , and Testors Dullcote clear aerosol

Cost: $$

Talent: Novice

Scales: HO, N, S, O and G

Space: 2x10 inches

Tip: Always match the weathering on your model to a photograph of a similar prototype locomotive, car, or structure. Use a brush dipped in water to produce really dark stains. Be willing to repeat the entire process if the Dullcote fades the weathering too much.

? WHY: Every real railroad locomotive looks dirty within hours of being freshly painted. Clean paint is often a certain sign that it's a model and an inaccurate replica of the original.

COMPLEMENTARY PROJECTS: 42, 44, 45, 47, 89, 92 and 94

1 A freshly painted HO scale model before weathering. This EMD SD60M is a combination of Athearn and Railpower parts.

If you wish to capture all of the realism of a particular prototype locomotive, car, or structure, you need to go beyond what is usually considered "modeling" and think of your miniature as "art." The model manufacturer has done nearly all the work of creating the form, but even the best forms lack some of the look of the real thing—namely, the dirt, grime, and sunbleaching that begins to discolor the locomotive, car, or structure almost the moment the paint dries. Modelers call the technique of capturing the real colors of the prototype "weathering."

As mentioned in Project 13, weathering, along with scenery building, is truly an art among the techniques that model railroaders might wish to learn. As with other art, you have your choice of pastels, lacquers, enamels, acrylics, and even oils. Some modelers combine two or even three of these media when weathering their models. Step one is to find a photograph depicting a diesel locomotive of about the same vintage as the locomotive you wish to weather. You do not need a photograph of the exact prototype, although it is a plus for a really accurate model. There are literally hundreds of full-color books on real railroads and one of them will have the photo you seek.

Art supply stores sell a variety of pastels, but most are oil based; the ones you want are chalk-based pastels. These pastel chalks can be reduced to powder by simply rubbing them on a piece of fine-grit sandpaper; oil-based pastels will merely form lumps of goo if you try to sand them. Buy light gray (not white), black, burnt umber (dark brown), burnt sienna (reddish brown), and ochre (yellowish beige) sticks of pastel chalks. It's also handy to have a few small paint jars with lids to store the powdered pastel chalks.

2 Subtle weathering effects make the same model look as if it's only been out of the paint shop for a few weeks.

3 Pastel chalks are available at most art supply stores. One common brand is Nupastel. Buy black, light gray, burnt umber, burnt sienna, and ochre, as well as five small empty paint jars to store the powered chalks. Rub the chalk over a piece of fine sandpaper to reduce it to powder.

6 There's a lot of beige dirt in the West, where this model's prototype ran, which gave it a yellowish cast. I applied the ochre to all the gray areas, including the trucks, fuel tank, and snowplow. If you're modeling a railroad from another part of the country, the dirt may be reddish brown (burnt sienna), dark brown (burnt umber), or black.

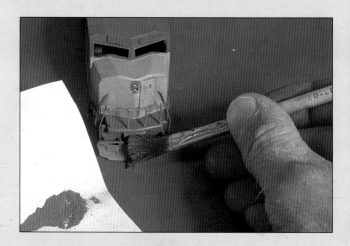

7 Wet the couplers and any other areas that may appear rusty. Brush a thick layer of burnt umber over these still-wet areas and let it dry. Keep the powder away from the moving areas of the couplers, however.

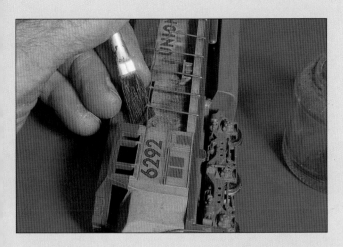

4 Find a color photograph of the prototype you are duplicating. It need not be exactly the same locomotive, but it should be of the same vintage. Use a number 1 paintbrush to apply the powders. Start by brushing the dark brown or burnt umber into the grills and around the panel openings to accent the shadows.

5 Use black inside the roof fans and stacks. If you need a darker black, especially around the exhaust stack and the nearby roof areas, wet the brush with warm tap water and apply the powder as a mud. Let it dry before you decide whether you've applied too much or too little. If you're unhappy with the color, scrub it off with a wet paintbrush or cotton swab and start over.

8 You can always go back and add more weathering. I decided the exhaust fans needed more shadow detail, so I applied more black with a wet brush.

9 The light gray is the final color. Its primary purpose is to simulate the effects of the sun bleaching the colors. It also helps tone down some of the dark brown, rusty brown, or black you've applied previously. It looks white at first, but most of it will not stick to the model.

10 Use a cotton swab to remove any excess weathering from the model. In some areas, particularly around the sides, rubbing the surface can help accentuate the panel lines and other molded-in details. When you're satisfied, spray the model with Testors Dullcote. Install any clear plastic windows after the clear flat is dry because the paint may etch the clear plastic.

PROJECT 55 • WEATHER A DIESEL WITH AN AIRBRUSH

 Time: 1 to 2 hours

 Tools: Airbrush, air compressor, and respirator

 Materials: PollyScale Rust, Dust, Dirt, Black, and Grimy Black paints; Pollyscale Thinner; and a number 00 paintbrush

 Cost: $$

 Talent: Novice

 Scales: HO, N, S, O and G

 Space: 2x10 inches

 Tip: Always match the weathering on your model to a photograph of a similar real-life locomotive.

 WHY: Every real railroad locomotive looks dirty within hours of being freshly painted. Clean paint is a certain sign that it's a model, not an accurate replica of the original.

COMPLEMENTARY PROJECTS: 44, 45, and 52 through 54

Real diesel locomotives are often the cleanest pieces of equipment on the railroad. However, even the most maintenance-conscious railroad only washes its locomotives occasionally, and repainting occurs only once or twice a decade. So, yes, there are a few out-of-the-shops-clean diesel locomotives out there, but most are pretty sun faded, grimy, and weather-beaten. You can use an airbrush to simulate all three of these weathering effects.

1 This O scale Red Caboose diesel was weathered with an airbrush to simulate units that had only been in service for a few months.

2 Apply a thin coat of PollyScale Dust to further lighten areas that would be bleached by the sun and that might receive mud splashes. This diesel was weathered with a final "splatter" effect (achieved by increasing the air pressure to around 30 psi) to simulate the effect of rain-soaked desert dust that attaches itself to the rain-wetted surfaces of locomotives. Practice on an old box lid, varying the air pressure and even the mix of paint to thinner until you achieve the desired effect. For spatter, try pushing and releasing the airbrush button in a vibrating motion.

3 Some areas of a black locomotive need more black. I recommend using the greenish black Grimy Black from PollyScale. Again, mix equal parts paint and PollyScale Thinner. If you make very quick passes with the airbrush (moving up and down the height of the sides and ends) you can soften the contrast between bright silver lettering (in this case) and the black body. Be careful, here, because you don't want to have to reletter the locomotive. If you apply too much, immediately wipe the area with thinner. After the weathering is complete, you can apply a very thin coat of black, perhaps with three parts thinner to one part paint, to blend the various shades of weathering and to soften the brighter colors.

4 Here, the trucks are receiving a light brown color to represent sun-bleaching. Mix PollyScale's Dirt paint with equal parts PollyScale Thinner, or substitute similar Badger Modeflex colors and thinner. (I adapted a jar lid to my airbrush to accept the PollyScale jar lids, but you can use the paint jar that came with your airbrush.) If you can, adjust the air pressure to about 20 psi and hold it about 3 inches from the model. Experiment on a piece of cardboard to get the mix, the pressure, paint flow, and distance right. Try passing the airbrush over the model at a variety of speeds, too. Your goal is a thin, barely visible tint of color with no spatters or runs. When you find the combination that works best, make a note.

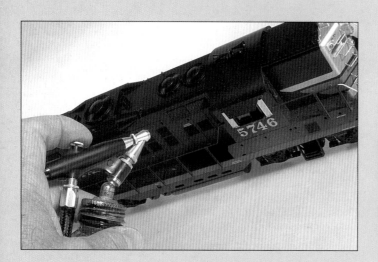

5 There are a few places where you can use solid black. Spray a gentle mist of three parts paint to one part thinner around the exhaust stacks to simulate exhaust stains. When using black, it's best to err on the light side and apply more the next day than to apply too much initially. You can also use black straight out of the bottle, applied with a number 00 paint brush, to simulate fuel dribbles from the fuel tank fillers and grease around the edges of the truck journals.

6 Use PollyScale Rust to apply a thin wash around the edges of the wheels, where dust and rust would appear. Adjust the airbrush to deliver as fine a pattern as possible and, if necessary, lower the air pressure—you want to be able to spray a dot about the size of a pinhead. Also spray the knuckles of the couplers and a few of the center areas of the steps where the paint would be worn through.

WEATHERING

PROJECT 56 • WEATHER A STEAM LOCOMOTIVE WITH PASTEL CHALKS

Time: 1 to 2 hours

Tools: Fine sandpaper, number 00 and number 1 paintbrushes, and cotton swabs

Materials: Artist's pastel chalks in black and light gray and Testors Model Master Semi-Gloss clear aerosol paint

Cost: $

Talent: Novice

Scales: HO, N, S, O and G

Space: 2x10 inches

Tip: Always match the weathering on your model to a photograph of a similar real-life locomotive, car, or structure. Use a brush dipped in water to produce really dark stains. Be willing to repeat the entire process if the clear semigloss paint fades the weathering too much.

WHY: Every real railroad locomotive looks dirty within hours of being freshly painted. Clean paint is often a certain sign that it's a model, not an accurate replica of the original.

COMPLEMENTARY PROJECTS: 46, 47 and 57

1 Here is the USRA "Heavy" 2-8-2 Mikado from Projects 46 and 47, weathered with powdered pastel chalks and an airbrush to match a specific prototype steam locomotive. Compare this photograph with the freshly painted model on Projects 46 and 47.

Steam locomotives are far more difficult to weather realistically than freight cars or even diesels. With diesels and freight cars, the primary weathering results from nature, with a dusting of soot or exhaust and kicked-up dust from the roadbed. For your first weathering attempt on a steam locomotive, start with the powdered pastel chalks described in Project 54. These wash off easily with warm water so you can correct any mistakes you make. You can go on, at a later date, and weather the locomotive with an airbrush as described in Project 57. The airbrushed "dirt" applied later will simply help to blend the powdered pastel weathering. I used

both techniques on this model, working with pastels first, then the airbrushing.

Use a number 1 paintbrush to apply streaks of black powdered pastel chalk that simulates the stains resulting from rain washing the soot off the top of the boiler and down the sides. Wet the brush with water to get enough color to stick to the model. This weathering is, of course, most visible on the silver smokebox, but it appears on the other portions of the boiler as well. Next, use powdered gray pastel chalk to simulate the stains from the boiler residue that drools down from the whistle and pop valves. Similar stains appear on the sides of the cylinders, around the pipes and valves beneath the cab, and in other areas. Again, study prototype photographs carefully to see where these stains appear and duplicate their patterns and colors with a number 00 paintbrush.

A third type of stain on steam locomotives is the result of occasional dribbles and drools of oil, steam, or boiler compound from various valves. Here, I used acrylic paints to more easily simulate the fluid nature of these stains—and also so I can wash them off immediately if I made a mistake, without disturbing the underlying paint.

2 Simulate rain-washed streaks of soot with black powdered pastel chalks. Wet the brush with water. Be sure the streaks are perfectly vertical.

3 Use light gray powdered pastel chalk to simulate the residue left by escaping steam. These stains appear on the cylinders and below the steam dome, where the whistle and pop valves release steam. Apply with a number 00 paintbrush dipped in water. Protect the surface with a final light coat of Testors Model Master Semi-Gloss clear aerosol.

WEATHERING

PROJECT 57 • WEATHER A STEAM LOCOMOTIVE WITH AN AIRBRUSH

Time: 1 to 2 hours

Tools: Airbrush, air compressor, and respirator

Materials: Floquil SP Lettering Gray, Engine Black, and Grimy Black; thinner; and Testors Model Master Semi-Gloss clear aerosol paint

Cost: $$$

Talent: Novice

Scales: HO, N, S, O and G

Space: 2x10 inches

Tip: Always match the weathering on your model to a photograph of a similar real-life locomotive.

WHY: Every real railroad locomotive looks dirty within hours of being freshly painted. Clean paint is often a certain sign that it's a model, not really an accurate replica of the original.

COMPLEMENTARY PROJECTS: 46, 47 and 56

1 This HO scale model looks like a real steam locomotive because it was first painted in the same semigloss hue as the prototype, then weathered not only with powdered pastel chalks, but also an airbrush to simulate the dust and rain-washed grime of the real world.

Prototype steam locomotives looked like the painted model in Projects 46 and 47 for about the first 50 feet of their trip from the paint shop. From then on, soot stained the top of the locomotive a flat black, the drivers and wheels kicked up mud and more soot, and steam and oil dribbled from various orifices to streak the sides.

This particular model is a based on a Colorado & Southern prototype, but the steps are similar for matching any steam locomotive models to their prototypes.

Weathering patterns can vary, depending on whether the locomotive burned oil or coal. The patterns can also vary with geographic location—a locomotive that spent its life running across California deserts would not have the same weathering patterns or colors as one that spent its life laboring at 15 miles an hour beneath a cloud of soot in the Alleghenies. With some research, however, you will always find a prototype photo that you can use to direct your artistic endeavors.

Start the weathering with a coat of flat black mixed with about three parts thinner to one part paint. Adjust the airbrush and air pressure from the compressor to deliver a mist about the size of a dime. Steam locomotives were soon coated with

139

black soot carried back with wind and washed down with the rain. That coating, however, appeared first on just the top of the boiler, cab, and tender. It took months for the soot to wash down the sides. Note, for example, that the once–bright red roofs on most of these Burlington steam locomotives were quickly coated eave to eave with soot. However, in some photos, only the top of the boiler appears to have the dull, blackening effects of soot.

The next major effect of weathering is the result of mud thrown up onto the wheels and drivers by the wheel flanges. That mud also finds its way to the trailing trucks, pilot, the front and rear of the cylinders, and the undercarriage and lower areas of the tender sides. These stains usually add a brownish-green tint to the black. This tint can be very close to the popular Grimy Black, although it isn't always. I started with the stock Rivarossi chassis color, which is very close to Grimy Black, then I mixed an earth shade (Armor Sand) with about three parts thinner and tried to duplicate the mud-splash patterns from the photographs of the prototype.

The final weathering effects can be re-created using either diluted paint or powdered pastel chalks as described in Project 56.

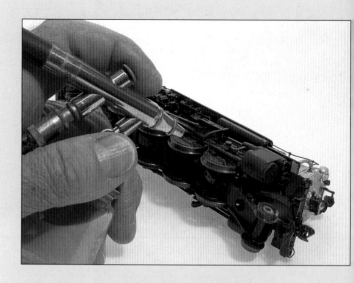

2 Mix one part Engine Black with three parts thinner and gently dust it onto the top of the boiler, cab, and tender. Match the patterns of light and dark from a photograph of the prototype. Adjust the paint and air flow so you can paint a pencil-point-thin line and work with rapid strokes, again focusing the "soot" on the inside and behind the stack. Mix one part Grimy Black with about three parts thinner and blend splashes of mud onto the cylinders, drivers, and pilot wheels, as well as the bottom edges of the tender, the tender undercarriage, and the tender trucks. Use the technique to simulate oil and grease stains around the truck journals, too.

3 Simulate the sun-bleaching effects on the cab roof and the top of the tender with the thinned Floquil SP Lettering Gray (or a similar shade of light gray). With the same technique used to simulate the mud splashes on the cylinders, drivers, and pilot wheels, soften the streaks from the whistle and pop valves.

PROJECT 58 • SHADOW-PAINT MOLDED-ON LADDERS AND GRABIRONS

Time: 1 to 2 hours

Tools: Hobby knife, airbrush, air compressor, and respirator

Materials: Ultrafine felt-tip black pen, black paint, and thinner

Cost: $$$

Talent: Novice

Scales: HO, N, S, O and G

Space: 2x10 inches

Tip: Blend the inked-in shadows with a bit of thinned black paint from an airbrush.

WHY: To make molded-on grabirons and ladders appear to be free-standing parts.

COMPLEMENTARY PROJECTS: 54, 55, 59 and 60

1 Before . . .

2 . . . and after. This HO scale Accurail car has ladders and grabirons molded onto the sides of the body. With a fine-pointed ink pen like those sold in stationery and art supply stores, molded-on ladders and grabirons can be made to appear to be standing free from the sides of cars.

Many model freight cars have ladders and grabirons molded onto the sides of the car. With a bit of subtle shading and weathering, those ladders and grabirons can look as if they have free-standing wire rungs. Is the final effect as realistic as individual grab irons and separate ladders? You decide. It is certainly a lot less work, however, than shaving off those parts and replacing them with individual wire grabirons, ladders, and steps.

This same ink and paint technique will work well on stock Athearn cars, as well as models from Accurail, MDC, C&BT Shops, LBF, Bowser, Mantua, Con-Cor, Rivarossi, and Walthers that have similar molded-on grabirons and ladders.

3 Use one of these pens to draw thin lines in the grooves below each ladder and grabiron rung. Trace thin black lines the length of the ladder just to one side of each ladder support.

4 To make the stirrup steps appear almost as thin as replacement detail parts, tra along their inner edges with the black pen.

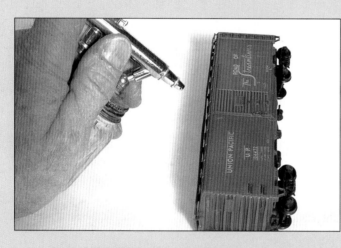

6 Mix four parts thinner to one part black paint. Adjust the air pressure to about 20 psi and spray the mixture at an acute angle to the bottoms of the sides and ends of the car. This will produce shadows along the bottoms of the ladder rungs and grabirons, and even along the bottoms of the rivets and other detail lines, making them appear to have more depth and detail. Spray a much thinner amount of the black over the roof to simulate accumulated soot and exhaust residue. Next, spray a mixture of one part Reefer Gray (or beige) and four parts thinner over the car, aiming the spray at an acute angle to the tops of the car's sides and ends. This coat provides lighter shading on the tops of the ladder and grabiron rungs to simulate sunlight.

7 Gently scrape the very edges of each ladder and grabiron rung to expose a hai thin line of the original (unweathered) paint color. This helps make the inked shadows and airbrushed highlights more effective.

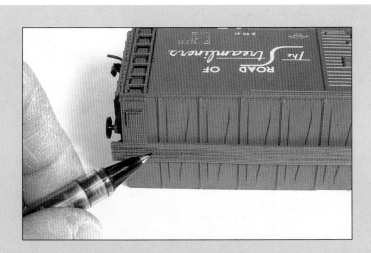

5 If the model has a simulated open-mesh, antiskid type of metal roofwalk (rather than simulated wood), rub over the surface with the pen and quickly wipe all excess ink from the surface to leave ink only in the cavities.

WEATHERING

PROJECT 59 • SUPERDETAIL N SCALE FREIGHT CARS WITH INK

 Time: 1 to 2 hours

 Tools: Ultrafine felt-tip black pen

 Materials: Black ink, cotton swabs, and facial tissue

 Cost: $

 Talent: Novice

 Scales: N

 Space: 2x10 inches

 Tip: Blend the inked-in shadows with a bit of powdered pastel chalk as shown in Project 60.

? **WHY:** To make molded-on details, seams, grabirons, and ladders appear to be freestanding parts.

COMPLEMENTARY PROJECTS: 54, 56, 58 and 60

1 Test a number of fine-tip felt-point pens to find the one that makes the sharpest and thinnest line. Use the pen to draw "shadows" beneath the grabirons and ladder rungs and up one side of each vertical ladder support.

Nearly every N scale freight car has as much potential for detail as an HO scale car. Many of the details on N scale cars, however, are molded onto the sides or roof rather than being freestanding details found on better HO models (and prototypes). You can make these more obvious by accenting them with black ink.

The steps in Project 58 show how to accent the ladders, grabirons, and steps on an HO scale model. The techniques are the same for any scale. When working on an N scale car, however, the black "shadow" line obviously needs to be even finer. In addition, you may choose to accent the molded-in panel lines around plug doors, and even the rivets on lighter-colored cars. Simply rub a small amount of ink from the tip of the pen onto the details and wipe off the excess with a damp facial tissue before the ink has a chance to dry. Even if you are not adding details, you are making the details that are already there much more visible. The rather harsh lines and shadows will look more realistic if you weather the car to blend the lines into the overall weathering as shown in Project 60.

144

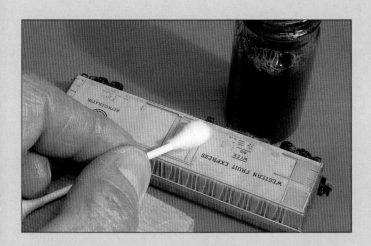 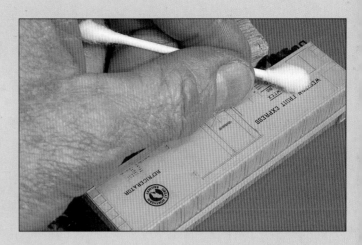

2 Draw over all the panel lines and around door latches and hinges with the fine-tip pen. Wipe the excess ink from the areas with a damp cotton swab, so the ink remains only in the recessed areas of the detail parts.

3 You can accent rivet and panel lines by rubbing just a trace of black ink over the surface with a cotton swab. Have a clean, damp facial tissue ready to wipe off any excess ink — you want just a trace to accent the parts. The final coat of Testors Dullcote that seals the weathering will also protect the black accent ink from being smudged when the car is placed in operation.

WEATHERING

PROJECT 60 • WEATHER N SCALE FREIGHT CARS WITH PASTEL CHALKS

Time: 1 to 2 hours

Tools: Fine sandpaper and a number 1 paintbrush

Materials: Artist's pastel chalks in black, light gray, burnt umber, burnt sienna, and ochre; Testors Dullcote clear aerosol; and cotton swabs or facial tissues

Cost: $

Talent: Novice

Scales: N

Space: 2x10 inches

Tip: Always match the weathering on your model to a photograph of a similar real-life locomotive, car, or structure. Use a brush dipped in water to produce really dark stains. Be willing to repeat the entire process if the Dullcote fades the weathering too much.

WHY: Every real railroad freight car looks dirty within hours of being freshly painted. Clean paint is a certain sign that it's a model, and not an accurate replica of the original.

COMPLEMENTARY PROJECTS: 58 and 59

1 Reduce the pastel chalk to a powder by rubbing it on fine-grit sandpaper. Store each color in a separate jar.

Some modelers find it easier to weather N scale cars and locomotives with powdered pastel chalks than with an airbrush, because it is a bit easier to control how much "weathering" is applied. You can duplicate many of the effects produced by weathering with an airbrush (see Projects 55, 57 and 59) with powdered pastel chalks. Buy some burnt umber, light gray, black, and yellow ochre colors of chalk-based artist's pastel sticks. The burnt umber will make the lettering appear to be faded. The light gray will simulate sun bleaching, while the black simulates soot and dirt, and the yellow ochre adds highlights and a "Southwest desert" look.

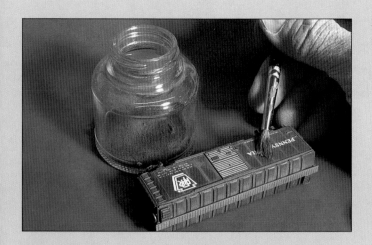

2 Brush the powder over the sides, ends, and roof of the car. Vary the amount of each color to match photos of prototype cars.

3 Use a piece of facial tissue or a cotton swab to spread the powdered pastels deeply into the cracks and around the rivets. The gray will help promote the sun-bleached look on the ends and roof of darker cars. The lower portions of the ends are usually darkened with dirt kicked up by the wheels and wind beneath the train. When the weathering is complete, protect it with a light spray of Testors Dullcote. The Dullcote will reduce the intensity of the weathering colors, so you may need to apply more powdered pastel chalks (and another final coat of DullCote) to achieve the effect you desire.

PROJECT 61 • WOODEN DECKS FOR PLASTIC FLATCARS

Time: 1 to 2 hours

Tools: Razor saw and a number 1 paintbrush

Materials: Masking tape, light gray aerosol paint, black India ink, artist's pastel chalks in medium gray and burnt umber, Testors Dullcote clear aerosol, and cotton swabs or facial tissues

Cost: $$

Talent: Novice

Scales: HO and N

Space: 2x10 inches

Tip: Take a good look at a real railroad's wooden flatcar deck and try to duplicate the color and texture you see.

WHY: To make the most visible portion of any wooden-deck flatcar more realistic

COMPLEMENTARY PROJECTS: 54, 59 and 62

Most HO and N scale flatcars are fitted with plastic decks, grooved to simulate wood. Most of these decks look, at best, like re-creations of some kind of strange steel sheets. It is relatively easy to "distress" a plastic flatcar deck so it has the look of rough woodgrain. Paint the roughened deck gray and weather it to match the prototype decks and you'd never guess it was plastic.

1 Form the masking tape into loops with the sticky side out. Press the tape loop onto a scrap of wood and stick the plastic pieces to the tape. The parts shown are the separate plastic wood deck pieces from Walthers HO scale 53-foot 6-inch flatcar kit. You can use this same technique with any other plastic flatcar kit in any scale, including those with decks molded into the sides, like Athearn and most N scale models.

4 The deck pieces can now be cemented in place on the car. Use a thickened cyanoacrylate cement to hold the parts in place.

2 Use a razor saw to scratch simulated woodgrain into the surface of the plastic. Hold the blade near the teeth and rake it firmly across the plastic, wiggling it as you drag to impart the wavy effect of real woodgrain. Use the very tip of the blade to work a woodgrain into the edges of the parts.

3 Use a damp facial tissue or cotton swab to wipe over the ink-covered pieces before the ink has a chance to dry. The ink will cling to the lines you scratched with the razor saw to simulate woodgrain.

5 Buy a stick of medium gray and a stick of dark brown or burnt umber artist's pastel chalks. (Oil-based pastels do not work.) Reduce the chalks to powders with fine sandpaper (see Projects 54 and 60). Brush the light gray over the entire deck of the car to produce a sun-bleached effect on the "wood" and the visible metal portions of the deck. Rub the powder into the surface with a cotton swab or a piece of facial tissue. Use the chalk to highlight the trucks, sides, and ends of the car, too.

6 Dust a thin coating of dark brown over the deck, sides, ends, and trucks. The dark brown simulates airborne dirt and grime, and it should appear in a rather random pattern. You can darken the effect by dipping the brush into water.

7 Seal and protect the weathering with a light spray of Testors Dullcote clear flat paint. The clear will reduce the intensity of the weathering, so you may want to go back and apply more of the powdered pastel chalks, followed by a final spray of Dullcote.

WEATHERING

PROJECT 62 • WEATHER FREIGHT AND TANK CARS WITH AN AIRBRUSH

 Time: 1 to 2 hours

 Tools: Airbrush, air compressor, and respirator

 Materials: Floquil SP Lettering Gray, Engine Black, and Grimy Black; thinner; and Testors Dullcote clear aerosol paint

 Cost: $$$

 Talent: Novice

 Scales: HO, N, S, O and G

 Space: 2x10 inches

 Tip: Always match the weathering on your model to a photograph of a similar real-life freight car.

 WHY: To accurately match the colors and textures of real railroad freight cars

COMPLEMENTARY PROJECTS: 56 and 57

The blowing action of an airbrush makes it easy to duplicate the windblown and rain-washed effects the environment has on tank and freight cars. Tank cars, however, are excellent models on which to learn the art of weathering because it's nearly impossible to get them dirtier than the prototype cars.

1 Tank cars are exposed to the same windblown and rain-washed grime as other freight cars, so start the weathering process by "dusting" an earth color around the trucks and on the tops of the running boards. Mix equal parts thinner and paint and adjust the paint flow so it barely mists on the color. It is easier to build up several coats than to remove an overdone coat. This is a light beige earth shade, but cars that traveled in the South would have a redder color, cars in the Midwest a brown shade. For all these techniques, keep the airbrush moving, so paint does not accumulate in splotches or highly visible streaks. Weathering is a subtle blend of colors that you must study closely to replicate exactly the changes to the original colors.

2 Black paint weathers to a dull dark gray in the sun. Simulate that effect with a wash of equal parts thinner and medium gray. Apply a mist to the tops of the tank and dome and the running boards; run a few light passes around the circumference to simulate rain-washed oxidization.

3 Because the effect of diesel exhaust settling on still-wet splashes of gasoline or oil is less pronounced than that of smoke and soot from steam locomotives, tank cars from the diesel era are likely to exhibit more gray from sun-bleaching than cars of the steam era.

4 Obviously, tank cars assigned to carry crude oil to a refinery would be far blacker than new cars carrying gasoline. Still, the soot from steam locomotives and some diesel exhaust accumulates on spilled gasoline to give all but the newest tank car a black hue. In fact, it is almost always difficult to read the lettering on tank car carrying petroleum products. Use the same proportion of half thinner and half paint to simulate stains from the dome by holding the airbrush just an inch or so from the car, so the paint actually runs down the dome and the sides. Simulate additional, but older spills from the top of the car down the sides with the same technique, but with the airbrush a f inches from the car.

5 For a final touch, apply some streaks and dribbles of undiluted black paint down the sides of the dome and, in some cases, down the sides of the tank, to simulate still-wet oil or gasoline spills. If the car "carries crude oil," use gloss black and tone down the shine with raw thinner.

6 Placed in a scene based on a prototype oil depot, the weathered tank cars are nearly perfect re-creations of the prototypes.

SECTION TEN
ADVANCED TECHNIQUES

The availability of ready-to-run models and snap-together kits makes it possible for you to be an accomplished model railroader without even building a model. We do not call this hobby "model railroad building" because the "building" part is optional. If you want to use ready-to-run models and snap-together track with built-in ballast—probably 70 percent or more of today's model railroaders have never built anything more complex than a snap-together kit. If you want to try building some models from kits, perhaps even altering or kit-converting some structures so your layout doesn't look like any other, you'll need to purchase a few special tools. Every one of the specialized modeling tools in this section is essential if you really want to get the most enjoyment from the hobby of building a model railroad.

PROJECT 63 • SPECIAL TOOLS FOR MODEL RAILROADERS

Time: 1 hour

Tools: Tweezers, screw-gripping screwdriver, small-tip needle-nose pliers, razor saw, cabinetmaker's file, hobby knife, sprue cutters, and a pin vise

Materials: Whatever you have on hand

Cost: $$

Talent: Novice

Scales: HO, N, S, O and G

Space: 6x10 inches

Tip: Invest in a small assortment of specialized tools that can make all aspects of model railroading easier and more enjoyable.

? **WHY:** To make it less frustrating to perform fundamental modeling techniques

COMPLEMENTARY PROJECTS: 22 through 43 and 64 through 79

You certainly do not need a machine shop or even an extensive assortment of tools to build most model railroad kits. There are, however, a few rather specialized tools that can make kit assembly and kit conversions far easier and more enjoyable. These are not the tools you would normally find in a home toolbox, but they are tools that I feel should be in every model railroader's tool drawer or rack.

1 I consider these essential tools for anyone who wants to assemble a plastic model car or locomotive kit or structure. Several are used in this book. This photo does not include common tools like small screwdrivers, needle-nose pliers, diagonal cutters, hand drills, soldering guns, or airbrushes, but I recommend that you purchase the tools shown (from left): pointed-tip tweezers, screw-gripping screwdriver, small-tip needle-nose pliers, razor saw, cabinetmaker's file, hobby knife, sprue cutters, and a pin vise with an assortment of drill bits.

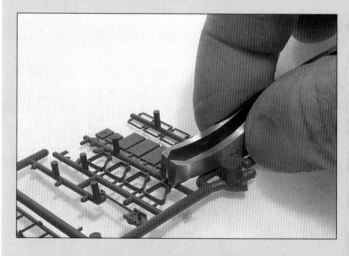

4 P-B-L and InterMountain Railway offer special sprue cutters that are, essentially, right-angle tweezers with sharpened points to cut plastic. This is the only tool to use when removing small plastic parts, like ladders and grabirons, from the molding sprue. Fingernail clippers work on a similar principle but are much too thick to reach inside the sprues. Keep the sharp cutting edges protected with a plastic bag and use the tool only for cutting small plastics to preserve the delicate cutting surfaces. Testors and Maxon make a much larger tool that is really a smaller version of a flush-cut diagonal cutter. These are useful for larger parts, but the P-B-L or InterMountain sprue cutters are the ones to use to remove ladders, grabirons, and similar tiny parts from the sprues.

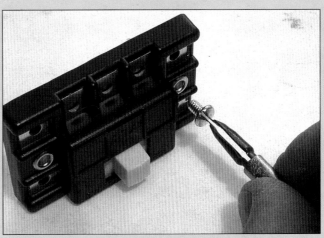

2 The small-tip needle-nose pliers are one of the most useful tools, because they offer the precision of most tweezers with the gripping force of pliers. Use them for bending grabirons or handrails, straightening rails and turnout switch points, and a host of other applications.

3 Self-gripping screwdrivers are sold at most auto parts and electronics supply stores, as well as by dealers like Walthers. This one has a split blade that spreads to grip the inner faces of the screw's slot. Even for simple tasks like inserting screws in Atlas electrical switches (shown here), the tool is useful. It can be even more helpful for installing truck-mounting screws, coupler pockets, and locomotive assembly screws.

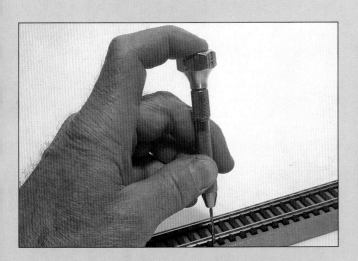

5 The pin vise is a modeler's-size hand drill. There is no need for an electric drill when drilling into plastic. The pin vise requires a minimum amount of force, and you have complete control over the location and size of the hole. Hold the pin vise as shown and twist it between you thumb and finger while maintaining downward pressure on the bit. Buy an assortment of drill bits, including numbers 42, 50, 51, 55, 58, 60, and 78, as well as 00-90, 00-80, and 2-56 taps to thread holes. The pin vise will also hold the taps.

6 The cabinetmaker's file is a 12-inch flat file with four parallel sides (there is no taper). One large side and one small side have fine teeth, one flat side has medium-cut teeth, and the other small side is smooth. The flat surfaces make it easier to file the joining edges of plastic buildings. The toothless side allows you to more accurately file inside corners. The tool is available at large hardware stores and shops that sell floor and countertop tile.

ADVANCED TECHNIQUES

PROJECT 64 • SET UP A PIN VISE

 Time: 1 hour

 Tools: Pin vise

 Materials: A straight pin and whatever you need to drill

 Cost: $

 Talent: Expert

 Scales: HO, N, S, O and G

 Space: 2x2 inches

 Tip: Use the pin vise and straight pin to impress a dimple in the exact place where you want to drill the hole.

 WHY: To drill holes in plastic track, cars, locomotives, and structures with ease and complete control

COMPLEMENTARY PROJECTS: 22 through 43 and 64 through 79

In this day of power tools, it seems absurd to drill holes with a hand drill, but a pin vise is basically that: a miniature hand drill. I suppose they call it a "pin vise" because it can hold drills as small as a pin. Your hobby dealer should be able to supply a variety of pin vises from firms like X-Acto, Maxon, and Gyros. Most pin vises include four different jaws, each a bit larger than the next, to hold drills from as small as a number 80 (a little larger than a human hair) to about 1/8 inch. You can also use the pin vise as a punch to provide a pinpoint-size dimple to locate the hole you want to drill. And the pin vise can also be used to hold small taps for cutting the common model railroad–size 00-90, 00-80, and 2-56 threads in metal or plastic.

1 Insert a straight pin through the bottom of the smallest of the four chucks included with most pin vises. The tip of the pin should protrude about 1/4 inch from the chuck. If the pinhead is in the way, simply cut it off with diagonal cutters.

2 Locate the position of the hole you want to drill with precision by simply touching the exact spot with the pointed tip of the pin, then increasing the pressure to leave a 1/64-inch or less depression in the surface of the plastic. If you try to drill without this locating dimple, the tip of the drill will wander and the hole will not be in precisely the location you desire.

PROJECT 65 • DRILL HOLES WITH A PIN VISE

 Time: 1 hour

 Tools: Pin vise; 42, 50, 51, 55, 58, 60, and 78 drill bits; 00-90, 00-80, and 2-56 taps; and a straight pin

 Materials: Whatever you need to drill

 Cost: S

 Talent: Novice

 Scales: HO, N, S, O and G

 Space: 2x2 inches

 Tip: Test the pin vise on a scrap of plastic to be sure the drill is mounted squarely in the chuck.

 WHY: To drill holes in plastic track, cars, locomotives, and structures with ease and complete control

COMPLEMENTARY PROJECTS: 22 through 43 and 64 through 79

1 Most pin vises include four chucks to accommodate drill bits from a number 80 all the way to a 1/8-inch diameter.

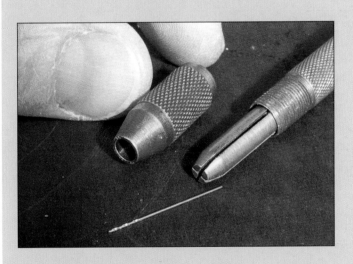

2 Use the drill chuck with the smallest opening in the center for the smallest drill bit like this number 78 drill bit.

I use a hobby knife and small screwdrivers more than any other tools, other than a pair of pointed tweezers. My pin vise, however, also gets a lot of use. The tiny holes for attaching grabirons, ladders, and other small parts in diesel and freight car kits are often partially filled with paint. In order to install the parts without breaking off their mounting pins, you sometimes need to drill out the holes to their original size using the pin vise and a drill bit. You also need to drill holes to mount superdetail parts and, sometimes, to route wires from the track through the tabletop.

The pin vise also holds taps to cut threads, which can be very useful if you want to replace a press-in pin with a 2-56 screw to hold a coupler or a set of tracks on a freight car.

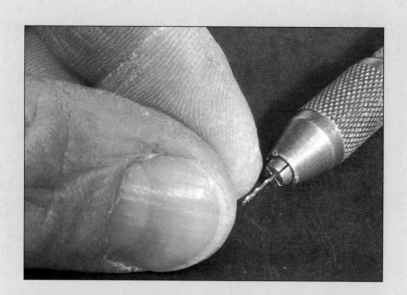

3 It can be tricky getting the smallest bits centered in the smallest chuck. Gently move the bit back and forth while you tighten the knurled knob and the bit should center itself. Spin the pin vise to be sure the drill bit is centered and, if not, repeat the process.

4 Hold the pin vise between your thumb and first finger and use the palm of your hand to push the drill into the material. Usually, you can use just the pressure from the two fingers holding the pin vise.

PROJECT 66 • TRICKS WITH SUPER GLUE

 Time: 1 hour

 Tools: Straight pin, toothpicks, respirator, and eye dropper

 Materials: Pacer Technologies & Resources, Inc. Zap-A-Gap, Zap CA/Super Thin, and Kicker (cement accelerator); Z-Debonder or Satellite City Hot Stuff Super T and Special T; Spray 'N Cure; Debonder Solvent; baking soda; and a jar with a tight-sealing lid

 Cost: $

 Talent: Novice

 Scales: HO, N, S, O and G

 Space: 2x2 inches

 Tip: Store your cements in a sealed glass jar in the refrigerator for longer shelf life.

 WHY: To allow instant glue joints without gluing your fingers to the model.

COMPLEMENTARY PROJECTS: 68 through 80 and 96

1 You can increase the shelf life of any cyanoacrylate cement by storing it in a large-mouth glass jar, then storing the jar in a refrigerator (not the freezer).

The aerospace industry's gift to model railroaders is cyanoacrylate cement, the clear liquid frequently sold under the brand name Super Glue. You can buy several different thicknesses or viscosities of cyanoacrylate cement. The thinnest or "standard" cement will only flow and cure in very tight areas of precise fit. For most modeling work you need the thicker variants. Your hobby dealer can usually offer a choice of different brands that are specially formulated for use by hobbyists. A word of caution: always wear a disposable respirator mask when working with cyanoacrylate cement because it does give off fumes that can be harmful.

I recommend you buy a bottle of standard cyanoacrylate cement, another bottle of thickened cement, a pump bottle of cement accelerator that makes it cure instantly, a bottle of cement remover, and a small box of baking soda.

Use the standard thin cement when you have a very tight fit and want the least-possible amount of cement. You can touch a single drop to the edge of tight-fitting joints and capillary action will usually carry the cement all the way around the joint, as far as 6 inches from where you apply it. You can also use the standard cement for creating "fillets" with baking soda.

The thickened cement is, to me, the most useful for modeling projects. It stays put better than the thin stuff, which means there's less chance you'll also glue your fingers to the model. I also recommend a cement solvent for cyanoacrylate cement, because you *will* eventually glue yourself to the model. In such an instance, a solvent will soften the bond, allowing you to wiggle a hobby knife blade between your skin and the model and break the bond without breaking your flesh.

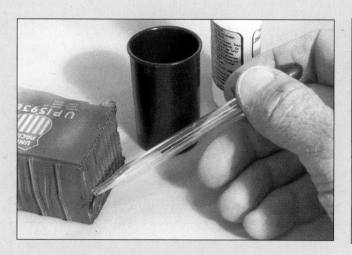 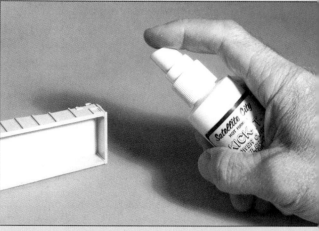

2 Baking soda can be used to fill in large gaps or to make fillets where extra strength is needed. First, apply the baking soda, then shape it just the way you want it and apply a couple of drops of cyanoacrylate cement. The whole mass will be rock-hard in an instant.

3 Cyanoacrylate cements, even the thickened kind, do not dry instantly unless there is a lack of air, such as you might find at a supertight joint (and, of course, at the points where fingers are gripping the model). I use thickened cyanoacrylate cement for most model work and create an instant joint by spraying the cement-filled joint with an accelerator spray of the type offered by most makers of cyanoacrylate cement.

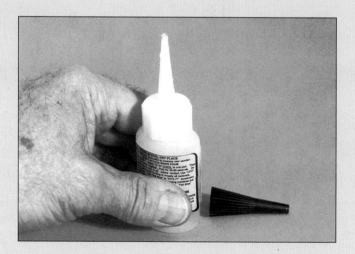

4 You can minimize the chance of cement clogging the nozzle if you stand the bottle upright on the table and gently squeeze it until air, but no cement, flows out the opening. Wipe off any cement that does come out and gently release the squeeze while still holding the bottle upright. The goal is to flow air through the nozzle to clear it of any cement before replacing the cap. Store the bottle in an upright position too.

PROJECT 67 • TRICKS WITH PLASTIC MODELS

Time: 1 hour

Tools: Hobby knife, 4-inch scrap of 1x2 hardwood, and sprue cutters

Materials: Any one of these thickened cements: Testors Liquid Cement for Plastics, Vollmer Super Cement, Kibri Plastic Cement, or Faller Super Expert Cement; one of the following cements for gluing ABS and similar "tough" plastics: Amboid Plastic Welder, Plastruct Plastic Welder, or Tenax Plastic Welder; Testors liquid cement; and Testors tube-type cement for large or very long joints

Cost: $

Talent: Novice

Scales: HO, N, S, O and G

Space: 2x2 inches

Tip: Thickened cements, especially those with needle-type applicators, are the best ones to use for most plastic-gluing projects.

WHY: To assemble a plastic model with strong joints but without great smears of glue

COMPLEMENTARY PROJECTS: 68 through 80

1 Testors Liquid Cement for Plastics has a brush built into the bottle cap. The brush, however, is too large and allows you to apply far more cement than you need. Use a hobby knife to cut off all but about five bristles, so you can apply a small drop of the cement at a time.

In the old days, everyone assembled every kind of plastic kit with a tube of cement. Things have changed. There are now some more specialized cements that can make joints in plastic models easier, quicker, and neater. Because it dries slowly, tube-type cement is still useful for cementing very large models of structures, with joints that might be up to several feet long. Tube-type cement also provides a bit of filler, so the joint does not need to be as precise as when gluing with thinner cements. The disadvantages of tube-type cement are that it can take weeks to dry completely and it can dissolve thinner plastics.

Modelers who assemble aircraft and armor models have used liquid cements for decades, because these kits have parts that fit together tightly enough so that no filler is needed. However, there's still a need for the thin cements like Testors Liquid Cement for Plastics, which is useful for attaching very small parts and very thin parts that thicker cements can dissolve.

No plastic cement I know of will cement the flexible plastic handrails that are fitted to most HO, O, S, and N scale diesels. Use Goodyear Pliobond or Walthers Goo if you need to glue these slippery plastics. Also, some kits have small parts molded from a tough plastic often called ABS. Older modelers might recommend MEK, or methyl ethyl ketone, for this, but I recommend that you do not because MEK is extremely toxic. Some special cements, including Amboid Plastic Welder, Plastruct Plastic Welder, and Tenax Plastic Welder, work just as well with ABS.

2 When adding trim to a building made of styrene plastic sheets and strip, cement overlength pieces of trim into place using the thin Testors Liquid Cement for Plastics. Let the cement dry for a few minutes, then cut the trim to size with large sprue cutters.

3 Cabinet and furniture shops can usually supply scraps of hardwood. I cut a diagonal corner off a 4-inch piece of 1x2 so I could position the block of wood inside two walls to ensure a square joint. The 1/4-inch diagonal cut keeps the block of wood away from the cement at the joint. Assemble the model on a flat surface like a 1x1-foot piece of 1/8-inch Plexiglas.

BUILDINGS

Real railroads use many of the same locomotive, freight car, and passenger car types, with only changes in paint and few details to differentiate one railroad's equipment from another's. In fact, if you want the most realistic trains possible, consider buying three or four identical cars with the markings of your favorite real railroad, rather than three or four different cars, because that's what you see on most real freight trains. Structures, however, are a different story. It is unusual to see more than one identical industry, store, or even house along a right-of-way (McDonalds, 7-11, and such being the exceptions).

But there is a relatively limited number of kits for model railroad structures; with experience, you can spot identical structures on nearly every model railroad in the country. To make your structures as unique to your railroad as they are to the railroad you are re-creating, you may need to build the structures from scratch. Modern styrene plastic sheet and strip stock is available at most hobby shops. You can, with practice and the techniques described in this section, build a model of just about any real world structure in little more time than it would take to build a kit. Assembling your own models from raw materials—scratchbuilding—is much easier than you might think.

James Schall and Phil Brooks' 3x12-foot NTRAK module set.

PROJECT 68 • ASSEMBLE PLASTIC KITS

 Time: 2 hours

 Tools: Hobby knife, 4-inch scrap of 1x2 hardwood, sprue cutters, and a cabinetmaker's file

 Materials: A thickened cement like Testors Model Master Liquid Cement for Plastics, Vollmer Super Cement, Kibri Plastic Cement, or Faller Super Expert Cement; white glue; and paint

 Cost: SS

 Talent: Novice

 Scales: HO, N, S, O and G

 Space: 2x2 inches

 Tip: Test-fit every part and check every inch of every joint for a tight fit before cementing the model.

 WHY: To assemble a plastic model with strong joints but without great smears of glue down the outside of the model

COMPLEMENTARY PROJECTS: 63, 67, and 69 through 80

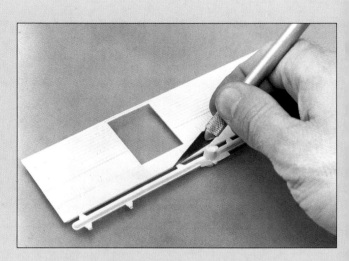

1 Use a hobby knife or sprue cutters to remove the sprues from the parts. Do not try to break the parts from the sprue, because a portion of the part may break off with the sprue.

The manufacturers of plastic structure kits assume that you already know how to assemble the kit. They usually offer an exploded view of where the parts are supposed to fit, but they leave up to you the task of getting the parts into shape for that final assembly.

The parts in most plastic kits are packaged just as they are ejected from the huge machines that mold them. The parts have long strips of scrap plastic called "sprues" or "runners" that are used in the molding process to channel the flow of hot liquid plastic into the cavity of the mold that creates the part. The sprues must be removed and their attaching points smoothed with a large flat file to make each part ready for assembly. A

cabinetmaker's file like the one shown in Project 63 is the best tool for this.

Take the time to test-fit each and every part before you assemble the model. This will help you understand where the parts belong so you don't use similar parts in the wrong places. Look carefully at each joint as you test it for fit to see if the joint needs to be filed to fit more closely. Use the cabinetmaker's file to smooth each joining edge and surface. This has two advantages: first, it will remove any slight ridges or depressions that result from the edges of the parts cooling faster than the center, and, second, it will remove the shiny "skin" from the plastic so the plastic cement can achieve a quicker and better bond.

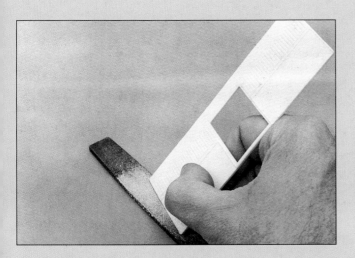

2 Use a cabinetmaker's file to smooth all the edges where the sprues were attached. File each joint, before assembly, to ensure a tight fit and provide a better surface for the cement to grip.

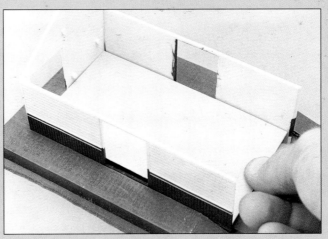

3 Always test-fit each part before assembly. Use thicker plastic cements in needle-applicator bottles, like Testors Model Masters Liquid Cement for Plastics, to assemble the parts. If the model has two-color trim, it's easier to paint the parts before assembly.

4 If you plan to provide interior lighting, paint the insides of the walls before adding the roof or window glazing. Any plastic cement will frost or "craze" clear plastic windows, so use white glue to install those parts.

PROJECT 69 • REAL GLASS FOR WINDOWS

 Time: 2 hours

 Tools: Hobby knife or scribing tool, steel ruler, cotton gloves, and eye protection

 Materials: Clover House window glass or microscope slide glasses and cyanoacrylate cement or white glue

 Cost: S

 Talent: Novice

 Scales: HO, S, O and G

 Space: 2x2 inches

 Tip: BuiMeasure the glass right on the window, rather than using a ruler.

 WHY: To make windows have that special reflective quality that only comes from real glass

COMPLEMENTARY PROJECTS: 63 and 67 through 80

1 Real glass has a quality that you cannot duplicate with clear plastic. Each of the windows in this HO Evergreen Scale Models building is fitted with real glass. Test-fit the glass before you cut it, using the window frame to mark the glass.

I know of no model kit that includes real glass for the windows; rather, kits usually include some kind of clear plastic. It would, obviously, be more difficult to package real glass without it breaking in the box, and clear plastic is enough to satisfy most modelers. If you really want the look of genuine glass, however, there's really no substitute for real glass. For the glass to be visible, though, you need to be fairly close to the model and the window panels need to be fairly large—it's not worth the trouble to install real glass windows in a model that's 2 feet from the edge of the table or in most N scale models, for that matter. For a foreground model, however, it is definitely worth the trouble.

You can buy glass microscope slides at stores that sell school supplies or supplies for college chemistry classes, and at some drug stores. Clover House offers prepackaged sets of real glass panels for modelers. You should also buy a scribing tool from a machine tool supply store or from Clover House. The scribing tool really is just a hardened pinpoint with a handle that will scratch the surface of the glass.

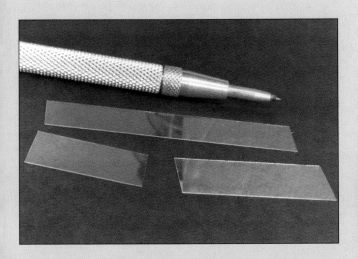

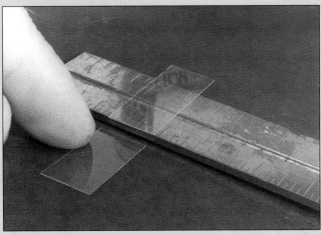

2   To cut the glass, simply scratch a perfectly straight line along its face, using a scribing tool and a steel ruler.

3   Bend the glass over the sharp edge of the ruler and it will break cleanly along the scribed line. Be sure to wear cotton gloves and eye protection, on the odd chance that the glass might shatter, rather than break. If the line you scribed is straight and the edge you use for bending is sharp, the glass should break cleanly every time.

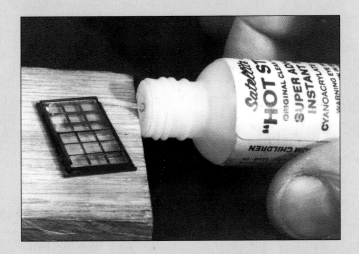

4   Test-fit each panel again before gluing. Hold each glass panel in place with a drop of cyanoacrylate cement or a bead of white glue.

BUILDINGS

PROJECT 70 • INTERIOR LIGHTING

Time: 2 hours

Tools: Hobby knife, wire strippers, small screwdriver, and soldering iron or gun

Materials: 3- to 12-volt bulbs; sockets and brackets from Bachmann, Life-Like, Busch, Faller, or Kibri to hold the sockets; a 12-volt transformer; 20-gauge insulated wire; electrical tape; solder; and aluminum foil

Cost: $

Talent: Novice

Scales: HO, S, O and G

Space: 2x2 inches

Tip: Test each light to determine if you need to add interior walls or panels. Be sure to keep light bulbs at least 2 inches away from plastic walls and to provide some opening in the roof to ventilate any heat.

WHY: To make model buildings look like they are actually occupied

COMPLEMENTARY PROJECTS: 63, 67, 68, and 69 through 80

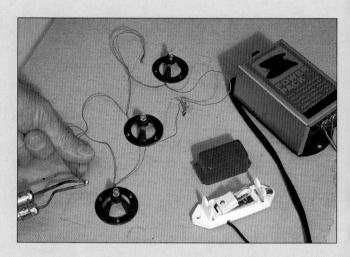

1 Bachmann, Life-Like, Busch, Faller, and Kibri all produce light supports like these three circle-shaped units. You can also use an inexpensive 12-volt automotive-trailer bulb (lower center). Strip the wires and solder each connection, then wrap the joint with electrical tape. These three lights are wired in series with a used toy transformer to reduce the voltage going to each light.

Lighting provides another dimension of realism and is one of the best ways to make models look more realistic. The concept of a "welcoming light" is frequent in all types of fiction, and it implies that warmth, comfort, and, most likely, human companionship wait at the source of the light. Those same feelings arise when you see the interior of a model building illuminated.

LIGHTING TRICKS

You can do several things to make lighting more realistic inside a model building. The first "trick" is to be sure that the bulb itself is not visible from any normal viewing angle. Bachmann, Life-Like, Busch, Faller, and Kibri all offer special interior lighting kits that include the light bulbs, sockets, and a plastic bracket to elevate the lights about 2 inches from the floor of the model. The trick is to raise the light bulb so it is just high enough that it cannot be seen through the windows. In some taller buildings (like churches) you may need to support the light bracket on a small stand made from scrap plastic.

I also recommend that you find some way of providing a hole in the roof so heat from the lights can escape. You can usually drill an unobtrusive 1/8-inch or larger hole beside a chimney or next to a vent.

You may also want to add interior walls to some structures so it is not so apparent that there is nothing inside. You can make these from sheets of styrene or even cardboard. Just be sure to keep the interior walls at least 2 inches from light bulbs.

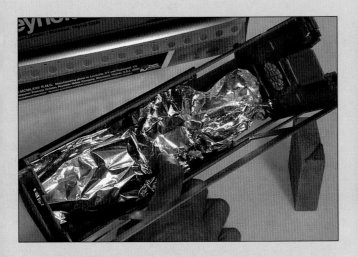

2 Diffuse and reflect the illumination inside larger structures, and protect the plastic from the heat of the light bulbs, by covering the inside of the roof with aluminum foil, inserted shiny-side down.

3 Stained glass windows can be simulated by photocopying pictures of real windows onto the clear plastic that is used for overhead projector images.

"SCALE" LIGHT INTENSITY

With full power, all of these model railroad lights are far too bright. The effect you want is that of a glow, not of a room illuminated brightly enough for a television crew to work. Most model railroad power packs have an "accessory" terminal that will deliver 12 to 18 volts of current to the light bulbs, and most light bulbs sold for model railroads are rated at 12 to 18 volts. The lighting will be far more realistic, however, if you reduce the voltage to as little as 3 volts, but no more than 6. You can provide reduced voltage by using a separate power pack or transformer with a lower rating, such as those sold by Radio Shack and similar electronics hobby stores, or by wiring the lights in a "series" like old-fashioned Christmas tree lights. Series wiring merely means that you connect one wire to the power pack, then to the first light. The second wire from that light goes to the next light, and its second wire to the next light, and so on until the last light's second wire is connected to the other terminal on the power pack. (Most Christmas lights nowadays are wired in parallel, with both wires from every light leading directly to the power pack or wall outlet.) The more lights you put on the string or "series," the fewer volts that are available to any single bulb. You have to experiment to determine how many lights you need to reduce the brightness to less than half of a single light.

PROJECT 71 • SIMULATE WOOD WITH PLASTIC

 Time: 2 hours

 Tools: Hobby knife or single-edge razor blade, razor saw, and a 3-inch scrap of 1x4 hardwood

 Materials: Evergreen Scale Models or Plastruct styrene plastic strips, commercial wood stains and thinner, rags, and a 1/4-inch flat paintbrush

 Cost: $

 Talent: Novice

 Scales: HO, N, S, O and G

 Space: 2x2 inches

 Tip: Test the stain on a scrap before applying it to the entire piece of plastic.

WHY: To make plastic indistinguishable from real wood

 COMPLEMENTARY PROJECTS: 63 through 68, 73 and 99

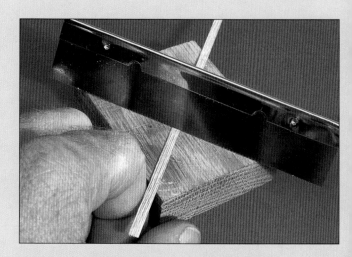

1 Hold the piece of styrene plastic on a 3-inch piece of 1x4 hardwood while dragging the teeth of a razor saw blade down the length of the wood. Wiggle the blade abruptly as you drag it to impart the wavy look of woodgrain. When satisfied, use a hobby knife blade to scrape away any wisps of plastic "hair" that resulted from using the razor saw blade.

Some modelers insist that only real wood can look like real wood. With a few painting and distressing techniques, however, you can make plastic indistinguishable from real wood. I made this project, a wooden fence, from both wood and styrene just to see if anyone could tell the difference. The fence-building is continued in Projects 72, 73, and 99. You can use these same techniques to build entire structures and platforms from styrene.

Milled styrene strips available from Evergreen Scale Models and Plastruct are made to match HO scale lumber, ranging from a tiny 1x2 to a 6x12 (about 1/16x1/8 inch). Fractional sizes are also available, so you can match N, S, O, or G scale lumber sizes with styrene strips. Craft supply stores offer stains in small bottles, or you can use mixtures of brown and black ink. Experiment on some scraps to determine how much thinner to use and what color stain. For really weathered wood, you might consider using a fairly dark burnt umber stain, then brush on a coat of light gray paint mixed with an equal part of thinner to impart the weathered appearance.

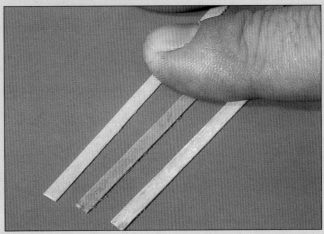

2 Use a hobby knife or single-edge razor blade to slice the ends of some of the boards to simulate deteriorating and splintering wood.

3 This is real basswood (left), painted light gray (right), then weathered with thinned dark oak stain (center).

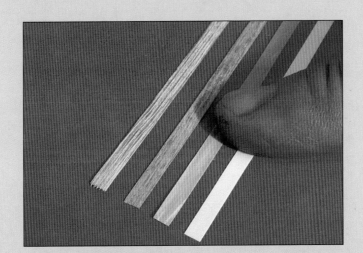

4 This photo shows a bare plastic strip that was painted with a light coat of gray (far right), then stained with a brushed-on coat of dark oak stain (right center), "distressed" by scraping its length with a razor saw blade (left center), and finally stained with another coat of dark oak stain to fill in the "grain" scraped by the razor saw teeth. Plastic "wood" can be painted with a second coat of light gray thinned with an equal part of thinner to simulate weather-faded whitewash.

BUILDINGS

PROJECT 72 • BUILD A BOARD FENCE

 Time: 2 hours

 Tools: Northwest Short Line "Chopper," tweezers, single-edge razor blade, fine-point felt-tip pen, steel ruler

 Materials: Evergreen Scale Models or Plastruct 4x4 and 1x6 styrene plastic strips; Testors Model Master Liquid Cement for Plastics, Vollmer Super Cement, Kibri Plastic Cement or Faller Super Expert Cement; masking tape; drawing paper; and waxed paper

 Cost: $

 Talent: Novice

 Scales: HO, N, S, O and G

 Space: 2x12 inches

 Tip: The "Chopper" makes it easy to build a precise model.

 WHY: To make an often-overlooked piece of scenery

COMPLEMENTARY PROJECTS: 63 through 68, 71, 73 and 99

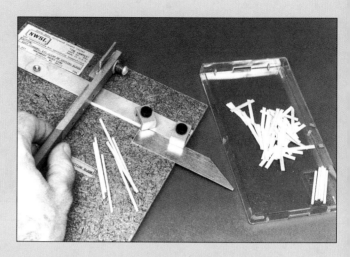

1 The NorthWest Short Line "Chopper" is a guillotine-like device with adjustable stops. It allows you to cut as many pieces of wood or plastic as you want to the exact same length with perfectly square ends. (The tool pictured is the original Chopper; the newer Chopper is a bit more rugged with a high-impact plastic table.) Before beginning, make a full-size sketch of the fence with a fine-point felt-tip pen and ruler. Depict the posts, rails, and pickets so you know exactly how long to cut each component. Adjust the stops on the Chopper to cut the 1x6s for the pickets and the 4x4s for the posts and rails. Allow an extra inch on the lengths of the posts so you have something to "plant" in the scenery. Stain the plastic or wood before cutting, so you only have to touch up the cut ends on the finished model.

The concept of making something from raw materials, or, as modelers call it, "scratchbuilding," is one of the more rewarding aspects of model railroading. This wooden fence is one of the simplest of all scratchbuilding projects and it's one that's pretty hard to mess up. You are, after all, trying to re-create a sloppy and broken down piece of scenery. You can use either basswood or styrene strips that are distressed and stained to look like wood as shown in Project 71. From here on, the techniques for either material are nearly identical.

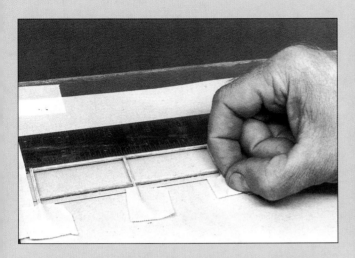

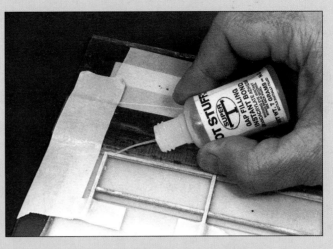

2 Use your drawing as a template for positioning the posts, rails, and pickets. Cover the work surface with waxed paper and tape a steel ruler to the paper to serve as a guide. Tape the 4x4s to the waxed paper and apply Testors Model Master Liquid Cement for Plastics or its equivalent to each joint.

3 If you use wood for the fence, cement the joints with thickened cyanoacrylate cement and make the joint "instant" by spraying it with one of the accelerators described in Project 66.

4 Use tweezers to install the 1x6 pickets on the 4x4 framework. If using plastic strips, use the thinner Testors Liquid Cement for Plastics (the thicker Model Master cement can melt thin plastic) to affix each 1x6 one at a time using the sketch as a guide. The steel ruler will give you something to butt the ends of the 1x6s against. Let the cement dry overnight. Use a single-edge razor blade to remove the parts from the waxed paper.

BUILDINGS

PROJECT 73 • WEATHER A BOARD FENCE

Time: 2 hours

Tools: Single-edge razor blade, electric drill, and bit

Materials: Dry transfers or decals, artist's matte medium, and a brown fine-point felt-tip pen

Cost: $

Talent: Novice

Scales: HO, N, S, O and G

Space: 2x12 inches

Tip: Study photos of real fences to match their colors and textures.

WHY: To make an often-overlooked piece of scenery

COMPLEMENTARY PROJECTS: 50 and 51, 63 through 68, 71, 72 and 99

1. Use a dark brown fine-point felt-tip pen to apply the barest traces of pinpoint-size dots to simulate rusted nail heads. Practice a bit, and you can even leave a trace of "rust" streaming down the board for a few scale inches.

The fence in Project 72 can be considered a work in progress. There's more to be done, including applying graffiti or old placards, weathering, and, of course, "setting" the fence posts. All of the decal and dry transfer makers mentioned in Projects 50 and 51 offer letters, ads, and even scale-model graffiti from every historical period. You can, in fact, use the fence to help "date" your railroad by applying appropriate-to-the-era posters (or torn pieces of old posters) and graffiti.

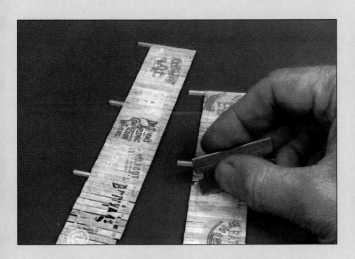

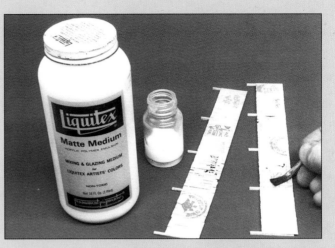

2 This fence was lettered with a combination of Microscale 87-243 decal "graffiti" and 1900s-era billboards from Vintage Reproductions. Use decal solvent to force the decals into the "grain" of the wood or plastic. Slice through the decals or dry transfers at the joints between pickets and apply another coat of decal solvent.

3 Protect the dry transfers or decals with a coat of artist's matte medium mixed with an equal part water. When that has dried, weather the fence with colors to match the earth it will rest in and, if it's near tracks, rain-washed soot and grime, using the airbrush or pastel chalk techniques from Projects 50 and 51.

4 When the fence is weathered, install it by drilling holes just a bit larger than the 4x4 posts. Use the fence itself to locate exactly where to drill the holes. Use a larger bit to allow room for one or more of the posts to be moved if the fence does not sit properly. Fill in around the holes with the same real dirt, sifted through a tea strainer, that you use for the surrounding scenery. Do not, however, cement the dirt in place: leave it loose so you can remove the fence if you wish. More photos of this fence in place appear in Project 99.

BUILDINGS

PROJECT 74 • PHOTOCOPY YOUR OWN SCRATCHBUILDING PLANS

Time: 2 hours

Tools: Fluorescent light; HO, N, S, O, or G scale ruler; hobby knife; 12x12-inch sheet of 1/8-inch Plexiglas; and a small machinist's square

Materials: Paper, Evergreen Scale Models or Plastruct sheet styrene, and doors and windows to match the prototype you are modeling

Cost: S

Talent: Novice and Expert

Scales: HO, N, S, O and G

Space: 2x6 inches

Tip: Use .020- to .040-inch styrene so you can see through it.

WHY: To quickly and easily transfer plans to styrene sheets for scratchbuilding cars and buildings

COMPLEMENTARY PROJECTS: 75 through 83

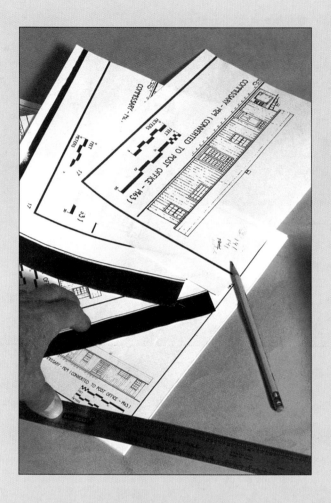

1 Reduce or enlarge the plans or photographs to match your scale as described in the text. When you check the plans with your scale ruler, be sure to start with the "0" markings on the scale and the ruler.

If you want your structures to be as true to reality as your rolling stock and locomotives, you will likely need to learn to scratchbuild at least some of them. Once you learn the simple "scribe-'n-snap" techniques, you can scratchbuild a structure almost as quickly as you can assemble a kit. The techniques shown on these pages have been developed over decades of trial and error and utilize all the best properties of styrene plastic, while avoiding the material's drawbacks.

SCALE-SIZE PHOTOCOPIES

Use the reduction and enlargement settings on a photocopy machine to alter any plan or photograph to the scale of the structure you want to build. If you know the scale of the plans, you can get close to the proper reduction or enlargement with simple mathematics. First, check the size of the plans with a scale ruler to see if they match a common modeling scale. If not, it may be possible to determine the scale for yourself. For this example let's say that you discovered the plans were drawn to 1/160 scale, the common size for N scale. To build the structure in HO or l/87 scale, use a simple fraction, putting N above HO, or 160/87, which divides to become 184 percent. Position the enlargement setting on the photocopier to 184

2 Lay a piece of 1/8-inch Plexiglas over a portable fluorescent light fixture. Place the plans (or a matched-to-your-scale photocopy of a photograph) over the Plexiglas. When you lay the styrene plastic you will use for the walls over the plan, you will be able to see the outline of the plan through the plastic. You can trace the outline with a pencil, but it's far quicker to use a hobby knife, guided by a steel ruler, and simply skip the pencil-marking step. I traced over the scribed lines with a pencil so they are visible, but you can skip that step.

existing building and have no scale-size plans, you can make "photo plans" by simply taking a picture of each side of the structure as close to dead-on, with the camera at right angles to the wall and positioned as close as possible to the exact center of the wall. Take a few measurements of the width and height of a window or door on each side. Use those measurements as the "standard" to reduce or enlarge photocopies of the photographs until you have photocopies in your exact scale.

TRACE—DON'T REDRAW—PLANS

One property of .040-inch or thinner sheet styrene is that when you place it in front of a fluorescent light you can see through it. You can use that property to trace plans or scale-size photographs of your prototype directly onto the styrene. I use an old two-bulb fluorescent fixture that I can lay on the workbench. Purchase a 12x12-inch piece of clear Plexiglas from a shop that sells window glass and lay it over the florescent fixture as shown in the photographs.

Place the photocopy of the plan or photograph of one side of the structure on top of the Plexiglas. Lay a sheet of .040-inch styrene over it. Use a machinist's square and a steel straightedge to guide a hobby knife as you trace the outline of the structure. Use the square edges of the Plexiglas and the machinist's square, not just the plans, to be sure each corner is perfectly square.

SURE-FIT WINDOW AND DOOR OPENINGS

Do NOT use the window openings on the plans or photograph. Use actual model doors and windows that you will install as templates, and mark each window and door outline with a light scribe line made with the hobby knife, always guided by a machinist's square and steel straightedge. It's easiest to use molded plastic windows (like those sold by Grandt Line, Micro Engineering, Campbell, Rix, Pikestuff, or metal windows from SS Limited, Alexander, Dyna-Model, or Sequoia) than to attempt to make your own from strip styrene. In some cases, it may be necessary to use windows that are not exactly the correct size, or to settle for a different number of panes.

As you trace the plan, use the windows and doors on the plan or the photograph merely as locations for the model windows and doors. Scribe the openings to match the model parts, rather than the plans, and the windows and doors should fit perfectly in their openings. Later, you'll learn how to

percent and make a copy. Double-check the resulting plan with a scale ruler. If a scale is not marked on the plan, assume that doorways are 6 feet, 6 inches high.

If necessary, reduce or enlarge the photocopies until you get the printed scale to match an HO scale ruler or the doorways to be that 6-foot, 6-inch height.

NO-PLAN PLANS

The subject for this and Projects 75 through 79 and 86 and 87 is a small oil depot. If you model an use the simple "snap" portion of the "scribe-'n-snap" technique to finish the walls, roof, and floors.

WALL SURFACE OPTIONS

The prototype for this particular structure has board-and-batten siding, so I opted for .040-inch siding scribed every .100 inch. The scribed lines will be used as built-in guidelines to lay .015x030-inch battens. Yes, Evergreen does make milled board-and-batten siding, but it is more difficult to use for walls with windows because each batten must be carefully carved to clear the tops and bottoms of the window frames.

This technique will not work with injection-molded plastic walls or roofs like those in most kits, or with the simulated brick, corrugated steel, shingle, or stone sheets sold by Pikestuff, Kibri, and Brawa—these materials must be cut through with a razor saw. You can, however, use the technique with Plastruct or with Holgate and Reynolds vacuum-formed styrene brick–, stone-, and shingle-textured plastic sheets.

BUILDINGS

PROJECT 75 • SNAP-OUT WALLS FROM STYRENE PLASTIC

Time: 2 hours

Tools: Fluorescent light; HO, N, S, O, or G scale ruler; hobby knife; 12x12-inch sheet of 1/8-inch Plexiglas; and a small machinist's square

Materials: Paper, Evergreen Scale Models or Plastruct sheet styrene, doors and windows to match the prototype you are modeling, and waxed paper

Cost: $

Talent: Novice and Expert

Scales: HO, N, S, O and G

Space: 2x6 inches

Tip: Use the model windows as templates for the holes in the walls.

WHY: To quickly and easily transfer plans to styrene sheets for scratchbuilding cars and buildings

COMPLEMENTARY PROJECTS: 74 and 76 through 83

1 On this model, only the bottoms of the windows need to be snapped out of the walls. Mark each window or door opening with a different number or letter so you remember which opening goes with which window or door. Mark the exterior faces of the walls so they can be assembled with the marks visible. (The marks can be erased easily after the walls are completed.) Search catalogs to locate windows and doors that are as close a match as possible to those of the prototype. You can modify most windows by removing the mullions or, if necessary, removing one row of panes by slicing straight down through the window, guillotine-style, with a single-edge razor blade. The vertical slices that define the widths of the walls and the window and door openings were sliced into the surface to be as parallel as possible to the vertical scribed lines in the styrene. If you use shiplap or other surface finishes with horizontal lines, these slices should be horizontal.

It's possible to prepare the walls for a scratchbuilt structure so you can literally snap them into pieces and reassemble them, like a puzzle, in just minutes.

The .040-inch styrene is the best thickness for HO scale structure walls, and .030-inch styrene works just as well for most N scale structures, with their smaller window and door openings. Either thickness must, however, be firmly supported with interior bracing. If you want a detailed interior, make two separate layers of walls, preferably using either smooth styrene or styrene with scribed lines running at 90 degrees to the exterior surface finish lines for the interior walls. This will minimize the chances of the plastic walls bowing in or out along the scribed lines. If you don't need a detailed interior, simply brace the walls with .100 x .125-inch Evergreen styrene strips. Use the techniques explained in Project 76 to assemble the walls.

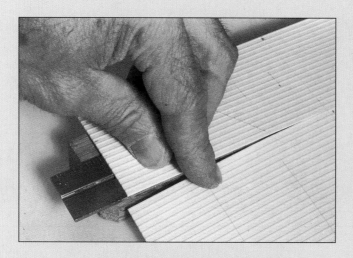

2 Mark the corners of each window and door over their proper locations, then use the hobby knife and machinist's square to scribe the outlines of the windows and doors. Carefully position the white plastic so a sliced edge of a wall is precisely along the edge of a steel ruler supported by a scrap of 1x2 wood. Press the plastic firmly over the edge of the ruler. Keep pushing and work your fingers along the break in the plastic until the plastic rests at the angle shown. Continue to press down with your fingers and it will snap cleanly along the sliced line that marks the edge of the wall. With practice, you can snap out all four walls, and all the windows and doors in 10 minutes or less.

3 If you copied the peaked roofs at the two ends of the structure so they shared one sloped side, you can snap off a sloped side of each at once with one long diagonal slice. Then finish the remaining sloped side of each by scoring and snapping off the shorter triangles as shown.

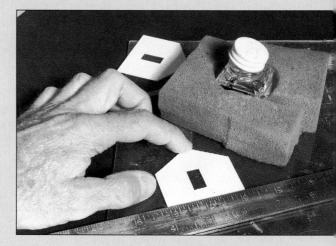

5 Here is a typical end wall with a single window. The portion of the wall above the window and the portion of the wall below the window will be reassembled with Testors Liquid Cement for Plastic.

6 Press the parts of the wall firmly together with the detailed outside faces upward, using the numbers or letters you wrote on the parts in the first step. Apply a thin layer of the Testors Liquid Cement for Plastic to the seams and press the parts firmly on the waxed paper over the Plexiglas. Use a steel ruler to be sure that the top and bottom edges of the walls are perfectly straight. Push the parts firmly against the edge of the steel ruler while the cement is still soft. The cement will stick the wall to the waxed paper. Remove the wall from the waxed paper within a few minutes after the last of the liquid cement is applied. Use a single-edge razor blade to slice between the part and the waxed paper.

4 Use the edge of the steel ruler to bend the plastic to snap out the edges of the windows and doors. It's best to try to limit the length of the break to the height of the window or door. Bend the wall over the edge just far enough so you can feel the plastic give way along the sliced edge. Next, use a shearing motion to force the wall downward, breaking completely through the plastic. Repeat the bending, then the shearing process, along the other edge of the window or door to break the opening from the wall as shown. The plastic you break from the window opening will be in three pieces: the lower portion of wall below the window sill, the "window" area, and the portion of the wall above the window. Hold the broken-out window pieces over the edges of the steel ruler and bend, then break the lower sill and upper sill from the window.

BUILDINGS

PROJECT 76 • FINISH THE BASIC BUILDING

Time: 2 hours

Tools: HO, N, S, O, or G scale ruler; hobby knife; 12x12-inch sheet of 1/8-inch Plexiglas; and a small machinist's square

Materials: Evergreen Scale Models or Plastruct sheet styrene; doors and windows to match the prototype; Testors Model Master Liquid Cement for Plastics, Vollmer Super Cement, Kibri Plastic Cement, or Faller Super Expert Cement; and waxed paper

Cost: $$

Talent: Novice and Expert

Scales: HO, N, S, O and G

Space: 2x6 inches

Tip: Use a machinist's square or squared blocks of wood to be sure all corners are in alignment.

WHY: To quickly and easily re-create any prototype structure

COMPLEMENTARY PROJECTS: 74, 75, and 77 through 83

1 A close up of a typical corner. The HO scale 1x2 strips used for the corner trim on this model (and on its prototype) were positioned so that the overlapping end walls would appear to be the edges of bats (from the board-and-batten walls). Again, test-fit each window and door. Do not cement any of them in place, as it will be much easier to paint them a second color if they are not installed in the walls.

When the walls and roof of your structure are snapped out as described in Project 74, you are ready to begin assembly of the structure. Test-fit the walls so you know whether the end walls fit inside the front and rear walls or vice versa. The interior braces must be short enough so they do not interfere with the fit of each corner. Assemble the walls on the bare Plexiglas, using the machinist's square to ensure that each corner is perfectly square. Apply the cement to both mating surfaces and gently work the parts up and down about l/64 inch with some force to dissolve the plastic and form a truly welded bond at each corner. You can adjust the fit of the walls for several minutes after the cement is applied.

2 If the structure will rest on the ground without a concrete, brick, or stone foundation, install a "basement" from strips of .010x.250-inch Evergreen Scale Models or Plastruct styrene strip. The strips should extend about 1/8 inch below the bottom of the structure.

3 When the model is installed on the layout, the extended "basement" strips will be covered with a layer of real dirt and/or flocking held in place with artist's matte medium.

PROJECT 77 • MAKE TEXTURED ROOFS FOR PLASTIC BUILDINGS

 Time: 2 hours

 Tools: HO, N, S, O, or G scale ruler; hobby knife; razor saw; 12x12-inch sheet of 1/8-inch Plexiglas; small machinist's square; and a cabinetmaker's file

 Materials: Faller, Grandt Line, Pikestuff, Kibri, or Vollmer injection-molded plastic roof sheets; Testors Model Master Liquid Cement for Plastics; thickened cyanoacrylate cement; and waxed paper

 Cost: $$

 Talent: Novice and Expert

 Scales: HO, N, S, O and G

 Space: 2x6 inches

 Tip: Make the razor cut about 1/16 inch from the final edge of the roof to allow for "file to fit" room.

 WHY: To quickly and easily re-create any prototype structure

COMPLEMENTARY PROJECTS: 74 through 83

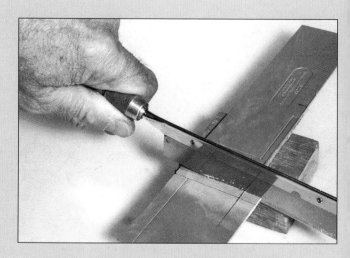

1 Measure each side of the roof carefully, allowing enough material for overhang on both ends as well as the bottom. With a ruler as guide, use a hobby knife to scribe a line indicating exactly where to cut. Hold the plastic roof material to a scrap of 1x4 wood with one hand while you cut through the scribed line with a razor saw.

The roof for your scratchbuilt structure can be made of styrene sheet just like the walls, if you model a structure with a tarpaper or standing-seam metal roof. You can also use paper shingles, like those offered by Campbell, or wooden shingles, like those from Evergreen Hill, on a plain styrene roof. In addition, Williams Brothers makes pressed aluminum roofing that is perfect for simulating metal-covered roofs.

If the prototype structure you model has a shingled or tiled roof, however, consider using injection-molded sheets of roof sold by Faller, Grandt Line, Kibri, or Vollmer. They are usually about 1/16 inch to 3/32 inch thick and have HO scale shingles or tiles molded into their outer surface.

The length of the roof can be determined from the plan's front or rear views. However, the width can only be determined by referring to the plan's end views.

I used Faller's injection-molded plastic shingle roof cut to size with a razor saw for this model. For the warehouse in the oil depot diorama, I used Evergreen Scale Models' 4544 .040-inch board-and-batten siding with .125-inch bat spacing to simulate the standing-seam roof of the prototype. With this material, use some extra force to slice through the thickness of the bats. Use the "scribe-'n-snap" steps shown in Project 75 to break the roof along these slices.

2   Use a cabinetmaker's file to shape the upper edges of the roof so they will join snugly for their entire length. Use the same technique to match and join dormer and gable roofs to main roofs.

3   Use a thicker liquid cement for plastic in a needle applicator bottle to join the two roof panels at their peak. Apply the cement to both surfaces and use as much force as you can to rub the two joining surfaces back and forth about l/64 inch, dissolving the plastic in the cement and literally welding the parts together. The roof can be painted as a separate piece and attached to the walls with thickened cyanoacrylate cement. First, test-fit the roof over the walls to be sure the angles are right.

BUILDINGS

PROJECT 78 • CREATE TELEPHONE POLES AND WIRES

Time: 2 hours

Tools: HO, N, S, O, or G scale ruler; hobby knife; razor saw; rectangular jeweler's file; pin vise; tweezers; needle-nose pliers; and a number 50 drill bit

Materials: SS Limited 2393 or Dyna-Model Products 2025 Telephone Pole Crossarms; Clover House or Northeastern 3/32-inch or 1/8-inch wooden dowels; "invisible" sewing thread; HO scale track spikes; thickened cyanoacrylate cement and accelerator; and waxed paper

Cost: $$

Talent: Expert

Scales: HO, N, S, O and G

Space: 2x6 inches

Tip: Scrape the pole with a razor saw to produce a simulated rough grain.

WHY: To re-create an obvious but often overlooked detail

COMPLEMENTARY PROJECTS: 74 through 77 and 79 through 83

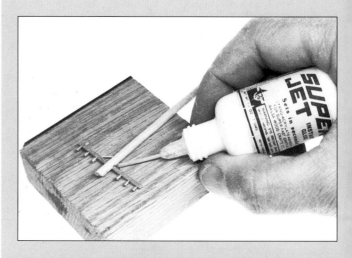

1 Match the poles you are modeling to a specific real site, making your best guess as to the height and diameter of the prototypes—height typically varies from about 15 to 40 feet, diameter from 7 to 12 inches. Cut the wooden dowel about an inch longer than necessary to leave some room to "bury" the end of the pole in the layout. Cut the dowel with a razor saw, incorporating an angle or peak on the top of the pole to match the prototype if necessary. Use a rectangular jeweler's file to cut notches for the crossarms. Cement the crossarm in place with thickened cyanoacrylate cement.

4 These scenes are part of a diorama constructed by Bob and Lynn Lunde. They took particular care to be sure that at least some of the wires actually lead to buildings. The insulators on the structures are cut from spare crossarms.

Telephone poles and wires are among the most common items in any real railroad scene. There are dozens of brands of plastic telephone poles that can be fit with wires as shown here. For the most realistic poles, however, consider assembling your own from cast-metal crossarms and insulators. You can choose SS Limited 2393 or Dyna-Model Products 2025 Telephone Pole Crossarms for HO scale, with Clover House or Northeastern 3/32-inch or 1/8-inch wooden dowels for the poles. Use HO scale railroad spikes for the climbing spikes that are fitted to poles with transformers. The transformers themselves can be cut from some of the Atlas, Life-Like, or Bachmann plastic poles.

Decide if it is worth the trouble to install the telephone wires, keeping in mind there is no other detail that can add as much realism to a scene,

186

2 Telephone and power poles with transformers usually have spikes so linemen can climb them. Use a pin vise with a number 50 bit to drill the holes, and install scale railroad spikes with needle-nose pliers.

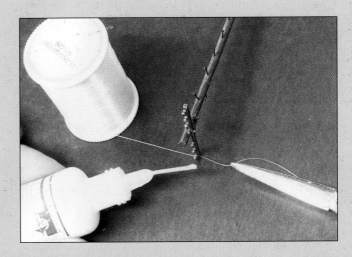

3 Fabric stores sell a fine nylon "invisible thread" that works well for simulating telephone or power lines. If you wish, use Rit clothes dye to color the thread to match a specific prototype, or you may be able to find the thread in black. Install the thread only after all the poles are in place. (Here, the step is illustrated on a plain background for clarity.) Pull the thread taut with tweezers and apply a drop of thickened cyanoacrylate cement to hold it in place. To speed up the work, spray each joint with accelerator.

5 Yes, it can get complicated, but this is an incredibly realistic scene. With practice, you'll learn to install the lowest wires (threads) first and work your way out and up. If you install a line along three or more poles, stretch the line taut, then cement it to the insulators on the extreme end poles first, then to the insulators on the center poles.

especially one set from 1920 to 1980, before many wires were buried. There is also no detail more vulnerable to a modeler's elbows. With some care, however, you may be able to locate the poles and wires in places that are out of reach, even if they do not precisely match the prototype.

PROJECT 79 • BUILD A CHAINLINK FENCE

Time: 4 hours

Tools: HO, N, S, O, or G scale ruler; hobby knife; razor saw; 12x12-inch sheet of 1/8-inch Plexiglas; rectangular jeweler's file; pin vise; tweezers; needle-nose pliers; number 50 and 72 drill bits; small scissors; airbrush; air compressor; and filter mask

Materials: Gold Medal Models chainlink fence kit for N and HO scales, Scale Scenics kit for HO scale, or Builders In Scale kit for HO scale; thickened cyanoacrylate cement and accelerator; Weldbond cement; aluminum or silver paint; waxed paper; and light gray paint

Cost: $$

Talent: Expert

Scales: HO and N

Space: 6x12 inches

Tip: Use excess lengths of tulle "chainlink" and cut it to size after gluing it in place.

WHY: To re-create a realistic replica of one of the most commonly seen fences

COMPLEMENTARY PROJECTS: 74 through 77, 82, 86 and 87

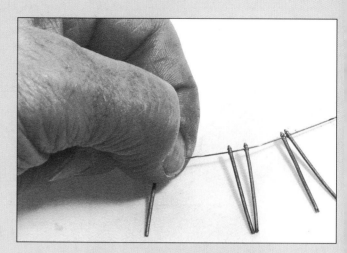

1 Begin by drilling through all the fence posts (including the corner posts— those with dimples at 90 degrees rather than 180, like the standard posts) with a number 72 bit in a pin vise. If the tops of the posts snap off, save them and cement them back in place when the fence is installed. I find that the tulle supplied by Builders In Scale allows the fence to be built in sections of about 48 scale feet, or seven posts, long. String seven of the posts on the .030-inch steel wire provided with the kit.

Chainlink fences are common along real railroad rights-of-way and around industries served by railroads. Gold Medal Models offers an etched-brass chainlink fence kit for N and HO scales and Scale Scenics has a kit with metal mesh for HO scale. For this diorama I used a Builders In Scale kit that features dressmaker's lace (called "tulle") for the chainlink, thread for the barbed wire, and cast-metal posts.

The Builders In Scale chainlink fence kit contains enough material for about 14 inches of fence, including two large gates and one walk-through gate. I used two of the kits for this 5 1/4x21 1/4-inch oil depot diorama, but I supplemented the kits with additional fence posts and top railings made from wire—there was just enough tulle for the entire fence. I deviated from the Builder In Scale instructions in several places, so decide before you begin whether to follow my instructions or those in the kit.

You can also build the fence from scratch using tulle with piano wire for the posts—tulle is available at any fabric store. The lace is very close to HO scale chainlink, but it can also pass for O, S, or even N scale. Cut the strips to match the height of the fence in scale feet.

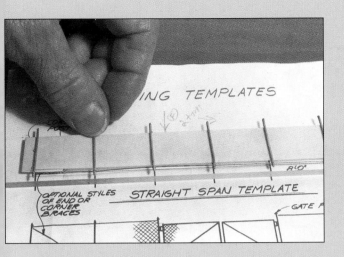

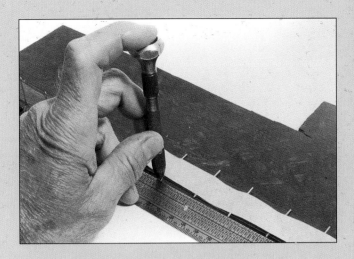

2 Lay a piece of Plexiglas over the Builders In Scale plans. Fold a piece of 3/4-inch masking tape over itself with the sticky side out and press it over the plan. Press the posts firmly onto the tape, using the plan as a spacing guide. Place each post so the hole you drilled is even with the top edge of the masking tape. Add a drop of thickened cyanoacrylate cement to each post-and-wire joint, and spray a bit of accelerator on each joint. Leave any excess length of top railing wire protruding from the ends of the posts for now. Carefully peel away the tape, leaving the posts and wires attached.

3 Use a pencil and straightedge to mark the location of the fence on the diorama. Lay the string of posts on the pencil line, using the tops of the posts as a guide for drilling the holes. (The tops are cemented to the top railing wire, so their spacing should remain constant.) Use a number 52 bit to drill a hole for each of the Builders In Scale posts, or use a number 66 bit if you make your own posts from .030-inch wire. Carefully insert each of the posts in its appropriate hole in the diorama. The 3/4-inch tape will help you know how far to push each post into the diorama. When all the posts are installed, look down the length of the fence and push or pull the posts so the railing is perfectly horizontal and exactly 3/4 inch from the top of the diorama. You can also bend the posts in or out so the fence does not lean. Take some extra time to get all the posts in perfect alignment.

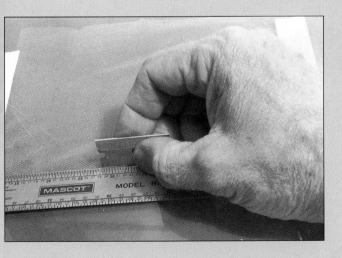

4 Stretch the tulle just enough to remove the wrinkles. Press it onto a piece of Plexiglas and tape the last 1/4 inch of each side of the tulle to the Plexiglas with 3/4-inch masking tape. Use a steel ruler and a new single-edge razor blade to cut the tulle in strips exactly 27/32 inch wide.

5 Use an all-purpose cement like Weldbond to attach the tulle to the fence posts. Spread the cement the length of the posts with a toothpick, but do not spread it along the top railing. Coat only enough posts to match the length of the "chainlink" and work quickly so the cement is still moist when you get to the last post. Hold the tulle by the masking tape strips on each end and gently pull it to its full length without pulling hard enough to stretch it. Dab the tulle lightly with a fingertip to push it into the still-wet cement. Because it's easier to hide joints in the tulle along straight sections of fence, plan the installation so you can wrap the tulle around the corners.

6 Allow the cement to dry for an hour before applying the next section of tulle. When the first section is dry, trim it flush with the vertical edge of the posts, using small mustache scissors.

7 Use Builders In Scale gates to determine the exact spacing of the gate posts. Note that the gate post with the hinges is yet to be installed. Mark the location of the necessary post and install the necessary posts and railings. Be sure to position the gate so the "chainlink" is on the same side of the gate as it is on the rest of the fence. Spread a thick coat of Weldbond over the entire face of the gate. Cut some of the leftover tulle about 1/4 inch larger than the gate and apply it while the cement is still wet. Let it dry for an hour, then use a single-edge razor blade to trim the tulle flush with the top, bottom, and sides of the gate.

10 The edges of this diorama are detailed with clumps of flocking fiber, as described in Projects 43 and 93. The walk-through gate is cemented to the hinge post in an open position.

11 This chainlink fence is part of an oil depot diorama that appeared in *Railmodel Journal* in the 1990s; most of the steps are shown here and in Projects 74, 75, 76, 77, 82, 86, and 87. You could also substitute the wooden fence in Projects 71 and 72. The fence defines the edge of the lift-out diorama, and it helps to hide its "removable" nature, especially when the bottom of the fence is sprinkled with fine ground green foam to hide the joint and simulate weeds.

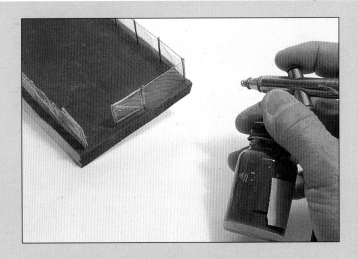

8 The Builders In Scale tulle material is a light gray. If you purchase tulle from a fabric store, buy light gray—it will look more realistic when given a wash (equal parts water and light gray paint) with an airbrush. Use the same technique to paint the posts, railings, and gates.

9 Use a wash that matches the dirt surrounding the fence to simulate rain-splashed mud on the bottom scale foot or so. Projects 86 and 87 show how to apply dirt and weeds. Alternately, the diorama can be painted a light gray and marked with inked-in lines to simulate a concrete pad.

PROJECT 80 • ASSEMBLE AND PAINT RESIN KITS

Time: 4 to 8 hours

Tools: Hobby knife, 12x12-inch sheet of 1/8-inch Plexiglas, cabinetmaker's file, rectangular jeweler's file, number 0 and number 1 paintbrushes, and a respirator

Materials: Design Preservation Models (DPM), SS Limited, or another cast-resin structure kit, thickened cyanoacrylate cement, regular cyanoacrylate cement, baking soda, accelerator or kicker for the cement, white glue, flat black and brick-color aerosol paint, PollyScale or Modelflex acrylic white and light gray paint, mild liquid detergent, masking tape, and facial tissue

Cost: SS

Talent: Novice

Scales: HO, N, S, O and G

Space: 2x6 inches

Tip: Be prepared to correct mistakes painting trim with brick-colored paint.

WHY: To increase your choice of structure kits by including cast-resin models

COMPLEMENTARY PROJECTS: 63, 66, 69, 70, 77, and 81 through 83

1 Use a cabinetmaker's file as described in Project 63 to file the joining edges of each of the walls until they fit together perfectly.

Design Preservation Models (DPM) and SS Limited produce a variety of interesting cast-resin structure kits in HO scale. DPM also makes a series of cast-resin N scale structures, while other makers offer limited-production cast-resin structure kits in all scales as advertised in a number of model railroad magazines.

Most of these kits have the windows and doors molded right into the walls, so you simply assemble the walls and roof and the model is complete. The corners of most of the kits do not, however, fit as tightly as most injection-molded styrene plastic kits, so you must be prepared to do a bit of filing and fitting to get tight-fitting corners. You can use white glue or epoxy to assemble the walls, but thickened cyanoacrylate cement, as shown in Project 66, is the quickest and easiest, especially if you use an accelerator or kicker spray to finish the joints. If the joints cannot be fitted perfectly by filing them, apply a filet of baking soda and a drop of conventional cyanoacrylate cement to fill in the larger gaps.

PAINTING BRICK WITH A WASH

This technique allows you to apply the mortar color in a single step as a "wash" of dilute mortar-colored paint. If the brick wall you are trying to re-create has different shades of bricks (and most do), touch up the individual bricks using the "dry brush" technique described in Project 81.

Some real-life structures have window and door frames painted the same color as the walls, so you do have the option of just spraying the cast-resin walls a single color. For most structures, however, you will want to paint the door and window frames a contrasting color—it is far easier to paint them while the walls are still unassembled.

Touch up the glue joints at the corners after the model is completed.

2 Use masking tape to protect the filed edges. Fold the masking tape into loops to hold the walls to a scrap of wood you can use as a handle while you spray the parts. Spray the inside of all the walls flat black to eliminate the slightly translucent appearance of some cast resins. The black is especially necessary if you intend to illuminate the interior, as shown in Project 70.

3 After the flat black is dry, turn the walls over and stick them back onto the masking tape to spray the fronts. You can probably find an aerosol paint to match the brick you're modeling. The "military" paints come in several appropriate shades. I used Testors Model Master Rust for this building. You can also use bottled paint applied with a brush.

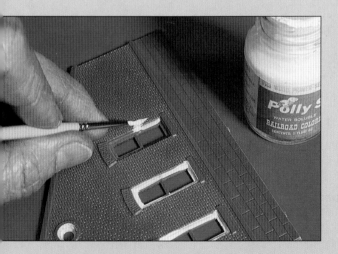

4 Acrylic paint works well for painting the windows and doors. If you are careful, you can even paint the window frames one color and the windows another color. Start with the outer window frames. Always work from the corners, pulling the paint along the edge of the window with the brush. Start with the lower corners of the window frames as shown. Stop about 1/4 inch from the beginning of your brush stroke.

5 Turn the wall 180 degrees. Start at the upper corner of the frame and pull the paint down to connect with the just-painted area The paint will almost flow by itself, thanks to capillary action. If you make a major mistake, the acrylic paint can be washed off with water. If the mistake is minor, you can touch it up with the brick color after the trim dries.

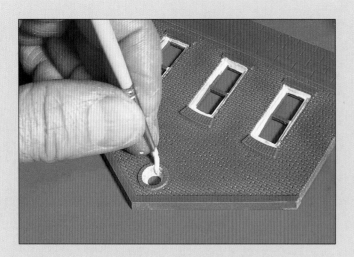

6 Circular windows require the same technique of pulling the paint. Here, however, you can rotate the entire wall a full 360 degrees as you paint, finishing the trim in one or two continuous pulling strokes.

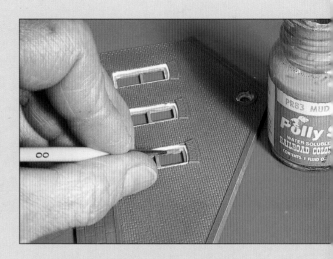

7 Allow the frames to dry overnight. The second color is optional, because man industrial buildings used the same color for both windows and sashes. The technique is the same as for the frames—just use a bit less paint.

8 When the windows are painted and any errors touched up, apply the "mortar." Mix about one part light gray (or whatever the mortar color is on the prototype structure) with about five parts water. Add a drop of liquid detergent to break the surface tension of the water and allow the diluted paint to flow easier. The paint should automatically settle into the seams, leaving just a trace on the flat faces of the brick to help tone down their color. If you apply too much mortar color, just wipe off the excess with a dry facial tissue.

9 I used a mix of equal parts gray and water to paint the foundation stones so they would look like a lighter version of the bricks. On most structures, you can paint the foundation a different color from the bricks, then apply the same mortar color.

BUILDINGS

PROJECT 81 • PAINT BRICK SURFACES

Time: 4 to 8 hours

Tools: Number 0 and 1 paintbrushes

Materials: PollyScale or Modelflex brick color, white and light gray paint, and masking tape

Cost: $$

Talent: Novice

Scales: HO, N, S, O and G

Space: 2x6 inches

Tip: For extra realism, use a number 0 brush to hand-paint a few dozen darker or lighter color bricks in a random pattern.

WHY: To capture the appearance of real brick walls

COMPLEMENTARY PROJECTS: 69, 70, 77, 80, 82 and 83

1 Spray the entire brick-textured wall the color of the mortar you select. When the mortar color is dry, apply the brick color using the side of the paintbrush. When you dip the brush into the jar, wipe off most of the paint on the inside edge of the jar as you remove the brush. Use a quick, whisking motion to just barely touch the paint to the model. If you get it right, the paint will only adhere to the raised surfaces of the bricks, leaving the mortar lines untouched. The technique is called "dry brushing," and it can be used with the "wash" technique in Project 80 to achieve the variegated effect that is common to most brick walls.

2 Mike Hulbert used the "wash" technique from Project 80 for the major wall surfaces on these N scale structures. Then, he went back and applied a beige color, using the "dry brush" technique from this project, to color the stones on the window arches.

You can choose from two techniques when painting the brick surfaces of an injection-molded plastic or cast-resin model. The first technique is described in Project 80, in which you paint the wall with the brick color of your choice, then flow on a "wash" of thinned mortar-colored paint.

The alternative is to paint the walls the color of mortar and then dry brush the faces of the bricks, leaving the mortar untouched. This second technique is far more difficult for most people because it takes skill and practice to avoid getting the brick-colored paint into the mortar joints. If you do, you

can paint the mortar back in and reapply the brick color to that area.

This technique's primary advantage is that it allows you to vary the colors of the bricks more easily, which can be especially useful when trying to re-create the look of brick walls. You can also use this technique to apply color to individual bricks that have been painted with the "wash" technique.

BUILDINGS

PROJECT 82 • WEATHER BUILDINGS WITH AN AIRBRUSH

 Time: 1 to 2 hours

 Tools: Airbrush, air compressor, and respirator

 Materials: Floquil, PollyScale, Modelflex, or similar model railroad paint in gray, an "earth" color (see text), Engine Black, and light gray; also, thinner

 Cost: $$$

 Talent: Novice

 Scales: HO, N, S, O and G

 Space: 2x10 inches

 Tip: Closely examine the weathering colors and patterns on a structure similar to the one you are modeling.

 WHY: To create structures that capture not just the look, but the colors and shading of the prototypes

COMPLEMENTARY PROJECTS: 65, 68 through 70 and 81

1 Find the color that most closely matches the dirt where the finished structure will rest. You may need to tone down the earth color with as much as an equal part of white paint. I recommend about four parts thinner to one part paint, so there's less chance of applying too much weathering. Set the air pressure to about 15 to 20 psi and adjust the pattern to deliver a spray about an inch in diameter with the nozzle about 2 inches from the model. Apply the earth color around the base of the model where rain would splash dust onto the surface. Dirt accumulates under the eaves of older buildings, too—use the thinned earth color to lightly coat the eaves, as well.

In the real world that you re-create in miniature, the elements have a visible effect on every car, locomotive, and building. Homes may receive regular maintenance, but industries and railroad-related structures are seldom cleaned or repainted. The effects of the weather are visible within weeks after a new structure is complete and can dominate its colors within a few years. Wind, rain, and the bleaching effects of sun combine to affix dust, soot, dirt, grime, and smoke to structures. While rain splashes dirt onto the lower walls, the sun hardens it into mud and bakes it into the paint. Similarly, soot and smoke are washed onto rooftops and down walls by rain. And the sun continuously bleaches and oxidizes paint.

All of these effects can be duplicated with an airbrush. For faded colors, simply mix about one part white to two parts paint to match the walls of the structure. Then, add about three parts thinner to one part of this lighter paint and spray the walls to duplicate the effects of the sun. Duplicate rain-splashed dirt by mixing paint to match the earth that will surround the model with about four parts thinner. Use this mix for "splashes" near the foundation of the structure, as well as rain-washed airborne dust to run down the roof and walls. Finally, use a dark gray like Engine Black mixed with about four parts thinner to duplicate stains from rain-washed soot and smoke, especially on roofs, but often under eaves and anywhere else rain might wash down chimney soot.

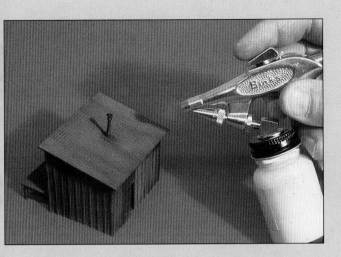

2 Mix one part dark gray (Engine Black) to four parts thinner and spray fine streaks of rain-washed soot and smoke to the roof as shown here. You can go back, after applying the black, and spray on a bit more of the earth color to reduce the harsh effects of the black streaks.

3 A mix of four parts thinner to one part light gray is used to simulate the effects of the sun-bleaching. Dust the roof liberally to fade the surface and to highlight any standing-seam roofing. The gray will also help to lighten any areas where you applied too much black powder. Use the gray, too, to dull bright trim colors. Here, the mix is used to "fade" the tanks that are part of the oil depot diorama.

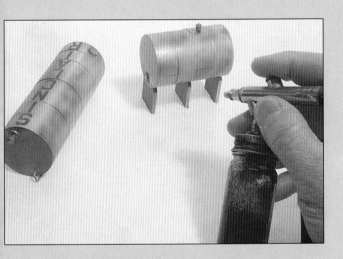

5 This is the oil depot diorama that also appears in Projects 74, 75, 76, and 79. The railroad side of the structure is dirtier than the truck-loading side, to duplicate the effects of the soot and exhaust from the locomotives. The finished model looks far more like the real structure when it is weathered to match the actual colors and patterns of color on the prototype.

4 You would expect to find lots of grungy black oil stains around an oil depot. Although the ones I studied were far more faded than stained, there was an occasional puddle of oil near drains and sometimes a stain leading from vents. You can duplicate those stains by dropping the air pressure to about 15 psi and adjusting the paint flow to produce a thin line of dark gray. You may even want to go back and apply a bit more light gray to "fade" the stains.

BUILDINGS

PROJECT 83 • SIMULATE PEELING PAINT

 Time: 1 to 2 hours

 Tools: Airbrush, air compressor, respirator, hobby knife, tweezers, and a number 1 paintbrush

 Materials: Floquil, PollyScale, Modelflex or similar model railroad paint in Box Car Red, gray, an "earth" color (see text), Engine Black, and light gray; thinner; and Walthers Magic Masker or Microscale Micro Mask

 Cost: $$$

 Talent: Novice

 Scales: HO, N, S, O and G

 Space: 2x10 inches

 Tip: Closely examine the weathering colors and patterns on a structure similar to the one you are modeling.

? **WHY:** To create structures that capture not just the look, but the colors and shading of the prototype

COMPLEMENTARY PROJECTS: 56, 57, 59, 60 and 82

One of the more common signs of a worn structure is paint that has peeled to reveal the underlying color or, in some cases, rust or bare wood. You can duplicate the effects of peeled paint on a model with this technique.

1 First, determine what color you want to appear under the peeled paint. On this model, I wanted the original galvanized roof to be visible. On other models you might want rust or bare weathered wood. Spray that area of the model with Box Car Red to simulate rust or light gray to simulate weathered wood. Brush a thick coat of Walthers Magic Masker or Microscale Micro Mask on just the areas that you want to be revealed by peeled paint and allow the fluid to dry. Spray the entire area, including the masking fluid. Finally, weather the model as described in Projects 56, 57, 59, 60, and 82.

2 If you look carefully at the surface of the model, you will be able to see the rough edges of the dried Walthers Magic Masker or Microscale Micro Mask. Loosen one of the edges with the tip of a hobby knife, then grip it with tweezers and very gently pull it away. Work carefully so you do not tear the dried fluid; if you do, it can remain on the model as "real" peeled paint. The color that appears beneath the peeled-back masking fluid will be that which you applied as the first step in the process. On this model, it was aluminum paint to simulate galvanized metal.

SECTION TWELVE

DIORAMAS AND SCENIC BACKDROPS

Most model railroads are built indoors while virtually all real railroads operate outdoors. Given that ridiculously simple statement, it's easy to understand why it's necessary to re-create outdoor scenery if you want your model railroad to look like the real thing. Model railroaders have been building scenery for nearly 100 years. Over that time, they have devised some very simple techniques, while hobby manufacturers have developed some equally easy-to-use products that make realistic scenery easy to create.

Because the techniques change as new products appear, it is rare for anyone today to shape model railroad scenery with the door screen hills and plaster surfaces that were common in the 1960s and 1970s. Today, most modelers use paper towels or gauze soaked in Hydrocal plaster to shape hills and valleys or, if they prefer, they carve the hills and valleys into easy-to-cut stacks of blue Styrofoam insulation board. Both techniques are explained here so you can pick the one that seems best suited to your talents.

Don Cabrall's 15x18-foot HO scale Northwestern Pacific.

PROJECT 84 • PLASTER, PAPER, AND NEWSPAPER SCENERY

 Time: 1 to 2 hours

 Tools: Scissors, atomizer spray bottle, empty 2-pound coffee can (or similar-size container), tea strainer, 2-inch-wide paintbrush, and a wooden stick (to stir plaster)

 Materials: 2x2-foot piece of 1/4-inch plywood or chip board; industrial-grade paper towels; Hydrocal plaster or Woodland Scenics Lightweight Hydrocal; masking tape; old newspapers; earth-color latex wall paint; real dirt; Woodland Scenics, Life-Like, Noch, Plastruct, Vista, Easy Scene, AMSI, Sunlit Vistas, Busch, Heiki, Faller, or Kibri fine ground foam to simulate grass and weeds; and artist's matte medium

 Cost: $$

 Talent: Beginner

 Scales: HO, N, S, O and G

 Space: 2x10 inches

 Tip: Look closely at the shape of real hills to avoid making slopes too steep.

 WHY: To create scenery for a diorama or a complete model railroad

COMPLEMENTARY PROJECTS: 9 through 14 and 85 through 100

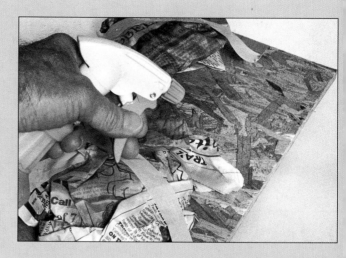

1 Begin a basic diorama with a piece of 1/4-inch plywood or chipboard. Cover the areas where you will want hills with wadded-up newspapers held in place with strips of masking tape. If the newspapers are too springy, spray them with a mist of water from a hand-pump atomizer bottle.

Scenery is often the most dreaded aspect of building a model railroad. I would guess that only about one model railroad in five has anything more than bare plywood or empty open grid surface. If you've been putting it off, consider building just a 2-foot-square diorama on a scrap of 1/4-inch plywood or chipboard. You can lay a piece of track down the center or on one edge and shape the remaining surface to represent a shallow cut, or you can shape the scenery into anything you want. You might even consider elevating the track 2 inches or more on a piece of 2x4 laid on edge, so you can model an earthen fill rather than a cut.

You can't make a very large mistake on just 2x2 feet. If you don't like what you see, chip it off and start over, or just pitch it into the trash and start with a fresh piece of plywood. The most important lesson is that, when constructing scenery, you don't need to preserve your mistakes—if you don't like it, toss it and start over. Once you understand the process and discover the mistakes that are unique to your own methods, you will have the confidence to cover your entire layout in scenery.

You can use common plaster of Paris from a hardware store for this project, but you may want to use the much stronger Hydrocal plaster. Hydrocal is actually a type of alabaster that dries almost rock hard, so you don't need wire screen supports like those you may have seen used with older plaster scenery. If you are likely to use Hydrocal for your actual model railroad, it's a good idea to use Hydrocal for this hands-on learning exercise.

You can also substitute plaster-impregnated gauze like that used for casting broken arms and legs. Plaster cloth is available at hobby shops as Activa's Rigid Wrap and Woodland Scenics or Faller Plaster Cloth. The cloth is less messy than powdered Hydrocal—just dip it in water and drape it over the scenery shapes.

2 Buy a package of industrial-grade paper towels, or superstrong home-style paper towels. Use a container like an empty 2-pound coffee can and pour in a quart of water. Gently sprinkle in Hydrocal plaster, stirring as you pour, until the mixture is about as thick as cream and there are no lumps. Dip one of the paper towels into the mix.

3 Drape the Hydrocal-soaked paper towel over your wadded-up newspaper hills, overlapping each paper towel, so you have at least two layers all across the diorama. Work quickly and, when working on a model railroad, only prepare about 3 or 4 square feet at a time. Smooth and shape the hills and valleys in the still-wet Hydrocal plaster—if you continue to rub the surface as it begins to harden, you can produce a rough texture. When you make more than a few square feet of scenery, it's a good idea to treat your hands with an ointment similar to those that mechanics use to protect their hands.

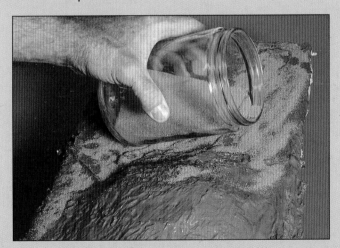

4 When the Hydrocal is hard, cover the scene with a thick coat of latex wall paint that closely matches the dirt from the area you are modeling. Have real dirt and ground foam to simulate weeds ready to sprinkle on while the paint is still wet.

5 Pour the sifted dirt over the still-wet latex paint. If you need to use more dirt than the paint will hold, you can brush on some artist's matte medium (a clear latex paint) and sprinkle more dirt onto the matte medium.

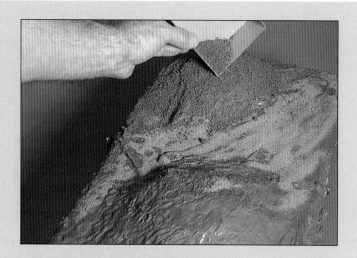

6 Woodland Scenics, Life-Like, Noch, Plastruct, Vista, Easy Scene, AMSI, Sunlit Vistas, Busch, Heiki, Faller, and Kibri all offer a wide range of finely ground foam rubber to realistically simulate the textures of leaves on weeds, bushes, and trees. It is available in a variety of green shades as well as autumn colors, so select colors that match the greens of the area you are modeling. Sprinkle it over any areas where you want to simulate grass and weeds.

7 When the foam is in place, give it a heavy coat of artist's matte medium mixed with an equal amount of water, sprayed through a hand-pump atomizer. The entire surface will have a milky appearance that will be clear and flat in a day or two. Be sure to flush the atomizer with clean water as soon as you are finished spraying. The diorama is now ready for ballasted track placed in the center.

PROJECT 85 • CARVE STYROFOAM SCENERY

 Time: 2 to 100 hours

 Tools: A Woodland Scenics Hot Wire Foam Cutter, Premium Concepts Tippi hot foam cutter, or hacksaw blade and holder; Liquid Nails "Projects and Foamboard" cement or Chem Rex PL300 Foam Board Adhesive; and a caulking gun

 Materials: 2-inch extruded polystyrene insulation board

 Cost: $$

 Talent: Novice

 Scales: HO, N, S, O and G

 Space: Between 2x2 and 60x100 feet

 Tip: Keep a vacuum cleaner and hose handy to remove the nearly weightless foam dust and scraps. Be sure to use extruded, not expanded, polystyrene insulation board.

 WHY: To provide the lightest possible weight for a portable model railroad

COMPLEMENTARY PROJECTS: 1 through 5, 7 through 21, 84, and 86 through 101

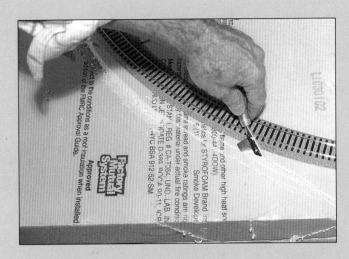

1 If you use Styrofoam for a layout base, you can carve valleys by merely working a razor saw into the surface of the Styrofoam with tight sawing motions. Any angles you cut should be 30 degrees or less.

Extruded polystyrene insulation board is an alternative to plaster and paper towels for shaping scenery. The two systems differ in that plaster and paper towels allow you to build up the scenery, while the insulation board method demands that you be willing to remove material until you have the shape you want. Either way, it's very similar to the work of a sculptor who either builds a piece from wet clay or chips away at stone until all that remains is the desired shape. Try them both to see which you prefer.

It is possible to carve scenery from white expanded polystyrene or "beadboard," but the material is, in my opinion, too soft. Extruded polystyrene boards are much tougher, and a little heavier. While they are usually colored to match each manufacturer's brand, the most common are the blue boards sold by Dow Corning under the "Styrofoam" label. These boards are available in 1-or 2-inch thickness in 2x8- or 2x10-foot panels, as well as a few other sizes.

If you build your model railroad on a Styrofoam base as shown in Project 6, you will have enough material to carve into valleys and simulated earthen fills. To shape mountains, merely cut some additional pieces of the Styrofoam to clear the edges of the tracks, roads, and structures, and cement them to the top of the table. You can stack as many layers of the Styrofoam as you need to gain the height of the mountains you wish to shape.

You can shape the Styrofoam with a hacksaw blade or a razor saw, but the work is quicker and easier if you use a hot knife. The Tippi is the only currently available hot wire cutter I have found that actually works like a knife. (The others have C-shaped handles like coping saws that make it difficult to work down into the surface.)

One advantage of working with Styrofoam is that you can replace areas where you have carved too deeply merely by cementing the just-cut piece back from where it came. When the cement dries, try again with a slightly shallower cut. Many modelers have decided that it is far more enjoyable to carve scenery into Styrofoam than to try to build up shapes in plaster. Whichever system you use, paint the surface and texture it with dirt and weeds as described in Projects 84, 86, 87, 93, and 94.

2 Wrap some masking tape around the last two inches of a 12-inch hacksaw blade and use it as an alternative cutting tool. Try both methods to see which you prefer.

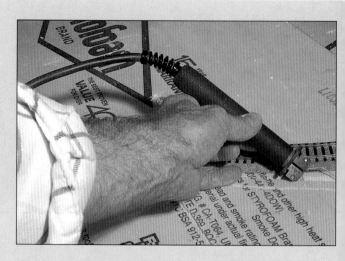

3 The quickest way to cut the Styrofoam is with a hot-wire tool like the blade-style Tippi shown here. Work quickly to slice through the material with the heated wire—if you work too slowly, the hot wire will melt into the Styrofoam and damage the tool.

5 When the valley is complete, paint the surface to seal it, apply dirt and weed textures, and ballast the track.

6 You can stack two or more layers of Styrofoam on the table to make mountains. Shape the edges at an angle to match the slopes of the real-world hills you are re-creating. When you achieve the desired shape, cement the layers together and texture the surfaces.

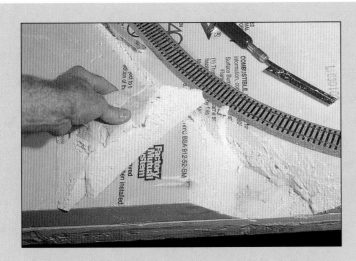

4 When the cuts from the top and the side meet, the "valley" piece should be free to lift away. You may have to make several shallower cuts to chisel out smaller chunks of the material. If you cut too much material, slice off part of the portion you just removed and replace it to raise the floor of the valley.

PROJECT 86 • BUILD A DIORAMA

 Time: 2 to 100 hours

 Tools: Tea strainer, atomizer spray bottle, and an ice cream stick or tongue depressor

 Materials: 2-inch extruded polystyrene insulation board, real dirt, artist's matte medium, and black ink

 Cost: S

 Talent: Beginner

 Scales: HO, N, S, O and G

 Space: Between 2x2 and 60x100 feet

 Tip: When the dirt has been sifted, pass a magnet over it see if any of the particles are magnetic; if so, find another source for the dirt.

 WHY: To create miniature dirt that is indistinguishable from real dirt

COMPLEMENTARY PROJECTS: 5 through 7, 84, 85, and 87 through 101

It's much easier to build complex scenes on a removable diorama than to try to add all the details to a scene built permanently into your layout. The removable diorama also provides the flexibility to change the era or scene as shown in Project 79, by substituting different details or buildings. And, if you decide to dismantle the layout, the entire scene, not just the structures, can be saved for a future layout. The major advantage of a removable diorama, however, is that you can add all the details to the scene on your workbench rather than leaning over the layout. The concept works particularly well with a complex array of buildings like this oil depot.

1 This diorama is bound by chainlink fence. Before I installed the fence, I painted the surface with a brown similar the color of the dirt I planned to use. When the brown paint is dry, brush artist's matte medium around the edges and beneath the fence. The artist's matte medium acts much like white glue, but is more flexible and less likely to crack; it dries with a flat finish.

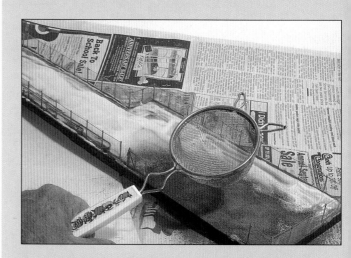

3 With a tea strainer, sprinkle enough dirt over the still-wet matte medium so no white is visible. While the matte medium and dirt are still wet, press all structures onto the diorama. Gently twist and wiggle each of the components to settle them into the mixture of sifted dirt and matte medium.

2 For a large diorama, pour the matte medium from the bottle to fill in the central areas. Use a 2-inch scrap of styrene or wood as a spatula to spread the matte medium in a layer just thick enough so more white than brown shows.

4 The installation of the buildings leaves some areas where the dirt has been scraped away; use an ice cream stick to spoon small piles of dirt into any areas where no dirt is visible. Finally, spray a light mist of water over all the dirt using an atomizer spray bottle. Add weeds around the bottom of the fence. Push flocking from Noch, Faller, or Woodland Scenics into the still-wet dirt and matte medium with your fingers. When the matte medium has dried for about 96 hours, turn the diorama on its side and shake off any excess dirt or remove it with a vacuum. (If you want to save the dirt, collect it with an old nylon stocking used to cover the end of the hose.)

PROJECT 87 • DIRT ROADS

Time: 2 to 100 hours

Tools: Tea strainer, atomizer spray bottle, hard rubber eraser, ice cream stick or tongue depressor, eye dropper, and a 1/4-inch paintbrush

Materials: Real dirt, 2-inch extruded polystyrene insulation board, artist's matte medium, and India ink

Cost: $

Talent: Beginner

Scales: HO, N, S, O and G

Space: Between 2x2 and 60x100 feet

Tip: Study the patterns that real trucks make in dirt parking lots and duplicate them on your model.

WHY: To capture that subtle difference between just plain dirt and a dirt road

COMPLEMENTARY PROJECTS: 5 through 7, 84 through 86, and 88 through 101

You can reduce dirt to model proportions by simply sifting it through a tea strainer as described in Project 86. To simulate the wear caused by passing vehicles, scrape the dirt to create lighter colors.

1 Sift real dirt through a tea strainer onto still-wet artist's matte medium, as described in Project 86. Allow 48 hours for the matte medium to dry completely, then remove any excess dirt with a vacuum cleaner. Determine the paths that vehicles would make across the dirt. On this oil depot diorama, the tank trucks would pull alongside the truck-loading platform to be filled with gasoline, kerosene, and fuel oil. Stake trucks would park alongside the warehouse platform to be loaded with cases of oil and auto parts, as well as beside the end of the barrel rack to be loaded with barrels. Simulate those patterns of wear by rubbing the dried surface with a tongue depressor or ice cream stick. Make marks at scale 4 1/2 feet apart to match the track width of most small trucks and automobiles. There would be more wear near the entrance than alongside the loading docks because every vehicle that left or entered would pass through that gate.

4 The gasoline, kerosene, and fuel oil would also leave stains near the valves where the unloading pipes are connected. Simulate those stains with the same flat black paint and thinner used for the dirt road surfaces.

2 Oil leaking from trucks and automobiles dribbles onto dirt wherever vehicles are parked. Here, vehicles waiting to be loaded at the fuel platform, the oil drum rack, and the warehouse would leave stains below the engines. Since this is an oil depot, there would also be stains where the fuel is spilled while loading the tank trucks. Expect stains, too, near the tanks where they have been overfilled. Mix a solution of equal parts flat black and thinner and apply it to the diorama with an eye dropper. Allow 24 hours for the paint to dry before you decide if more stains are necessary. The paint will dry about three shades lighter than it appears while still wet.

3 Since the parked vehicles will obscure some of the stains, leave some of the parking areas unoccupied. The worn dirt surface and the stains lend variations that make it appear more like the prototype.

5 These same techniques can be used on dirt-covered bridges and dirt roads.

PROJECT 88 • BUILD A MODEL OF YOUR MODEL RAILROAD

 Time: 2 to 10 hours

 Tools: Hobby knife and a scale ruler

 Materials: Basswood or styrene plastic strips, cardboard or sheet styrene, Testors Model master Cement for Plastics or thickened cyanoacrylate cement, and oil-based modeling clay

 Cost: $

 Talent: Novice

 Scales: HO, N, S, O and G

 Space: Between 24x8 and 40x80 inches

 Tip: Modify an existing published track plan if it's your first or second model railroad.

 WHY: To envision what the finished model railroad will look like

COMPLEMENTARY PROJECTS: 1 through 21, 75, 84 through 87, and 89 through 101

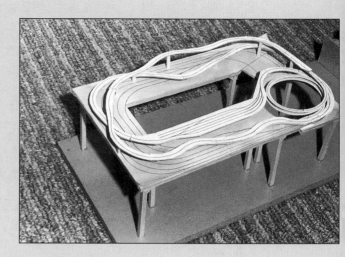

1 Paul Brennecke assembled this model of his N scale railroad layout. He enlarged his plan to 3/4 inch per foot in a photocopy machine, then cemented two copies of the plan to thin cardboard. (You can substitute .020-inch styrene sheet if you wish, cutting the plastic with a scribed line, as described in Project 75.) He assembled a table using 1/8-inch-square basswood for the legs and the frame. Paul's full-size layout features open-grid benchwork with 1/2-inch plywood subroadbed directly beneath the track only. For a mock-up, however, the flat tabletop is easier to work with. He cut the plans apart, leaving 1/8 inch on each side of the track's centerline, to allow room for the roadbed and track. Then he supported this subroadbed (with the track centerlines) above the tabletop on 1/4-inch-square strips of balsa wood, to provide room for bridges and earthen fills, even on the lowest level of the track. Paul duplicated the upgrades and downgrades by adding thicker pieces of stripwood between the bottom of the cardboard subroadbed and the tops of the 1/4-inch supports. Because there was no scenery inside the loop at the far right, Paul cut through the cardboard tabletop to re-create the access opening that would be in that area of the final layout.

When an architect designs a new house or office building, he or she almost always includes a scale model of the finished structure so the buyers can see what they are getting. You can do the same thing with your model railroad—build a model of the layout before you even start constructing the real thing. There's no real point in actually modeling every stick of benchwork, for example, because you are going to make dozens of minor (and major) changes as the work progresses. You can, however, prevent some mistakes even in the benchwork if you discover, for instance, that you want a canyon that extends almost to the floor, because you won't need benchwork in that area of the layout.

The mock-up is most useful if you have a lot of grades and, perhaps, several levels of track. The mock-up or model can show you whether those grades are practical or not.

Any modeler, even those just trying to build scenery for a 4x8-foot layout, can benefit from using a model of the model railroad to test scenery shapes and positions. Use oil-base modeling clay for the scenery so you can shift the shapes until they suit you. In fact, the mock-up for the scenery can be an extremely useful tool when building the actual scenery, because you will know where to position bridges and tunnels. Also be sure to include exact-scale footprints of every structure so you know the scenery will not encroach on their space. If you are really ambitious, you can take the time to cut mock-ups of buildings from scraps of balsa wood.

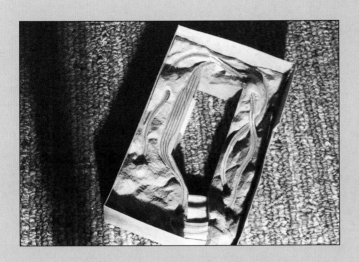

2 Paul added cardboard walls to support the sides of the clay hills. He worked oil-base modeling clay into the model, stuffing it below the subroadbed to create fills and around the subroadbed in the few areas where there were tunnels. By mocking up the scenery in clay, you can avoid the unrealistically steep slopes and canyons in the planning stage, before you actually slap on plaster or carve into Styrofoam.

PROJECT 89 • INSTALL A BRIDGE

 Time: 2 to 10 hours

 Tools: Saber saw, hacksaw blade, and steel ruler

 Materials: Bridge kit or built-up model, bridge abutments, scraps of wood or Styrofoam, and Micro Engineering or Walthers bridge track and guard rails (optional)

 Cost: $

 Talent: Novice

 Scales: HO, N, S, O and G

 Space: 4x8 and 40x80 inches

 Tip: Include bridges at the planning-on-paper stage.

 WHY: To include on your model railroad one of the more dramatic elements of real railroading

COMPLEMENTARY PROJECTS: 1 through 16, 84, 85, and 90 through 101

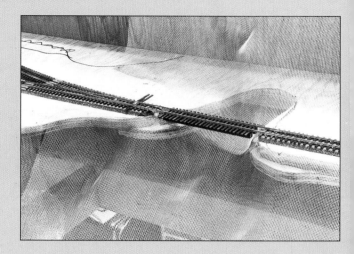

1 It is possible to add a bridge to a flat tabletop layout. The tabletop can be cut to produce the wavy edges of a small valley as shown. This modeler elected to use wire screen to support the plaster scenery, but you can also use Hydrocal and paper towels, as shown in Project 84, supporting the paper towels with a network of masking tape in place of the wire screen. The track that spans the gap has the ties spaced closer together. No provision has been made, however, for the abutments that will support the ends of the bridge. It would be easier to cut the tabletop parallel to the ties so the bridge abutments could be cemented right to the edges of the plywood. The Walthers catalog lists dozens of bridge abutments in wood, plaster, styrene, cast-resin, and foam. For this short bridge, however, you could simply stack three or four pieces of HO scale 12x12 timbers. The appropriate bridge, here, would be a through-girder like the Micro Engineering 75520, Atlas 885, or Campbell 766.

If you want the bridges on your model railroad to look like those on the real railroads, you need to plan for their installation when you design your layout on paper. When the benchwork is constructed, the subroadbed must be high enough above the tabletop to allow adequate space for an embankment or fill where the bridge will span. When you create the gap to be spanned, you also need to know the exact length of the bridge you want to use. With most bridges, you must increase or decrease the area to be spanned, because it's often difficult to change the length of the bridge itself. Also, when you cut the subroadbed or carve the Styrofoam, plan on leaving space below the bridge for the abutments that will support it.

You can buy kits to duplicate just about any type of bridge used on a real railroad. Walthers catalogs include nearly 100 different bridges and kits made from wood and card, injection-molded styrene plastic, cast resin, cast plaster, and molded foam. The dimensions of most of the bridges are included with their listing so you can determine what your options are for the area you wish to bridge.

Finally, consider replacing the length of track that crosses the bridge with special track that has the ties spaced more closely together, like those on most real bridges. Micro Engineering and Walthers offer the track in HO scale, and Micro Engineering offers it in N scale.

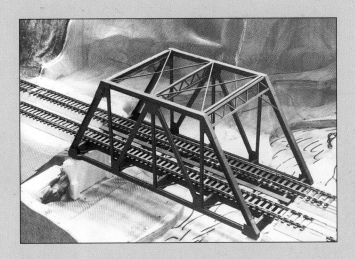

2 This bridge was planned at the time the layout was designed. The track is elevated about 2 inches above the top of the open grid benchwork. The 1/2-inch plywood subroadbed was cut parallel to the ties, and the span or opening was matched to the exact length of the bridge. A piece of plywood was installed on the bottom of the open-grid benchwork to support the lake or river that the bridge will span. The bridge is supported by scraps of Styrofoam that will be replaced by cast-resin bridge abutments from Chooch. The track that rests on the bridge will be replaced, too, with Micro Engineering track with closer-spaced bridge ties.

3 This is a Campbell 764 Double-Track Truss Bridge assembled from the kit with two of the four panels removed to make it shorter. The Walthers 3012 Double-Track Truss Bridge is similar, but is molded in styrene plastic.

4 Pieces of cast plaster with a stone texture were used as bridge abutments to support this short deck girder bridge. The "water" is a piece of plywood painted with Floquil Grimy Black paint and clear high-gloss floor paint, applied thick enough so it could be rippled slightly with a paintbrush as it dried.

PROJECT 90 • RUBBER-STAMP TREES

 Time: 1 hour

 Tools: Rubber stamps with tree images and ink pads

 Materials: Various shades of green ink and a cardboard backdrop

 Cost: $

 Talent: Beginner

 Scales: HO and N

 Space: 1x2 feet

 Tip: Test the technique on a scrap of cardboard painted the same color as the background sky.

? **WHY:** To create a two-dimensional backdrop that more closely matches the three-dimensional layout

COMPLEMENTARY PROJECTS: 84 through 97 and 99

Hobby shops can order a wide range of printed backdrops for your model railroad. In some areas of the backdrop, however, you may want to make your own scene, especially where hills reach right up the edges of the "sky." Craft stores offer a wide selection of rubber stamps depicting almost any kind of tree. The stamps are just large enough to make them useful for the background on an HO or N scale layout. Rubber-stamp stores have an even wider selection, and most have catalogs listing thousands of stamps that they will order for you. They can also supply stamp pads with green inks or dry stamp pads and inks so you can mix your own colors.

1 I found these stamps to match the trees I wanted on my backdrop. If you only want one or two trees from one of the larger stamps, use a hobby knife to slice through the rubber and peel away the trees you do not need.

4 These pine trees look as if they are shrouded in mist, which increases the feeling of depth. If you want a brighter image, touch up the trees by applying ink with a number 0 paintbrush.

2 Find a stamp pad with the shade of green ink you need for the types of trees you are modeling. You can also buy dry pads and inks to mix your own colors. Test the stamps on both white paper and on cardboard painted in the same color as the backdrop.

3 A single-tree stamp can be used to produce a forest of trees. Keep plenty of ink in the pad and vary the positions of the trees.

5 This row of trees really should be done with brown rather than green ink. Experiment with rubber-stamping bare trees, covering with artist's matte medium the areas where leaves would appear, and pressing fine-ground foam into place for texture.

DIORAMAS AND SCENIC BACKDROPS

PROJECT 91 • CREATE A HORIZON FOR YOUR LAYOUT

 Time: 2 hours

 Tools: Scissors, hobby knife, airbrush, and an air compressor

 Materials: Rubber cement, black foamcore board, poster stickers, light gray paint, and thinner

 Cost: $$

 Talent: Novice

 Scales: HO, N, S, O and G

 Space: 2x4 feet or more

 Tip: Use an airbrush with diluted light gray paint to dull down preprinted backdrop scenes.

 WHY: To make your layout stretch beyond the walls of the room

COMPLEMENTARY PROJECTS: 71 through 73 and 93 through 98

1 This back wall is painted a sky blue, but its plainness makes the scene look like the edge of a flat earth.

You can make your model railroad far more realistic by providing a horizon of scenery near eye level. Printed and photo mural backdrops are available from a number of sources, including Walthers, Faller, and Vollmer. You may also find suitable photo murals at a wallpaper store. Personally, I prefer photo murals to paintings. All backdrops, however, are far too bright to be backdrops. The Walthers 7070 "Desert to Country" painted backdrop in these photographs looks realistic enough in two dimensions, but it is far too colorful in person.

To make a background more realistic, mix about two parts thinner to one part light gray paint and airbrush it to lend that hazy effect that usually occurs with mountains or hills in the distance. You can further increase the sense of depth by cutting out the printed backdrop at the bottom of the printed sky and painting the sky directly onto the wall. Use rubber cement to attach the cut-out backdrop to a 1/8-inch piece of black foamcore, available from artist's supply and craft stores. Cut the edge of the foamcore board to match the scenery and attach it to the wall with poster stickers from a stationery store.

2 This backdrop lends the feeling that there is much more beyond the back edge of the table, but the transition from flat foreground to hills is just not credible.

3 Add a fence, a row of trees, a low rise, or a row of buildings at the back edge of the layout to disguise the transition to painted backdrop. This is the fence that is shown in Projects 71, 72, and 73.

DIORAMAS AND SCENIC BACKDROPS

PROJECT 92 • MAGIC WITH MIRRORS

 Time: 4 hours

 Tools: Screwdriver

 Materials: Mirror, mirror-mounting clamps, and screws

 Cost: $$

 Talent: Expert

 Scales: HO and N

 Space: 1x2 feet

 Tip: Position the mirror so there is no chance you can see any full-scale humans.

 WHY: To double the apparent size of your model railroad

COMPLEMENTARY PROJECTS: 84 through 99

John Allen is a legend of model railroading. John passed away decades ago, but his influence on the hobby in the 1950s and 1960s was profound. He advanced the art of model railroad scenery and effectively introduced weathering to the hobby. John was also a master at using mirrors to make his already massive layout seem even larger. It's fairly obvious that you can place a mirror across one entire end of your layout. What John perfected was inserting relatively small mirrors that almost defied detection.

It's best to place mirrors in the rear of wider layouts so you cannot get close enough to detect the thickness of the glass. You can also avoid this problem by purchasing "face front" mirrors; these have their reflective material on the front of the glass. They are extremely fragile and easily scratched, however, and must be cleaned with extreme care.

1 Jim Nodeler selected buildings and a truss bridge that would be most effective if their lengths were doubled by a mirror. He extended the mirror all the way into the far corner on the right, but disguised the upper edge with smoke and the far left edge (not visible here) by leading it into a tall mountain.

2 Steve Kryan used a mirror across one wall of his layout. It is almost impossible to tell where the model ends and the reflection begins. Only the buildings in the far upper right corner are reflected images. He positioned the mirror so there is no possible chance that you can see your reflection in it.

SECTION THIRTEEN
GROUND COVER, TREES, AND WATER

In my opinion, shaping hills and valleys, whether you use Hydrocal or Styrofoam, is the most difficult part of creating realistic scenery. Once you have the shapes right, the textures are easy, thanks to an incredible variety of materials designed just for the purposes of looking like scale-model dirt and vegetation. Look through the Walthers model railroad catalogs and browse your hobby shop to see which materials are most readily available. Some, like Super Trees, must be ordered by mail while others, like sagebrush twigs and weed roots, can be found in the real world. Combine the natural materials with special texturing products created just for making realistic model scenery, and you can have a scene as realistic as any in this book.

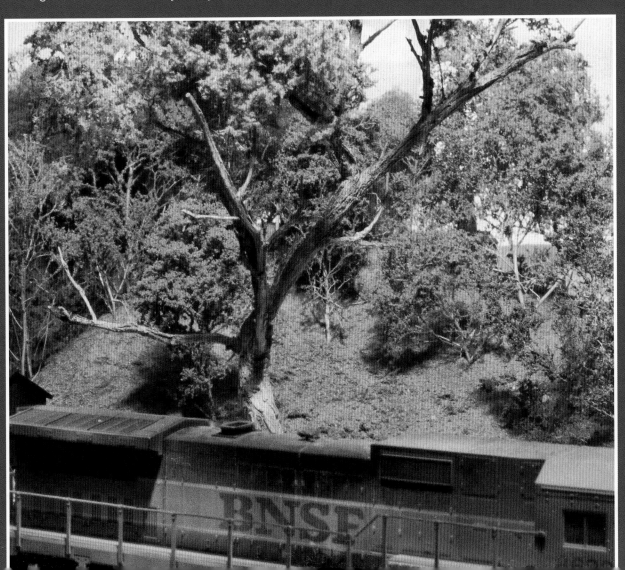

PROJECT 93 • WEEDS FROM WEEDS

 Time: 1 hour

 Tools: Scissors, tweezers, and a tea strainer

 Materials: Foxtails or cattail seeds, artist's gel medium, and dirt

 Cost: $

 Talent: Novice

 Scales: HO, N, S and O

 Space: 1x1 inches

 Tip: Keep the weeds pointing more or less upward and at the same angle.

 WHY: To re-create in miniature some more common types of weeds

COMPLEMENTARY PROJECTS: 43, 59, 60, 86 and 94

Weeds are as much a part of any real railroad right-of-way as ballast or ties. From a modeler's point of view, weeds fall into three easily modeled categories: leafy weeds (which can be modeled from various sizes and colors of ground foam), grassy weeds (which can be modeled from sweatshirt material as shown in Project 94 or with flocking), and tall weeds like those in this project.

Tall weeds can be trimmed from polypropylene twine (as shown with the "hay" in Project 43), pulled from inside fall cattails before their seed pods burst, or fashioned from the fibers of foxtails as shown here. For variety, use all three in small patches.

1 Tall weeds stand up better when stuck into thick cement. Artist's gel medium is thick enough to hold the weeds in position, and it's clear when dry. Coat just the area you want to cover with weeds. Place the weeds before you cover the scene with sifted dirt or, as shown here, as a later detail.

3 Sift real dirt through a tea strainer and save it in a jar or cup. Sprinkle the sifted dirt onto the gel medium while the gel is still wet. Cover the entire area so none of the gel is visible.

2 For these weeds, I cut some foxtail weed fibers to about 1/8-inch lengths. Use tweezers to insert the fibers into the still-wet gel medium.

4 The dry gel will be slightly glossy, but the dirt hides the gloss and makes the weeds appear as though they are actually growing out of the dirt.

GROUND COVER, TREES, AND WATER

PROJECT 94 • FIELDS OF GRASS AND WEEDS FROM SWEATSHIRT MATERIAL

 Time: 1 hour

 Tools: Scissors, tweezers, tea strainer, and a stiff-bristle brush

 Materials: Sweatshirt material, Rit Kelly Green and Yellow fabric dyes, acrylic contact cement, dirt, acrylic paint to match the dirt's color, and artist's matte medium

 Cost: $

 Talent: Novice and Expert

 Scales: HO, N, S and O

 Space: 1x1 inches

 Tip: Allow plenty of time for the contact cement to dry.

 WHY: To reproduce fields of weeds that look like they are actually growing out of the dirt

COMPLEMENTARY PROJECTS: 43, 59, 60, 86 and 93

Common sweatshirt material can be used to create incredibly realistic grass and weeds for fields and meadows. This is an adaptation of a technique developed by British model railroaders using materials more readily available in their part of the world. The process is easy enough to demonstrate, but you should practice a bit on some scrap boards to determine how much contact cement to use and what sweatshirt material has the hairlike cotton fibers that best reproduce the effect of standing blades of grass.

1 Search the larger fabric stores for white sweatshirt material—the thicker the better. Used sweatshirts won't do because the fibers tend to bunch into little balls after repeated washings. Cut the sweatshirt material to fit the area you will cover with "grass," adding about 10 percent to each dimension to allow for shrinkage. Experiment with some scraps of the material and small portions of dye to find the proper shade of green. I like the green color that results from equal amounts of Rit Kelly Green and Yellow dyes, but there are many other choices. The longer the material is in the dye, the darker the color—I left this material in for only about 2 minutes. Gently squeeze out the water and dye. Spread the wet sweatshirt material over plain paper grocery bags to dry. Do not use printed bags or newspaper, because the felt may pick up the inks. And be careful not to get the dye on your clothes! After the sweatshirt material is completely dry, fluff it up by shaking and lightly twisting it.

4 Here's where the magic happens! Peel the sweatshirt material away from the scenery surface, pulling the material back over itself to minimize the chances of tearing the surface loose from the plaster. The result is millions of tiny fibers the precise size, shape, and texture of scale-model blades of grass. Take a closer look. The thicker sweatshirt material produces blades of grass that are about 1/16 to 3/16 inch tall. If that's too tall, for a smooth grass field or for N scale, simply trim the taller fibers with manicure scissors.

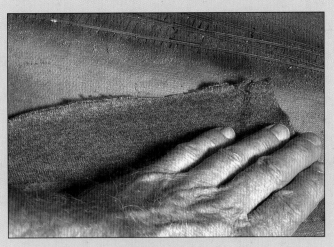

2 Paint the scenery with acrylic paint to match the dirt you will use and let the paint dry for at least a week. If your scenery is not yet complete, it is better to color the Hydrocal plaster with powdered pigments intended for concrete driveways—the Hydrocal is hard enough to withstand the pulling you will be doing later, which can also tear paint loose from the scenery. If you must paint, I find that a slightly rough Hydrocal plaster surface holds the paint best. You can roughen the surface by rubbing over it with your hands as the plaster is setting. Using a disposable brush, coat the areas you want covered with grass or weeds with a thick layer of water-base contact cement and let it dry for about 5 minutes.

3 Press the dyed sweatshirt material firmly into the contact cement with the fuzzy side down. Let it dry for about 24 hours.

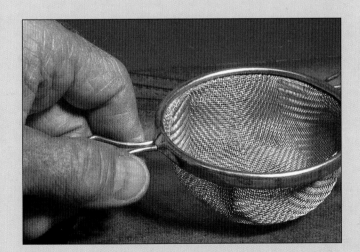

5 Meadow grass and weeds are usually surrounded by dirt. Sift it through a tea strainer right onto the "grass." For a thicker grass effect, sift just a trace of the dirt to provide texture and to hide the sheen of the dried contact cement. For a sparse or prairie grass effect, sift on more dirt.

6 Brush the grass with a stiff brush to force the dirt down onto the surface. To bond the dirt, spray it with a mixture of equal parts water and artist's matte medium, with a few drops of dishwashing detergent to break down the surface tension of the water. Let the matte medium dry for a few days.

7 The finished patch of weeds with an HO scale figure for size comparison. The rough texture can be reduced by trimming the taller fibers with manicure scissors.

PROJECT 95 • TREES FROM WEEDS

 Time: 1 hour

 Tools: Scissors, tweezers, metal pan, clothespins, rubber gloves, pin vise, and 1/16-inch drill bit

 Materials: Scenic Express Super Trees, Woodland Scenics Fine Leaf Foliage, or Noch 23800 or 23820 Natural Trees; gray or brown acrylic paint; artist's matte medium; gray spray paint; and cheap hair spray

Cost: $

 Talent: Novice

 Scales: HO and N

 Space: 1x1 inches

 Tip: Be sure the weeds hang straight from the clothespins while the artist's matte medium dries.

 WHY: To re-create the most realistic trees possible in N or HO scales.

COMPLEMENTARY PROJECTS: 43, 59, 60, 86, 93, 95 and 96

1 Scenic Express Super Trees are sold as individual pieces or in more economical foot-round clumps. The individual trees are usually curved slightly and they have a few leftover dead leaves. First, pick out the leaves with tweezers. Next, mix equal parts artist's matte medium and water in a metal pan so you can submerge the entire tree. You can also mix in a dozen drops of dark gray or dark brown acrylic paint, which allows the matte medium to color the light beige trunks. Hang the tree upside down with clothespins. Use one of the steel self-clamping tweezers as a weight for the tip of the hanging tree. Scenic Express offers a package deal that includes four of these tweezers, the weeds, ground foam, and instructions. Let the matte medium dry completely.

The Scandinavian weeds sold by Noch as Natural Trees and by Scenic Express as Super Trees provide the most realistic tree limb structures available in the hobby. These scale-model trees are actually part of a weed that looks a bit like a tumbleweed, but their fine structure is almost perfect for HO and N scale trees. You can use them as thye are for small- to medium-size HO scale trees, group them together for larger trees, or even attach them to sagebrush or other "trunks" for really large trees as shown in Project 96.

Scenic Express Super Trees must be treated with artist's matte medium and straightened; Noch Natural Trees are already straightened, but are much more expensive. Woodland Scenics Fine Leaf Foliage is straight and already has the ground foam applied. They, too, should be treated with artist's matte medium so they are not quite so brittle. The trees will, however, still be very delicate—position them where they cannot accidentally be brushed by an elbow.

2 If you prefer, paint the tree with gray or brown spray paint after it has been treated with matte medium and straightened. Try to keep the spray directed only at the trunk, so it does not coat the hairlike limbs and make them thicker. Let the paint dry overnight. Woodland Scenics Fine Leaf Foliage—already has the foam applied,

3 Spray the bushy part of the tree with the least-expensive hair spray you ca find. Sprinkle fine-ground foam over the tree while the hair spray is still w If you are modeling a tree in early spring, stop here. For trees in full foliage, however, repeat the process, spraying the foam-coated tree with the hair spray and sprinkling on another application of foam. On some trees, you may even want to rep the process a third time. Real trees have far fewer leaves than you might imagine, so be sure to stop adding foam before you fill in all the open spaces.

4 Use a pin vise or an electric drill with a 1/16-inch bit to drill holes to "plant" the trees.

5 Sift dirt through a tea strainer around the base of the tree to hide the hole.

PROJECT 96 • SAGEBRUSH AND WEED TREES

 Time: 1 hour

 Tools: Scissors, tweezers, clothespins, rubber gloves, pin vise, and 1/16-inch drill bit

 Materials: Sagebrush, Scenic Express Super Trees, Woodland Scenics Fine Leaf Foliage, gray or brown acrylic paint, artist's matte medium, gray spray paint, cheap hair spray, thickened cyanoacrylate cement, accelerator for the cement, 4-inch scrap of 1x4 lumber, and a nail

 Cost: $

 Talent: Novice

 Scales: HO and N

 Space: 4x4 inches

 Tip: Position the curved trunks of the Scenic Express Super Trees so the branch structure sweeps upward like a real tree.

 WHY: To re-create the most realistic large trees possible with simple techniques

COMPLEMENTARY PROJECTS: 95 and 97

The Scenic Express Super Trees, Woodland Scenics Fine Leaf Foliage, and Noch Natural Trees shown in Project 96 have some of the most realistic twig shapes and sizes you can find. If you want a larger tree, you can utilize the Super Trees for just the smaller twig structures with a natural weed for the trunk. Dead sagebrush can be found in most of the western states. If you "shop" carefully around these dead plants you will locate a variety of twisted limbs that look almost exactly like cottonwood and oak trees, right down to the bark. Some of the straighter pieces of sagebrush can be used to model ash, aspen, beech, birch, and large maple trees, provided the trunks are painted to match the real tree.

1 Straighter sagebrush limbs can be used as trunks and major limb structures to build replicas of ash, aspen, beech, birch, and large maple trees.

2 Use the more-twisted sagebrush limbs to make the trunks and major limbs of oak and cottonwood trees. Drill a 1/16-inch hole in the base of the sagebrush and another in a 4-inch piece of scrap 1x4 off which will serve as a stand while you work on the tree. Cut the head of the nail and use cyanoacrylate cement to hold it into the tree trunk with the pointed end down. Use the pointed end of the nail to push the finished tree into the scenery, and into the block of wood.

3 Paint some of the Scenic Express Super Trees and cover them with ground foam, as shown in Project 95, but do *not* straighten the trees—allow them to retain their natural curve. Lay the curved base of the Super Tree parallel to the limbs of the sagebrush trunk. Position the curved tree so most of its limbs point upward and hold it in place with a bead of thickened cyanoacrylate cement.

4 Spray the cement with accelerator for an instant joint.

7 The finished tree is a near perfect replica of cottonwood. If you remove some of the loose bark and paint the trunk, the same tree could be a replica of an oak. A darker green foam would be a better choice, however, for modeling an oak.

8 One of the wonders of using natural growths is that they automatically re-create nature. This tree, like most real trees, looks very different viewed from the opposite side.

5 Rotate the tree to determine how many of the separate Scenic Express Super Trees you want to fill out the structure of the tree. You can leave some of the sagebrush limbs empty to represent the dead limbs that are common on many trees. I used 10 of the smaller Scenic Express trees on this one cottonwood.

6 When you're satisfied with the tree, paint the glue joints with flat gray paint to match the color of the trunk. The limbs of the tree are a bit too thick in these areas, but the gray paint will help disguise that.

9 Push the nail on the base of the sagebrush trunk right into Styrofoam scenery. For plaster or plywood, drill a 1/16-inch hole to accept the nail. Fill the area around the base of the tree with real dirt sifted through a tea strainer. Do not glue the dirt in place, so you can remove the tree if you need to move the layout or do repair work in that area.

PROJECT 97 • DEAD TREES FROM ROOTS

Time: 1 hour

Tools: Hobby knife, razor saw, 1/4-inch paintbrush, and an empty 2-pound coffee can

Materials: Dried weed roots, automobile body putty, gray paint, and black India ink

Cost: $

Talent: Novice

Scales: HO and N

Space: 4x4 inches

Tip: Wait until after a rainfall to pick the weeds, so you won't break off their root structure when you pull them up.

WHY: To model what is rarely modeled—dead trees.

COMPLEMENTARY PROJECTS: 95 and 96

1 Three dead roots have been combined and their thick bases covered with automobile body putty to fill in the gaps.

One of the easiest ways to be sure your trees are realistic is to use natural growths. You will, however, find them in some rather unexpected places, including under the ground. Pull up large, bushy weeds during the early summer, wash the dirt off their roots, and let them dry. You can combine the roots from three or four weeds and mold them onto a trunk sculpted from automobile body putty to make a tree with several large limbs. The roots are best for simulating dead or winter trees, but they can also be dipped in an equal mixture of water and artist's matte medium and covered with ground foam to represent early spring trees. The general shape of these trees (depending, of course on the shape of the weeds) most resembles cherry, elm, and oak trees. Drawings of tree shapes and trunks for specific trees are shown in my book *Scenery for Model Railroads, Dioramas & Miniatures*, and in the NMRA's *data sheets* (available to members).

2 Break off any limbs that seem to extend too far from the center of the tree.

3 When the putty dries, use a razor saw to scrape a bark texture into the putty.

4 Paint the putty trunk with gray paint to match the color of the upper portion of the tree. If the limbs and branches are too light, spray the entire tree with an aerosol can of gray paint.

5 Fill a 2-pound coffee can or similar size container with water and pour in an ounce of black India ink. Submerge the entire tree into the can, remove it, and let it dry. The India ink will accent all of the hollows and the streaks of the natural roots.

6 The tree on the left is a single root, painted gray and dipped in India ink. The tree on the right is the one constructed in the previous photos.

PROJECT 98 • SHEET-PLASTIC LAKES

 Time: 2 to 10 hours

 Tools: Saber saw, hacksaw blade, steel ruler, and scissors

 Materials: Bridge kit or a built-up model, bridge abutments, scraps of wood or Styrofoam, and Kibri 4126 or Noch 60850 clear-plastic "water" sheets

 Cost: $

 Talent: Beginner

 Scales: HO, N, S, O and G

 Space: 4x8 to 40x80 inches

 Tip: Try to match the shape of the "lake shore" to that of a real lake or pond.

WHY: To make it as easy as possible to include reasonably realistic water scenes

COMPLEMENTARY PROJECTS: 1 through 16, 84, 85, and 90 through 101

Scenery does not really need to be permanent. If you want to be able to move the track around the tabletop to try new locations for sidings, reverse loops, or wyes, you need scenery that can be relocated as easily as the track.

For instance, the HO and N scale track with built-in ballast described in Projects 9 and 10 does not really need to be nailed or cemented to the tabletop. Also, you can use dark green felt to cover the tabletop and make "portable" scenery, stuffing wadded-up newspapers beneath the felt to create hills. It's a bit more difficult to create a valley this way, but you can certainly cut an irregular notch in the tabletop like that shown in Project 89. Or, if you use Styrofoam insulation board for a tabletop, you can slice a valley into the tabletop like that in

1 Make a cardboard template to determine the exact shape of the lake, so it fills the entire depression in the scenery. When satisfied with the shape, use the pattern to cut the Kibri 4126 or Noch 60850 clear plastic "water" sheet to the same size as the pattern.

Project 85. If the notch is less than 9 inches wide, you can span it with bare track and roadbed—bridges are strictly for realism, not strength.

Crumpled-up aluminum foil can be used to simulate water, but there is a far more realistic product; Kibri 4126 or Noch 60850 are similar sheets of clear plastic with very realistic ripples molded into their surfaces. Either product is useful to simulate a lake, even on a permanent model railroad. First, make the depression or valley in the tabletop. You can drape the felt into the depression. Notice the shape of the depression and use some scraps of cardboard to cut a few "lakes" to fit the area. With practice, you'll find a shape that suits the natural flow of the felt into the depression. If you've carved a depression in a Styrofoam tabletop, cut and fit cardboard until you determine the shape that best fills the carved depression with a minimum amount of gap around the edges. When you are satisfied, use the cardboard as a template to cut the clear plastic "water" to the same shape.

Simply drop the clear plastic water into the scenery. You can disguise the lack of a shoreline by surrounding the clear plastic with clumps of lichen ground foam.

2 Position the "water" in the depression and place clumps of lichen around the shoreline. This is a 1/2-inch plywood tabletop layout with a 6- to 12-inch notch cut into it and dark green felt used as a cover for the bare tabletop. The felt was merely pushed downward into the plywood opening before the track was put in place.

PROJECT 99 • QUICK WATER FROM ARTIST'S GLOSS MEDIUM

Time: 1 to 2 hours

Tools: None

Materials: Artist's matte medium, artist's gloss medium, artist's gel medium, wooden tongue depressors, paper cups, ground foam, flocking, and lichen

Cost: $

Talent: Beginner

Scales: HO, N, S, O and G

Space: 4x8 to 40x80 inches

Tip: Be sure to seal the bottom of the pond, lake, stream, or river with artist's matte medium so the gloss medium does not change its color.

WHY: To make realistic water scenes with the least amount of mess or smell

COMPLEMENTARY PROJECTS: 1 through 16, 84, 85, and 92 through 101

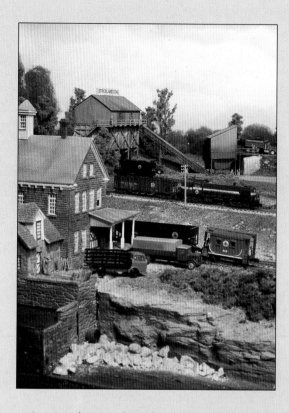

1 Use either artist's gloss medium or decoupage resin for shallow streams and ponds like the canal on James Schall's N scale modular layout. The bottom of the stream or pond can be painted with dark grayish green to simulate deeper water. Place partially "submerged" stones or other material in the fluid after it is poured but before it hardens.

Model railroaders often use two different fluids that look almost exactly like water: artist's gloss medium and the resins used for decoupage. Artist's gloss medium is the simplest for this project. Essentially a thick, clear latex paint, artist's gloss medium looks creamy or cloudy until it dries completely. When it does dry, however, it is as glossy as water. It is also a bit flexible, so it does not crack—that can be a major advantage when building a portable or modular layout that is moved frequently.

Artist's gloss medium is only useful for small lakes and streams that are less than 1/4 inch deep. If more depth is needed, use the decoupage resins shown in Project 92. Pour only 1/8 inch or less depth of the artist's gloss medium at a time. If you need a deeper lake or stream, allow the first pour to dry crystal clear before you add more. If you pour a deeper area than that, it can take weeks for the cloudiness to disappear. If cloudiness persists, it can often be eliminated by poking a pin through the surface of the gloss medium to allow air to reach the cloudy area. When it dries, brush on a thin coat of gloss medium to make the pin holes look like small ripples.

The surface of the gloss medium is not as tough as the decoupage resin, so it will eventually begin to dull. The shine can be restored by simply brushing on a thin coat of gloss medium.

If you try to use the gloss medium for steep streams and rapids, the fluid simply runs to the nearest low spot. For these steep slopes, apply artist's gloss gel with a paintbrush or wooden stick. This stuff is a bit like jelly and sticks to fairly steep slopes. Fill in any gaps between lumps by brushing on a thin coat of gloss medium.

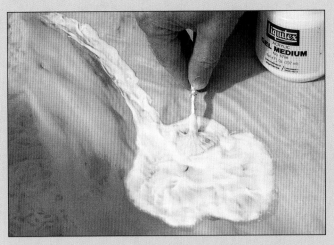

2 Seal the bottom of the pond or stream with a thick coat of artist's matte medium and let it dry for a few days. Pour the artist's gloss medium right into the pond or stream. If you want to simulate ripples, dab in a bit of the artist's gel medium. The gel medium will settle to about half its original depth when dry.

3 Place weeds, sticks, and/or pebbles along the shoreline while the gloss medium is still wet. These "weeds" are the fuzzy seeds from inside cattails picked in the autumn.

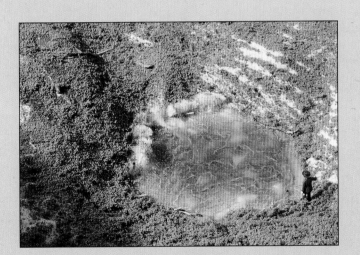

4 The final step in finishing the pond or stream is to add any loose dirt, flocking, grass, or ground foam weeds as texture around the edges. Use artist's matte medium to hold the loose material to the scenery.

PROJECT 100 • RESIN RIVERS, PONDS, AND STREAMS

Time: 1 to 2 hours

Tools: none

Materials: Decoupage casting resin, dark blue and dark green dye, artist's matte medium, wooden tongue depressors, paper cups, ground foam, flocking, and lichen

Cost: $

Talent: Beginner

Scales: HO, N, S, O and G

Space: 4x8 to 40x80 inches

Tip: Be sure to seal the bottom of the pond, lake, stream or river with artist's matte medium, so the gloss medium does not change its color.

WHY: To make realistic water scenes with the least amount of mess or smell

COMPLEMENTARY PROJECTS: 1 through 16, 84, 85, and 92 through 101

The bottom of the pond or stream must be completely sealed before the resin is poured. If there is any loose dirt or ground foam, small air bubbles will become trapped in the bottom of the resin that look like foam. To prevent this, pour a layer of artist's matte medium to seal all the little air pockets and let it dry for a few days before pouring the casting resin. Mix the resin and catalyst according to the manufacturer's instructions. Use a paper cup or the flexible plastic mixing pans that are included with some brands of resin. Place any pebbles, sticks, or other debris you want "underwater" before you pour the resin.

Decoupage casting resin is an alternative to artist's gel medium (Project 91) for creating water that looks wet enough to swim in but is as hard as plastic. This two-part resin is used primarily for covering decoupage projects and is sold by most artist's supply shops and craft stores. Most of these stores also sell dyes that can be used with the resin. A word of caution: while the artist's gloss medium and gloss gel can be cleaned up with water, only a few solvents work with casting resin. Work outdoors or in a well-ventilated area, and protect the floor and general area with newspaper and plastic drop cloths. I also recommend you wear rubber gloves to keep the stuff from sticking to your bare skin. There's very little smell, but the hardened resin is almost impossible to remove.

When working with casting resin, it is essential that the bottom of the pond or stream be sealed completely, because the resin seems to flow into places even water won't go. It takes about an hour to cure completely and that's plenty of time for it to drain completely through any pinholes that might be in the bottom of the pond or stream. Since it does flow so easily, it's also difficult to use for streams with rapids unless you can tilt the entire table so the stream is level until the resin cures.

The techniques for using decoupage casting resin are virtually the same as those described in Project 91 for artist's gloss medium. The decoupage resin, however, is a two-part material with a catalyst. Mix only about half of a small paper cup full of the fluid. You can pour dozens of layers, so there's no need to try to fill the entire pond or stream with one pour. You may also want to add a drop or two of dark green and dark blue dye to each half cup of the liquid to give more of a "watery" color.

If you need to pour a pond or stream deeper than about 1/4 inch, just continue to mix half cups of the resin, pouring each and allowing it to cure before pouring in another batch. I've seen cast-resin lakes as deep as 2 inches. The material is very hard, however, and very large areas will crack if the scenery flexes or if there are extreme changes in temperature. If you do get a crack, you can disguise it fairly effectively by pouring another thin layer of resin so it seeps into the crack. The crack will never completely disappear, however.

2 If you want ripples in the surface, jab at the resin with a wooden tongue depressor during the last few minutes of curing. The resin will have a jellylike surface for a few minutes before it hardens.

3 You can also stick some individual strands of flocking and more pebbles around the shore so they will be partially submerged in the still-fluid resin.

4 The members of the Midwest Mod-U-Trak Model Railroad Club near Chicago have a modular layout depicting typical Midwest scenes. This river is poured-decoupage resin with a bit of dark blue and dark green dye mixed in to increase the feeling of depth.

5 This pond, also on the Midwest Mod-U-Trak Model Railroad Club layout, was poured from dyed decoupage resin in two steps. First, the pond was covered within 1/16 inch of the top and allowed to cure. Next, the ducks (from Preiser) were put in place along with some of the willows cut from rope. A final 1/16 inch of clear decoupage resin was poured to partially submerge the ducks and the willows.

6 This waterfall on Ed Patrone's layout was made by pouring about six layers of decoupage resin down the slope. Each layer only added a paper thickness to the "water," but it does eventually accumulate.

SECTION FOURTEEN
RESEARCH

Once you decide that you want your model railroad to look like the real thing, this is the project for you. In fact, this is the project that you should turn to before you begin building or painting or weathering any locomotive, car, or structure; before you design your layout; before you install the track; and, certainly, before you begin work on any of the scenery. But before you can re-create reality, you need to know where to find reality. Whether you are modeling the past or the present, it's likely someplace far from your backyard.

PROJECT 101 • MODELING AND REAL RAILROAD RESOURCES

Time: Lifetime

Tools: Your choice

Materials: Your choice

Cost: $$$

Talent: Beginner, Novice and Expert

Scales: HO, N, S, O and G

Space: Your choice

Tip: Research can be as enjoyable as modeling. Try it.

WHY: To provide a real-world "model" for your railroad in miniature

COMPLEMENTARY PROJECTS: 1, 4, 12, 13, 30 through 38, 40 through 62, and 71 through 100

1 This white hotel is an HO scale Con-Cor model converted to match a prototype in Basalt, Colorado. The real hotel is still standing to provide dimensions. The proportions of the real hotel were used to create scale sketches to scratchbuild the red icehouse from styrene sheet and strips. Photos from several books on the real Colorado Midland provided the research resources. The models are part of a re-creation of Basalt on the Colorado Midland, circa 1906.

BASIC RESEARCH TOOLS

Before you can model anything, you need to know what kits and raw materials are available. Your first investment, then, should be a copy of *Walthers Model Railroad Reference Book*. Walthers publishes three editions: one each for HO scale, N scale, and the "large scales" (S, O, and G). These books are actually catalogs with a few bits of modeling information and a few dozen photos of model railroads included for "color." Nearly all of the products included in the "Scratchbuilders" (raw materials), "Paints," and "Publications" sections are duplicated in each of the three volumes, so you only need the one for your scale. Many of the books available

both on real railroads and model railroads are listed in the back of each Walthers catalog. That section alone will get you moving in a direction you may never have considered.

Your second investment should be a copy of the National Model Railroad Association's *Data Sheets*. The *Data Sheets* describe and illustrate most everything you would want to know about real railroads, from switches (turnouts), bridges, cuts, fills, ballast, signals, and yard or terminal design to tree species and rock formations, to the dimensions of city streets and baseball diamonds. There are no photographs in the *Data Sheets*, but you can find those in the history section of your local public library. The *Data Sheets* also illustrate "typical" real railroad construction, as drawn from specific real railroads. Keep in mind, however, that each railroad had its own standards for rights-of-way, bridges, buildings, operations, and yard design.

My third "essential" book is John Armstrong's *Track Planning for Realistic Operations*. John is the dean of model railroad designers and has also authored several books on real railroads. His book is

2 Steve Abernathy visited Juliette, Georgia, on the Southern Railway to measure the buildings. He assembled the HO scale replicas from styrene sheet and strip to match his own photos and sketches. Juliette was made famous in the motion picture *Fried Green Tomatoes*.

a quick course in just about everything a real railroad does and how you can duplicate track patterns that allow you to re-create their operations. After reading it, you may even discover there are real railroad situations you can only duplicate by selecting a real railroad beyond your present knowledge.

MODELING FROM A PROTOTYPE

Most modelers find it difficult, if not impossible, to pick just one favorite prototype railroad. However, if you find you prefer a specific prototype, you should join the historical society that specializes in that particular real railroad. Each June, *Railmodel Journal* publishes a listing of all active railroad historical societies, and the list is repeated on their website, www.railmodeljournal.com. In addition, *Mainline Modeler* magazine lists some railroad historical societies, and *Model Railroader* magazine publishes an annual listing, usually in their April issue. Some of the historical societies cater more to modelers than others, but there is useful information available from every one of them. The historical societies can also help you locate specific books

and other documents, often in their own files, about your favorite real railroads.

Your next source of reference for real railroads should be the thousands of books published about specific railroads. A variety of subjects, from specific portions of railroads, to books depicting nothing but freight cars, to books on just locomotives are available. The more specialized books tend to go out of print, so you may also need to do some searching through libraries. Larger hobby stores usually carry books; often the real railroad books they stock are dedicated to local railroads. If you model a railroad far from your home, it is worthwhile to check with hobby dealers in the area you are modeling for books with local color. Another source for books is railroad museums which, again, specialize in books about their particular railroad or area. Kalmbach's *Guide to Tourist Railroads and Museums* can be helpful in locating railroad museums.

For more specific information, check the Library of Congress' catalog of Sanborn Insurance maps. Available for nearly every portion of North America, and often available from decades past, Sanborn maps inventory the structures that existed for insurance purposes, showing the locations of virtually all railroad tracks and the footprints of nearly every structure.

And don't overlook word of mouth! Try to attend at least one of the annual National Model Railroad Association conventions and attend the clinics that are presented on your favorite topics. Also look for the Railroad Prototype Modelers (RPM) Meets at the NMRA conventions to find out if other RPM conventions are located near you, and attend the annual convention(s) of your favorite railroad historical society or societies. And, finally, if you *really* care, visit railroad employees and ex-employees in the area you are modeling to get their firsthand accounts.

3 You can create exact replicas of prototype scenes even on a portable layout. This is Gregg Fuhriman's 2x12-foot HO scale Free-Mo module set. You can see portable layouts as well as Railroad Prototype Modelers Meet models at most of the NMRA national conventions. That's where Gregg's modules, as well as Steve Abernathy's and the Railroad Prototype Modelers layouts, were photographed.

4 J. D. Smith is re-creating every siding on the Southern Railway's "Rathole Division" in HO scale in his 56x61-foot basement. Like many modelers, he uses actual dirt and crushed ballast from the real Southern Railway to provide the proper colors for his model right-of-way.

5 A typical collection of exact-scale models displayed at a Railroad Prototype Modelers Meet. The group has no dues, no bylaws, and no hierarchy. Modelers just show up at meets organized by RPM stalwarts to display their models, give clinics, and generally talk about modeling from the prototype.

APPENDIX

SOURCES FOR MODEL RAILROADING SUPPLIES

Although some model railroad manufacturers and importers offer catalogs (expect to pay anywhere from $3 to $15 for each), most sell only through hobby dealers. The best use for this list, then, is to provide your local hobby shop with contact addresses. If you do contact an importer or manufacturer yourself, be sure to send a self-addresses stamped envelope if you expect a reply.

A-Line
P.O. Box 2701
Carlsbad, CA 92018
www.ppw-aline.com

Accurail (Easy Scene)
P.O. Box 278
Ellburn, IL 60119-1202
www.accurail.com/accurail

Accurate Dimensionals
4185 S. Fox St.
Englewood, CO 80110-4564

Alexander Scale Models
Box 7121
Grand Rapids, MI 49510

American Limited Models
P.O. Box 7803
Fremont, CA 94537-7803
www.americanlimitedmodels.com

American Model Builders
1408 Hanley Industrial Court
St. Louis, MO 63144
www.laserkit.com

American Models
10087 Colonial Industrial Dr.
South Lyon, MI 48178
www.americanmodels.com

AMI
P.O. Box 11861
Clayton, MO 63105

AMSI (Architectural Model Supplies, Inc.)
P.O. Box 750638
Petaluma, CA 94975
www.AMSI-minilandscaping.com

Aristo-Craft Trains
698 S. 21st Street
Irvington, NJ 07111
www.aristocraft.com

Arizona Rock & Mineral Co.
P.O. Box 567
Paulden, AZ 86334
www.rrscenery.com

Athabasca Scale Models
771 Wilkinson Way
Saskatoon, SK S7N 3L8
Canada

Athearn, Inc.
19010 Laurel Park Rd.
Compton, CA 90220
www.athearn.com

Atlas Model Railroad Co. Inc.
378 Florence Ave.
Hillside, NJ 07205
www.atlasrr.com

Atlas O
603 Sweetland Ave.
Hillside, NJ 07205
www.atlaso.com/welcome.htm

Avalon Concepts (see Premium Concepts)

Aztec Manufacturing
2701 Conestoga Dr. 113
Carson City, NV 89706
www.aztectrains.com

Bachmann Industries Inc.
1400 E. Erie Ave.
Philadelphia, PA 19124
www.bachmannindustries.com

Badger Air-Brush Co.
9128 Belmont Ave.
Franklin Park, IL 60131
www.badger-airbrush.com

Bethlehem Car Works
363 Parkview Dr.
Souderton, PA 18964

Blair Line
P.O. Box 1136
Carthage, MO 64836
www.blairline.com

Bowser Manufacturing Co.
1302 Jordan Ave.
Montoursville, PA 17754
www.bowser-trains.com

Branchline Trains
333 Park Ave.
East Hartford, CT 06108
www.branchline-trains.com

Brass Car Sides
715 S. 7th St.
St. Peter, MN 56082
www.mria.org/companies/brasscarsides.html

Brawa (see Walthers)

Builders In Scale
P.O. Box 460025
Aurora, CO 80046-0025

Busch (see E-R Model Importers or Walthers)

C-D-S Lettering Ltd.
P.O. Box 65074
Nepean, ON K2G 5Y3
Canada

C 'n C Soft Metal Castings
8080 University Ave.
Fridley, MN 55432

Caboose Industries
1861 N. Ridge Dr.
North Babylon, NY 11703-0185

Campbell Scale Models
P.O. Box 5307
Durango, CO 81301

Cannonball Car Shops (see Model Railroad Warehouse)

Canon & Company
310 Willow Heights
Aptos, CA 95003-9798

Centerline Products
18409 Harmony Rd.
Marengo, IL 601152
www.centerline-products.com

Central Valley Model Works
1203 Pike Ln.
Oceano, CA 93445

Centralia Car Shops
1468 Lee St.
Des Plaines, IL 60018

Challenger Imports, Ltd.
P.O. Box 93244
Capital Square Station
Des Moines, IA 50393
www.challengerimports.com

Champ Decals
Division of Champion Decal Co.
P.O. Box 1178
Minot, ND 58702

Chooch Enterprises
P.O. Box 217
Redmond, WA 98072-0217

Chicago Model International
P.O. Box 170
Deerfield, IL 60015

City Classics
P.O. Box 16502
Pittsburgh, PA 15242

Circuitron
211 RocBaar Dr.
Romeoville, IL 60446

Classic Motorbooks
Galtier Plaza, Ste. 200
380 Jackson St.
St. Paul, MN 55101-3885
www.motorbooks.com

Clover House
P.O. Box 62M
Sebastopol, CA 95473-0062

The Coach Yard
P.O. Box 593
Del Mar, CA 92014-0593
www.TheCoachYard.com

Con-Cor International
8101 E. Research Court
Tucson, AZ 85710
www.all-railroads.com

Custom Finishing
379 Tulley Rd.
Orange, MA 01364

Dallee Electronics
246 W. Main St.
Leola, PA 17540
www.dallee.com

DeLuxe Innovations
P.O. Box 4213
Burbank, CA 91503-4213
www.deluxeinnovations.com

Design Preservation Models
Box 66
Linn Creek, MO 65052
www.dpmkits.com

Detail Associates
P.O. Box 5357
San Luis Obispo, CA 93403

Details West
P.O. Box 61
Corona, CA 94611

Digitrax, Inc.
450 Cemetery St., #206
Norcross, GA 30071
www.digitrax.com

Dimi-Trains
P.O. Box 70310
Reno, NV 89570-0310

Division Point
3415 Heidelberg Dr.
Boulder, CO 80303

Downtown Deco
4319 Rainbow Dr.
Missoula, MT 59803
www.downtowndeco.com

Dyna-Model Products
RR 1, Box 624
Sangerville, ME 04479

E-R Model Importers Ltd.
1000 S. Main St.
Newark, NY 14513
www.ermodels.com

Easy Scene (see Accurail)

Evergreen Scale Models, Inc.
18620-F 141st Ave. NE
Woodinville, WA 98072

F&H Enterprises
2562 Silver State Pkwy.
Building C, Ste. 3
Minden, NV 89423

Faller (see Walthers)

Fine N-Scale Products
P.O. Box 287
San Pedro, CA 90731

Floquil-Pollyscale Corporation (see the Testor)

Funaro & Camerlengo
Rd. #3, Box 2800
Honesdale, PA 18431

GarGraves Trackage Corp.
8967 Ridge Rd.
North Rose, NJ 14516
www.gargraves.com

GC&R Model Railroad Electronics
378 Taylor Ford Rd.
Columbia, KY 42725

GHQ Models
28100 Woodside Rd.
Shorewood, MN 55331
www.ghqmodels.com

Gloorcraft (see Walthers)

Gold Medal Models
1412 Fishermen Bay Rd.
Lopez, WA 98261
www.goldmm.com

Grandt Line Products, Inc.
1040 B Shary Ct.
Concord, CA 94518

Hallmark Models, Inc.
4822 Bryan St.
Dallas, TX 75204
www.hallmarkmodels.com

Heiki (see E-R Model Importers, Portman Hobby Distributors, or Walthers)

Highliners
P.O. Box 22435
San Diego, CA 92192

Hi-Tech Details
P.O. Box 244
Ukiah, CA 95482

HJJ Company
P.O. Box 60833
Boulder City, NV 89006

Hunt Corp.
2005 Market St.
Philadelphia, PA 19103

InterMountain Railway
P.O. Box 839
Longmont, CO 80501
www.intermountain-railway.com

International Hobby Corp. (IHC)
413 E. Allegheny Ave.
Philadelphia, PA 19134-2322
www.ihc-hobby.com

JAKS Industries
P.O. Box 1421
Golden, CO 80402-1421

JnJ Trains
P.O. Box 1535
Ottumwa, IA 52501

JV Models
P.O. Box 700
Artesia, CA 90702-0700

K-Line Electric Trains
P.O. Box 2831
Chapel Hill, NC 27515
www.k-linetrains.com

K&S Engineering
6917 W. 59th St.
Chicago, IL 60638

Kadee Quality Products
673 Avenue C
White City, OR 97503-1078
www.kadee.com

Kalmbach Publishing Co.
21027 Crossroads Cir.
Waukesha, WI 53187-1512
www.kalmbach.com

Kato USA, Inc.
100 Remington Rd.
Schaumberg, IL 60173
www.katousa.com

Key Imports
P.O. Box 1848
Rogue River, OR 97537

Kibri (see E-R Models, Portman, or Walthers)

Krause Publications
700 State St.
Iola, WI 54990-0001
www.krause.com

LBF Company
1931 NW Mulholland DR
Roseburg, OR 97470
www.lbfcompany.com

LGB of America
6444 Nancy Ridge Rd.
San Diego, CA 92121
www.lgb.com

LaBelle Woodworking
P.O. Box 391
Cheyenne, WY 82003-0391
www.labellemodels.com

Lenz Digital
P.O. Box 143
Chelmsford, MA 01824
www.lenz.com

Life-Like Products, Inc.
1600 Union Ave.
Baltimore, MD 21211-1998
www.lifelikeproducts.com

Lionel, LLC
50625 Richard W. Blvd.
Chesterfield, MI 48051-2493
www.lionel.com

Lonestar Models (see Plano Model Products)

Mantua
P.O. Box 10
Woodbury Heights, NJ 08097-0010
www.mantua.com

Märklin Inc.
16988 W. Victor Rd.
New Berlin, WI 53151
www.marklin.com

McHenry Couplers
1207 Pebble Point
Goshen, KY 40026

Micro-Mark Tools
340 Snyder Ave.
Berkeley Heights, NJ 07922-1595
www.micromark.com

Micro Engineering
1120 Eagle Rd.
Fenton, MO 63026

Microscale Industries, Inc.
18435 Bandilier Cir.
Fountain Valley, CA 92708
www.microscale.com

Micro-Trains Line Co.
P.O. Box 1200
Talent, OR 97540-1200
www.micro-trains.com

Midwest Products Co.
400 S. Indiana Blvd.
Hobart, IN 46342

Miller Engineering
P.O. Box 282
New Canaan, CT 06840-0282
www.microstru.com

Miniatures by Eric
RR #1
Busby, AB T0G 0H0
Canada

Model Die Casting (MDC) see Roundhouse

Model Power
180 Smith St.
Farmingdale, NY 11735
www.modelpower.com

Model Railroad Stone Works
13235 Summit Square Center
Langhorne, PA 19047

Model Railroad Warehouse
P.O. Box 411
Roanoake, IN 46783

Model Rectifier Corp. (MRC)
80 Newfield Ave.
Edison, NJ 08818-6312
www.modelrec.com

Modelflex (see Badger Air-Brush Co.)

Mountains-In-Minutes
I.S.L.E. Laboratories
P.O. Box 663
Sylvania, OH 43560

MRC (see Model Rectifier Corp.)

MTH Electric Trains
7020 Columbia Gateway Dr.
Columbia, MD 21046
www.mth-railking.com

N Scale Architect
48 Kensington Ct.
Hackettstown, NJ 07840

N. J. International
230 W. Old Country Rd.
Hicksville, NY 11801
www.njinternational.com

Noch (see E-R Models, Portman, or Walthers)

NEC Corporation
899 Ridge Road
Webster, NY 14580
www.ncedcc.com

NorthWest Short Line
P.O. Box 423
Seattle, WA 98111
www.nwsl.com

Northeast Decals
P.O. Box 324
Deerfield, MA 01342

Northeastern Scale Models Inc.
3030 Thorntree Dr.
Unit 5
Chico, CA 95973
www.nesm.com

Oddballs Decals
26550-227th St.
McLouth, KS 66054
www.members.tripod.com/mopac1/oddballs.htm

OK Engine Company
P.O. Box 355
Mohawk, NY 13407

Overland Models, Inc.
3808 W. Kilgore Ave.
Muncie, IN 47304
www.overlandmodels.com

P-B-L
P.O. Box 769
Ukiah, CA 95482
www.p-b-l.com

P&D Hobbies
31904 Groesbeck Hwy.
Fraser, MI 48026

Paasche Airbrush Company
7440 W. Lawerence Ave.
Harwood Heights, IL 60706-3412
www.thomasregister.com/olc/paasche/

Pacer Technology
94320 Santa Anita Ave.
Rancho Cucamonga, CA 91730

Peach Creek Shops
201 Main St.
Laurel, MD 20707

Peco (see F&H Enterprise or Walthers)

Pecos River Brass
560 E. Church St.
Lewisville, TX 75057

Period Miniatures
P.O. Box 1421
Golden, CO 80402-1421

Plastruct
1020 S. Wallace Pl.
City of Industry, CA 91748
www.plastruct.com

Plano Model Products
2701 W. 15th St., Ste. 113
Plano, TX 75075
www.planomodelproducts.com

Pollyscale Corporation (see the Testor)

Pola GmbH
Am Bahndamm 59
D-8734 Rothhausen
West Germany

Portman Hobby Distributors
851 Washington St., Box 2551
Peeksill, NY 10566

Precision Scale Co.
3961 Hwy. 93 North
Stevensville, MT 59870

Precision Masters (see Red Caboose)

Preiser (see E-R Models or Walthers)

Premium Concepts
P.O. Box 174
Presto, PA 15142

PSI (Power Systems, Inc.)
56 Bellis Cir.
Cambridge, MA 02140
www.tttrains.com/psidynatrol

Quality Craft (see Weaver)

Rail Power Products
7283 N. Stagecoach Dr.
Park City, UT 84098

Railmodel Journal
2403 Champa St.
Denver, CO 80205
www.railmodeljournal.com

Railworks
P.O. Box 148
Woodbury, NY 11797

Red Caboose
P.O. Box 250
Mead, CO 80542
www.red-caboose.com

Rapido (see E-R Models or Walthers)

Rix Products
3747 Hogue Rd.
Evansville, IN 47712
www.rixproducts.com

Roco (see E-R Models or Walthers)

Roundhouse (MDC)
5070 Sigstrom Dr.
Carson City, NV 89706

Run 8 Productions
P.O. Box 25224
Rochester, NY 14625

S-Helper Service
2 Roberts Rd.
New Brunswick, NJ 08901

San Juan Car Company
P.O. Box 1028
Durango, CO 81302

Satellite City (see Walthers)

Scale Scenics (see Circuitron)

Scalecoat Paint
P.O. Box 231
Northumberland, PA 17857

Scenic Express
1001 Lowry Ave.
Jeannette, PA 15644-2671
www.scenicexpress.com

Sequoia Scale Models
P.O. Box 47326
Seattle, WA 98126

Shoreham Shops, Ltd.
P.O. Box 22011
Eagan, MN 55122

Showcase Miniatures
P.O. Box 753-N
Cherry Valley, CA 92223

SignsGalore
9 Carlson Ln.
Palm Coast, FL 32137-8150
www.tttrains.com/signsgalore/

SmokeyValley Railroad Products
P.O. Box 339
Plantersville, MS 38862
www.smokeyvalley.com

SMP Industries
P.O. Box 72
Bolton, MA 01740

Soundtraxx
210 Rock Point Dr.
Durango, CO 81301
www.soundtraxx.com

Stewart Hobbies, Inc.
140 New Britain Rd.
Chalfont, PA 18914-1832
www.stewarthobbies.com

SS Limited (see JAKS Industries)

Sunlit Vistas
P.O. Box 278
Elburn, IL 60119-1202

Sunrise Enterprises
P.O. Box 172
Doyle, CA 96109
www.sunrisenterprises.com

Sunshine Models
P.O. Box 4997
Springfield, MO 65808-4997

Switchmaster (see Builders In Scale)

The Testor Corporation
620 Buckbee St.
Rockford, IL 61104
www.testors.com

Thayer & Chandler Airbrushes
28835 N. Herkey Dr., Ste. 205
Lake Bluff, IL 60044

Tippi (see Premium Concepts)

Tomar Industries
9520 E. Napier Ave.
Benton Harbor, MI 49022

Train Station Products
P.O. Box 360
Granville, OH 43023

Vintage Reproductions
2606 Flintridge Dr.
Colorado Springs, CO 80918-2274

W & R Enterprises
P.O. Box 3235
Alhambra, CA 91803

Walthers
5601 W. Florist Ave.
Milwaukee, WI 53201-0770
www.walthers.com

Wangrow Electronics
P.O. Box 98
Park Ridge, IL 60068
www.wangrow.com

Weaver Models
P.O. Box 231
Northumberland, PA 17857
www.weavermodels.com

Westerfield
55 River Ln.
Crossville, TN 38555

Wiking (see E-R Models or Walthers)

William Electric Trains
8835-F Columbia 100 Pkwy.
Columbia, MO 21045
www.williamstrains.com

Woodland Scenics
101 E. Valley Dr., Box 98
Linn Creek, MO 65052
www.woodlandscenics.com

X-Acto (see Hunt Corp.)

Xuron Corporation
60 Industrial Park Rd.
Saco, ME 04072

Ye Olde Huff 'n Puff
Rear 606 Knepp Ave.
Lewistown, PA 17044-1651

INDEX

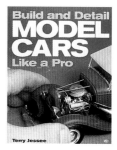

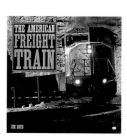